NEW YORK REVIEW BOOKS

POETS

VIVEK NARAYANAN's books of poetry include *Universal Beach* and *Life and Times of Mr S*. He has been a Fellow at the Radcliffe Institute at Harvard University and a Cullman Fellow at the New York Public Library. A full-length collection of his poems in Swedish translation was published in 2015 by the legendary Stockholm-based Wahlström & Widstrand. He currently teaches creative writing at George Mason University and is a member of the editorial board at *Poetry Daily*, where he helps to select poems and writes about world poetry.

D1548523

Vivek Narayanan

After

NYRB/POETS

 NEW YORK REVIEW BOOKS   *New York*

THIS IS A NEW YORK REVIEW BOOK
PUBLISHED BY THE NEW YORK REVIEW OF BOOKS
435 Hudson Street, New York, NY 10014
www.nyrb.com

Library of Congress Cataloging-in-Publication Data
Names: Narayanan, Vivek, (Professor of creative writing), author. |
    Vālmīki. Rāmāyaṇa.
Title: After / by Vivek Narayanan.
Description: New York: New York Review Books, [2022]. | Series: New York
    Review Books poets | Identifiers: LCCN 2021050595 | ISBN 9781681376462
    (paperback) | ISBN 9781681376479 (ebook)
Subjects: LCGFT: Poetry.
Classification: LCC PR9499.4.N365 A48 2022 | DDC 821/.92—dc23/eng/20211110
LC record available at https://lccn.loc.gov/2021050595

ISBN 978-1-68137-646-2

Cover and book design by Emily Singer

Printed in the United States of America on acid-free paper.
10 9 8 7 6 5 4 3 2 1

to Arshia Sattar

Contents

AFTER IS A COLLECTION OF POEMS inspired by Valmiki's *Ramayana*, a Sanskrit text quite different from the more devotional story that most Indians have in their heads. In the Sanskrit tradition, Valmiki is the *aadikavi* ("first, or foundational poet"), but the *Ramayana* today is often understood only as story, or even worse, as history. My principal aim here is to reanimate the *Ramayana*, in English, as poetry.

My method for this has throughout been open and evolving. I have explored the epic's terrain through a play of fragments and a kind of critical conversation with Valmiki. Every poem here is in some way a reinvention or *rewiring*, if you will, but I've still taken great care and worked from a close study of the sound and strategies of the original.

Those who would consider what I'm doing to be "tampering" should think of the long tradition of freedom in the the long traditions of *Ramayanas* that already exist. When, for instance, Kamban brings Valmiki into Tamil in the thirteenth century, or Tulsidas brings the text into a dialect of Hindi in the sixteenth century, one sees that in some moments the vernacular writers stick very close to the Sanskrit and at other moments make quite purposeful departures, cutting things out or changing them, incorporating stories from sources other than Valmiki, and so on. This is no accident or neglect. The point of bringing across has always been to make a source and its possibilities come fully alive in each new language and, importantly, each new era, to be answerable to the questions of the present. And the key to the Ramayana's greatness lies in its innate multiplicity, its resilience, and its potential for being retold.

Each of Valmiki's seven books, or *kandas*, invents a distinct emotional, narrative, and geographic landscape of its own. I've listed the kandas in the Notes and Sources section at the back of the book, along with my various sources, plot summaries that correspond to each of the four main sections of *After*, and some extra context and information about the world of the *Ramayana*. My hope, however, is that the poems themselves contain everything that is necessary for their reading and comprehension.

BOOK ONE

City and Forest

Pity causeth the forests to fail,
Pity slayeth my nymphs,
Pity spareth so many an evil thing.
Pity befouleth April,
Pity is the root and the spring.
                    —Pound, Canto XXX

feet and syllables in place
  with tone and time contained in it
only from sadness did the stanza shape emerge
        and not otherwise

        —*Balakanda*, Canto 2

Sit waiting for the fruition of your seed
till arrives the immortal bird that eats no fruit.

—Gopalakrishna Adiga, translated by M. G. Krishnamurthy

simple as the holy lotus is simple
  because it is edible

—Inger Christensen, translated by Susanna Nied

To Valmiki

cooing ram ram
                softly so softly   perched
on an upper branch the koel called
                                Valmiki
who drinks again and
                drinks again of that
                ram-saga-nectar
taking his own pain
        to those sorrow-seas

i

Valmiki Discovers the Shloka Meter

Balakanda, Canto 2

A pair of water birds subsumed in
   their lovemaking
A soldier in the woods
  whose venturing arrow found them
           on a turn of the Tamasa

    I'd gone there for my bath
  I heard the soul scream
     then saw pink ripples
         in ribbon light

    Why would He kill like that
   so pointlessly? Before I knew it
a curse had left my lips
    in the newest of meters:

Warrior   you'll live forever in infamy
   for snuffing half
     of a pair joined as one
   in the ritual of love

    Soon as I said it:
     regret
   But there it now was
    in a four-part meter & I

couldn't get the trifle out of mind
   Student Bharadwaj brought my clothes
We went back to the hut
   talked about random things but

it didn't go away   Then
      an elder who must have been
      Brahma in disguise
      dropped in for a visit

Still worried by the verse
      I blurted it out
Briefly mortified   But Brahma
just smiled & said

So you invented a verse form!
      What's the big deal? There's
      nothing to be worried about
Then he said: *I put it there*

You'll use it to tell the whole Ramayana

And so happened   that shoka
      turned to shloka
      that pain came trapped
      in a cage of forms

& when my students recited &
      memorized it
      was only more
      of whatever it was

Fawned in your bramble
that pricks
& protects
the rains lashed unabated
—the tanks filled
& communicated—
the loch below
the nothing
of that shrunken landscape

and you   and of you

Ganga

Dropped   from the blue-black
  of that sky

For stray millennia
  lost in Shiva's locks

bursting coil after coil
    with a grey weft when

in   in a trembling flash
    under stellar thunder he

shook open his hair and
    she wound toward the Earth

    where the gods &
    the demons & the seers

in caves could see that falling river
    coruscating like stone   blind   scorched

    black shoal of fish & whole
    root lashing in air &

blue oxen   whinnying thatch
  of huts stray block

  of village wall &
    such grit that

    when she finally had
been sated   & had her ground   with

    one last delayed
spell she had to leap

straight up to shuck off
all the matter that clung to her

so then pure and clear
with whispers

of consecration she
could rill fresh

Sita-furrows
into returning soil

Shiva

And Shiva's cum
  white and sticky
poured onto the nearest
  mountain and the white
reeds that shot
  up to make
their own shade and soon
  by extension was all the
world cum and the clouds
  pure unadulterated
cum foam the snowy
  little cum caps on the cum
peaks and the rivers pure hard
  coursing cum
and the grass made
  green by the sprouting of
cum on soil and sheets
  of cum fanning in the wind
and the people's bodies
  slowly congealed
  over the ages

and cows sculpted from
  cum and tigers come
to life from cum and
  tanks of cum
rolling down
  the cum-washed streets

sky-kissing apartments of cum
  cum palaces   suburbs
of cum undulating into
  the thirsty fields and far
shrines of cum

and the bodies
burning from the fire
    of cum   minds still muddled
under our blinding white
    sun of cum

Song for the Horse Sacrifice

Black horse   transport of the sun
as your last breath leaves   I'll lie with you
touch you where need to be touched

How far   what grassland or mountain did you test
and did you meet the two boys your story sung?
Black horse   I'll press you where need to be pressed

The fire burns   so does our gratitude accrue
You'll keep the land you've won   black horse
as your last breath leaves   I'll lie with you

You   are the envoy of the king   I   his wife
and your mistress   So let blood taste the air of lung
black horse   I'll kiss you where need to be kissed

and lick wherever you want to be licked
your flesh upon my tongue
O let the weak grow weaker   let the sick remain sick
black horse   as your last breath leaves   I'll lie with you

Rishyashringa

Come back to Eros   Rishyashringa—
the skin-split jamuns of the city
           call to you
the finger-whorled black
           of the land-grant temple
the generations of ground
           under the sacrifice

Come back   Rishyashringa
too long in the hut of your father
pressed twigs show a path
  we're not going far
 we'll draw a trace of us
to find our way back

Come back to Eros
  flit of red-tipped deer
even the brambles that spoke on you
           protect you

Come back   Rishyashringa
 the s in the pool is the water snake
the sitafals shriveled in your grove

Come back to the palace   you'll be
  safe among these walls
where the laughter never leaves
where the lamps are always lit

Here

Here   where by Shiva's laser eye
desire became a wisp of smoke
forever free from the body   where

in the tangle of trees
and in the limbs and shoots
that bind among them

the wind's fury entered the joints
of beautiful boys and girls
and bent them crooked   where

the sons of Sagara were born
to dig the soil
and tear the Earth in search

of a stolen horse   their progeny turned
to heaps of ashes
where the river Ganga brought the land to life

after such devastation
only that the asura angels
might hope on to some settled end

Here   where memory burns like fat
in the wildfires and in the altars
that seek to tame them

where the deer
is still afraid
and the hunter blind

This forest was never new   Rama
It's not yours
not even after
you've mastered it

Rama

Rama   that hero's hair dark as a crow's wing
     Your son is not your son
Rama   that boy still with the sidelocks curled
     Your son is not your son
Rama   that he-man of the heavy lotus eyes
     Your son is not your son
Rama   speechless and radiant with swords
     Your son is not your son
Rama   tiger among men
     Your son is not your son
Rama   that blank face turned to the face of Saturn
     Your son is not your son
Rama   may you never grow sick or tired
     Your son is not your son
Rama   three-headed cobra from behind
     Your son is not your son
Rama   that forest torn from the heart
     Your son is not your son
Rama   that sip of clearer water
     Your son is not your son
Rama   that empty gaping dark
     Your son is not your son
Rama   that corpse within the corpse
     Your son is not your son
Rama   your nipple in the rain
     Your son is not your son
Rama   that reason beyond reason
     Your son is not your son
Rama   that sleep beyond sleep
     Your son is not your son

Rama's Servants

Punisher's hooked discus	Dharma's bladed discus
Time's hooked discus	Vishnu's bladed discus
Indra's bladed discus	Vajra (h-bomb)
Siva's lance	Brahma's Crest
Aishika (guided missile)	Brahma's artillery
Time's noose	The Tower
noose of Dharma	Vengeance's noose
noose of chemical rain	The Drier
The Drencher	Pinakin's ballistic missile
Agni's long range fire thrower	Vayu's air to air missile
The Drainer	The Horse-head missile
Vilaapana (bomb)	The Wrester
Kankila (death machine)	The Peacemaker
Kaapaala (sniper rifle)	Mohana (poison gas)
Kankana (assault rifle)	Taamasa (cruise missile)
Nandana (gilded sword)	Saumana (tactical missile)
Varunastra (heavyweight torpedo)	Maanava (anti-tank missile)
BrahMos (hypersonic missile)	Prasvapana (anti-ship missile)
Sudarshan (laser–guided bomb)	Saura (thermobaric bomb)
Maayaadhana (cluster bomb)	Nirbhay (subsonic missile)
Dispossessor	The Cooler
Tvastr's deadly Sudaamana	Prithvi (short range ballistic missile)
Agni (intercontinental missile)	Sagarika (submarine-launched missile)
Raudra (rocket launcher)	Aindra (submachine gun)
Paasupata (interceptor missile)	Gaandharva (fire bomb)
Dhanush (anti-ballistic missile)	The Yawner
The Humidifier	Vidhwansak (anti-material rifle)
Aakash (surface-to-air missile)	Brahma's cordon
The Monster (missile)	Vaayavya (artificial weather machine)
Shivalik (multi-mode hand grenade)	Shaurya (glide missile)

Calling his servants in   Rama
caressed their heads   their
shoulders   their
elbows and knobs   blowing
lightly on their deadliest
points   their sharp
mouths still   licking
the thought of human
bodies with the last
life-sparks leafing
out of them   and when
as Rama's loyal
servants they drew
close letting themselves
be touched and touched so
he closed
his eyes
whispered

form into name into kill

Tataka

Sage   tell me   who is she   this
   disfigured one with the rage

and the force   of a thousand
   elephants? How does

a woman come to be so strong   that entire armies
crossing into her forest are simply torn

     to strips of skin and lumps
      of half-chewed flesh?

       Rama   she is Tataka
   once the most beautiful and kind woman

   in the world   jewel of a daughter
     to the virtuous and powerful Suketu

     wife to the gentle Sunda
   mother of the fearless Maricha

It happens that her husband
  was killed and

she and her son were cursed
  with these   the hideous

   unbearable forms you see
Now she hates Agastya and all of us

with every drop of her being

Sage   who killed her husband Sunda?
  Who disfigured Tataka's body?

Rama   you must never hesitate
to kill a woman   not

for a second   This is the
immortal unwavering

rule for a man charged with
the burden of kingship

Tataka

"I'll spare the woman   snip her nose
            & nipples first

& if that warrior's bluster
    has not yet left her

 I will kill her   then
    and only then. "

Tataka, the Yakshi

The most beautiful woman
in the world   some say   but strong

stronger than elephants
    and wise as any mother

and keen   With her son by her side

    the shapeshifting Maricha
        still a toddler

hand linked in hand they slipped
    through the forest they'd made

to the clearing
        of the settler's camps

    Sacrificial fires burned
there now   that had to be

stopped from taking hold
(Dawn steals upon them all)

Ahalya

The sage Gautama was fond
of intense   solitary meditations   Once when

he was out on a trip his
wife Ahalya was seduced by

Indra   "king of the gods"   whom she found
not half bad   When Gautama

caught and cursed them   Indra ended up
dropping his testicles and

needing a ram transplant   This isn't
a poem about Indra's balls

though   it's about Ahalya   "invisible
living on air   sleeping in the ashes"

Ahalya

A stone ringed by fine white sand
  but otherwise anonymous
           more than half-sunk
  into ground for all those years
   of negative subsistence
Not so much the sole of his reigning foot
as the wider change of season
it brought   leaf-rustle and
snap of twig   the low breeze
in the sun-shafted air

  and then you were there
reformed   but the same person
  who'd kept a secret
with the god in his lover's body

Ahalya   was the wine of him
          new as the first of nights

Were those long fingers
       familiar or strange?

Have thought and touch
       found each other yet?

Ayodhya

No one is poor in Ayodhya
No one is unhappy in Ayodhya
No one goes hungry in Ayodhya
No one is robbed in Ayodhya
No one is beaten in Ayodhya
No one is illiterate in Ayodhya
No one is an atheist in Ayodhya
No one is cruel or miserly in Ayodhya
No one is a slave in Ayodhya
No one is sick in Ayodhya
No one is old or crippled in Ayodhya
No one   in Ayodhya

Rama, the Husband

Ask of the husband what you will, he can only give what he has to give.

The husband who carries the bow and is scribed into it.

The husband who is the bow, the wood drawn back against its grain, its will.

The husband who arrives late to the wedding and to the funeral.

(And the dug pond behind the house where you bathed on the way to the temple, those leaves and febrile branches embroidering the sky.)

The husband with his back to the wall.

The husband as he who does not speak, who carries to you a bowl of fruit, withdrawing expression.

Known for his tears, known by his tears: angry and shimmering as the night in its fugitive stars.

For the Crowning of Rama

Gold & votive offerings
white flowers & puffed rice
honey & ghee kept separate
new clothes   & new
four-akshauhini army
A pair of fly whisks
a hundred fire-bright pots
bull with horns cupped in gold
a whole tiger-skin
the flagstaff &
                        the white umbrella

Manthaara, the Hunchback

Spoken to her servant by Kaikeyi, King Dasaratha's youngest wife

Manthaara   bent
like a lotus in the breeze

your humped back is a fount
of wisdom   I'll bring

my lips to it and kiss it
Manthaara   your

shining face
your chest that rivals

your shoulders   your
slim unassuming waist

your spiraled navel
generous hips

and wide behind
The tinkle of your girdle

the sturdy legs on
your slender feet

Your hump is a chariot wheel
I'll know your steadfastness by it

I'll hold you by it
I'll anoint you with gold

I'll cover you with gold
And one day when you walk

proudly   and still yourself
in the street   people will know at last

you are   you are more lovely
than the white orb

that limns
the sky at night

Kaikeyi

Kaikeyi   sky after all
the stars have set   tigress who brought

a king to his death   conducting
rod for pain   You are

unafraid to the fear
you've woken   You are

misfortune in search
of fortune   One day soon we

will all come to feel the pain
as you do   Kaikeyi   your name

is misery but in your heart holds
something that will not shake

Kaikeyi   your heart
cradle of truth

Lakshmana

Rama, snap out of it. Can't you see a coup would be the only righteous choice? You make a public announcement, I take care of the trouble-makers, give standing orders, *c'est fini.*

Rama, my abs bulging for the fight. Our father's like a baby, weeping for the future and the past.

Rama, a thousand fates alongside the one you've shown.

Rama, each blink of your eyes a fate, each foot scraped on stone.

Rama, blush of blue arms.

Rama, that always my true love for you keeps me alive.

like an injection penciling
under skin
only you   the assassin

Dasaratha

    Days
after Rama's departure Dasaratha
    on fours like a dog
and barking rubs his hair
 in dirt or dung rolls around
on the palace floor

 The cries are loud enough
to carry beyond the gates:

Damn you woman damn you!

Rama have me arrested
please just have me arrested!

  Empties the wine
 licks mithai from his fingers
sings *koro koro! kiri kiri!*
    then passes out

Put your hand on me Kausalya
   I can't see a thing

  Wakes briefly—
to the forgotten pleasure of light filling

the room warm heat
washing over Faraway sounds

with a crushing exactness:
   the snap of wheel on

rutted stone still water splashes
  Then young again

in the night woods
such a genius shot

   aimed an arrow
to follow intuition—

but the cry that came was not
  an animal's

           and at the bank
a young monk still a boy

  was splayed   black blood
    between his legs

Who'd do that? Who'd shoot
an innocent for kicks? I'm a penniless

renouncer   son of a Vaishya father
and Shudra mother   and if you've

killed me you've surely also killed
* my blind and decrepit parents!*

Dasaratha   whose arrival those unsteady elders
   mistook for their son's

until they touched his cold hand

  Dasaratha   fallen from the high seat
         into a pool of shit

then stepping out to sip from it

like a cap of sesame oil   smearing face
and skin with days-old rice

  diving back to the deep

Dasaratha   on blackened throne
surrounded by mocking women

and the gold censer that catches fire
and the body that hardens to aloe wood

and we take what's left
to the Ganga   and the ash fills

the evening and the song
of the aarti from the shore

and then   as if they were a ritual offering
    the bone-crumbs are nibbled by fish

Dasaratha

The rest of the family
had already gone to the village

for his wife's pregnancy ceremony—
seemantham—but your great-grandfather

Sreenivasa Iyengar   42 years old
stayed back in Madras an extra day

on government business
That evening it was just

the cook and he
in the huge old

Triplicane house   A pandit
came   as he did every week

to read out and gloss
the *Ramayana*   They'd come now

to the part where Dasaratha dies
Srinivasa cut the pandit short

He'd felt the verses too troubling
His mind was agitated

Later   in the middle of the night
he got up to grope his way

to the latrine   They found him like that
in the morning

keeled over   mid-squat

Bharata's Arrival

No   no no no   Nono
Aho   ho   Aho ho ho ho   Aho
Halahala   halaa   haa-la

Greyness drops on Ayodhya
        the skies grey
    and the flanks of the buildings too

    It's as if the fresh paint that adorns
    and brightens sculpture
            has been stripped

        away to show
      the fire-blackened
      stone below

Greyness drops—no one's in the street
      no diyas in the halls
    where hundreds gathered

    Greyness—which is also the cold
                        of a handle
        that will no longer turn

Bharata

The messenger never told him
his father was dead   He arrived

to reach & was numbed by the instruction
or the fear of consequence   The messenger

never told him his father was dead
The skies were darkening   and shrunk from him

on the long journey through woods and lands—
with the clarity of an underwater sun

the animals were credulous but afraid
& Ayodhya was completely cipher

silent & abandoned   The messenger
never told him his father was dead   Until

the preservation in sesame oil   the nurses were kind
but private: a cloth covered the penis   they refused

to remove it   The messenger never told him
his father was dead   The blankness of the expression

the eyes closed indifferent
as if the old man were still asleep

Clang of the crematorium door   dead weight
and the knowing of it   the city

given up but watching   the messengers
never told him his father was dead

The State

    Like the breath on a long trip
   outside the body is
the State   the gift we'd asked
    Dangled from all the windows
   echoed in the pot's hollow is
the State   with holy water drunk

   Let no harm to the king
   lest it fall on us
Let the wives be in concordance
   and the succession clear
Let parricide carve lightly into
    throne and scepter on
the State   from wrenching order born

Ayodhyakanda, Canto CXIV

"Traveling in his chariot, which moved with a deep and pleasing rumbling, the Lord Bharata of great renown quickly entered Ayodhya, where cats and owls were on the prowl, but men and women were not seen. It was enveloped by darkness, like a night on the dark half of the month, without stars; beset by a sorrow and suffering, like Rohini, the beloved spouse of the moon, whose glory enhances her brilliance when he is eclipsed by his enemy Rāhu; thin like the mountain stream in summer with its trickle of water, hot and turbid, its birds drooping in the heat, its fish, great and small, and crocodiles hidden from view; extinguished, like the smokeless, golden tongue of flame of the sacrificial fire when the milk oblation is poured into it; its very existence imperiled, like that of an army in a great battle, whose chiefs have been killed, whose fighters have lost their armor, whose elephants, horses, chariots and flags lie battered and mangled; silent and with little movement, like the great ocean-tide, foam-flecked and thundering, that has subsided with the fall of the wind; all the noise and bustle of it stilled, as they are about the sacrificial altar, denuded of the comely sacrificial implements and abandoned by the priests, when the extraction of the soma juice has been done; suffering and longing, like the cows forsaken by the lord of the herd, as they stand in the cow pen, their new grass untouched; deprived of its shining lights, like a new garland of pearls denuded of rare pendants like rubies, that delighted and dazzled in their brilliance; its lustre dimmed, like a star's fallen on earth from the sky, hurled from its place all of a sudden by the exhaustion of its religious merit; wilting like a sylvan creeper covered with flowers and alive with the hum of bees drunk on honey when it is enveloped by a quick-spreading forest fire at the end of spring; its roads deserted, its activities at a standstill, its shops closed, no sales being made, like the sky overcast with clouds while the moon and stars remain hidden; desolate and fallen into neglect, like a drinking saloon deserted by drinkers, with broken jugs, emptied of rare liquors... with the floor of its squares cracked and sagging like that of a disused watershed with its broken pillars and tumble-down roof..."

—Translated by N. Raghunathan, *Srimad Valmiki Ramayana of Valmiki*, vol. 1, *Balakanda and Ayodhyakanda* (Madras: Vighneswara Publishing House, 1981), 423–5.

Jabali

Ramkrishna Bhattacharya. "Reflections on the Jābāli Episode in the Vālmīki *Rāmāyaṇa* (Ayodhyākāṇḍa)," *Journal of Indian Philosophy* (2016) Volume 44, 597–615

iii

Dawn it is
too early for you

always a minute too early
Cross with me
to the other side

the boatman waits
for a signal

Alternate Titles, Alternate Epics

Sitayaś Caritam (Sita's Story)

Rāmāyana (Rama's Path)

Paulastyavadhan (The Defeat of Ravana)

These the sandals I'm obliged
   to keep these the errors

I must honour   stray breaths of his
   in me   Strange how well

  I fit the clothes   the messenger
never told me my father was dead

Does it matter
where you'd been sent

a party always went along
& the wandering concealed
a purpose:

to bring under control
the trees by the river

That day back from her bath
with her black black hair

slicked as torrid
rope folded

into inverse earth   that day
of the carnivorous
crow's beak—

It happens: a story
not sensing

where to go
turns token
Look:
her palms
inlaid
with astral bones

Chitrakuta

To that mountain paradise set on fire
   by the red blossoms of the kimsuka tree

honeycombs hanging like buckets
    marking-nut trees the cry of the moorhen

the peahen's bleat the herds
   of elephants & the echoing of birds

  they arrived with open eyes Sita
gathered firewood and fruit while the brothers

  caught & killed some quick deer rabbit
wild fowl Famished they ate on the riverbank

The next day readying for the long darkness
    ahead Lakshmana sacrificed a black antelope

with a splotch of red between its horns
  Arrows removed bleeding stanched the animal

 was gently strangled then laid down
    with its legs to north then stroked

and pleasured cleaned in all the openings
   through which its life-spirit had fled: mouth nose

     eyes ears navel penis anus hooves
In the beginning the gods accepted man

as victim Later the ability to be sacrificed
    passed from him into the antelope and horse

From horse into cattle from cattle
   into sheep from sheep into goat then from

goats into the earth   so all the world
   was touched by our humility   our

      complicity   Outside the leaf-thatched hut
the animal was raised on a spit and roasted

      until it had attained a deep   dark brown colour
Then   chanting the appropriate verses   taking care

      not to split the bones   Rama carved the animal
limb by limb   cut by cut   setting aside the grain

      of its hair   the pumice of its skin   taking into him only
the fire of the flesh   the fat of its marrow

The Jeweled Deer

And later
when you yourself chased
the deer

no one could hear
the single cry
the forest dark and

inexpressible   A little ways in

and you no longer knew
where the
floor was

The Jeweled Deer

Even Raghava's mind
liquefied in that creature's
unhurried gaze

emeralds & rubies & malachite
& highlights of gold & silver

the celestial deer in the sky
this one here on earth

Raghava wanted it
was entitled to it   probably killed a second
to reassure the fact:

तत् सारम् अखिलम् नॄणाम् धनम् निचय वर्धनम् |
मनसा चिन्तितम् सर्वम् यथा शुक्रस्य लक्ष्मण || ३-४३-३३
tat sāram akhilam nṝṇām dhanam nicaya vardhanam |
manasā cintitam sarvam yathā śukrasya lakṣmaṇa || 3-43-33 *

Mahabharata Udyoga Parva:
manushyebhya samaadatte shukrah cintaa aarjitam dhanam

(the dreams of everyday people
fill up Shukra's coffers)

*all the wealth of the forest / is the human king's to take for his own // just
as whatever Shukra thinks of / instantly lands in his vault

Lakshmana

Where do these messages go?
  Where do the antelope run?

Lakshmana his elder brother's slave
Lakshmana with sword and double quiver
Lakshmana unsleeping
Lakshmana the strategist
Lakshmana fixer
Lakshmana front and centre
                    never sidekick
Lakshmana married but single forever
Lakshmana architect of
                    their lavish hut

Surpanakha

[Nasik]

The cut bone
            of her nose—

where is it? Buried under
the video parlors & gambling shops
        of Tiwandha Chowk?
        And where's she herself
    that widow wandering the forest
        with her sad hunger?
    Gone   gone are the thick woods everyone
        says were here   vaporized
        into the name of a place
        Nasik   the intersections
            Tulsi's text sprouted
        from the great   sixteenth
        century rains   The truth is
            we will not forget
    the violence or bury it—how could we
        we will wrap the violence in grim
            sad compromise into our piety

    So was there an exact location where she was violated?
Perhaps here by the only temple to Lakshmana in the country
        where a bespectacled lady
        sits at a table with a hundi
    and announces the call for donations?

        On the wall   the stark cartoonish tableau:
    Surpanakha's shocked and bloodied face

        The incredible act of Rama's brother
    hunted by the distance of belief

Or maybe by the peepal tree behind the main shrine
wrapped in red thread

      Was it here
      the peace

of Lakshmana's meditation
disturbed by her appearance?

The yakshi   The beautiful Meenakshi
     The rakshasi that manifests only

in the beholder's eye—never to herself

Aaranyani

They say the goddess of love is steadfast   they lie:
I   Aaranyani of the wide fish eyes   whom Rama goaded so indecently

I'm Sita and then her opposite   by turns

They say the goddess of desire is young   they lie:
I   Aaranyani   the irresistible   who have lived so long in the forest
    can't even remember what towns are like

I take the men from their wives   I am what I am

They say the goddess of the jungle is unruly   they lie
I   Aaranyani   sweet with the scent of the dark   who made Sita
    cower and cling

I'm the faint breeze against the dew on your cheek

They say the goddess of beauty is weak   they lie:
I   Aaranyani of the long nails   who know the thousand forms of pleasure

I'll swoop down and swallow you with your juices

They say the goddess of poetry is fair-skinned   they lie:
I   Aaranyani   face bloodied by Lakshmana

I'm dark   and blue   a blue lotus bud

Sita's Arguments

Rama,

three are the evil addictive
products of desire in men:

the first   which you might call insincere talk
        is bad enough

    worse is a roving eye
    but worst is a pointless murderlust

Rama   you've never loved or looked at
        anyone but me   you've never lied

    and never will   but your closeness
    to your weapons corrupts you

    Do you remember that monk
who accepted the gift of a sword for safekeeping

    from that disrupter of ambition Indra
        dressed up as a soldier?

Taking the entrustment with great seriousness
        he kept the weapon close

even when walking the forest
    for fruits or tubers—

    by degrees   living with it
        he lost his mind and his selfhood

    The moment you see those unlike us
    entering the thickets   brother by your side

you itch to empty your arrows don't you?
　　It's true the crossbow　and the fuel

　of a burning fire can multiply
the powers of the one who deploys them

　　But where's the weapon? Where's the forest?
Where are the warrior's principles and the mendicant's code?

　Rama　let's respect the ways of the land
　　we've come to

I know I say all this
　　with a woman's weak and intemperate mind

but I love you and respect you and
　　fear for you　So don't take offence　consider

　　what I've presented

Sita

Sita   silt
of older
suffering   silt
of layers
of prayer
in the dawn-meadow
of our gathering
fawn of the furrow
the plough's blade
spared   now the mist
has arrived   time arrives
the new
stones arrive

and in the *Sitayana*
you come
to the verge
of speaking but for
the shrill wind
that keens over
the places where you
lived and were loved

The Jeweled Deer

Gathering in all his powers
every ounce of himself   Maricha

transmuted into a deer
face

mottled dark and light
blue and pink   alert ears like

sapphires   neck gently elongated
glowing moon belly

sides soft like the velvet
of the mahua flower

slim   slender legs
puffy tail tinged with all

the colours of the rainbow   And in
his skin studded everywhere with

diamonds and precious stones
he was both utterly deer-like

and unlike any deer that
had ever been seen

So with little
bleats he flitted

in and out of the   trees   made
his way to the grove where Sita

golden-skinned herself   plucked
flowers

In the clearing shone
with a sudden brightness that hurt

the eyes   Some of the other animals
　　　　　neared him and sniffed   then quickly

bolted   Hunter turned
　　　　to prey   he kept his calm

Completely still as he
was   it took a while for Sita's eyes

to find him but when they did
　　　　　she dropped her garland and stared
a full minute in awe   Then greed

or equally   just a hopeless yearning to be
　　　　　　　　fulfilled   took possession of her

Rama   that gleaming jeweled deer
nibbling at tender shoots   I must

have him   Whether as pet or
plaything   he would look so good

in our hut   Aren't we already
visited by herds of yak and spotted

antelope   apes   monkeys
and centaurs   And when

it's time to go
we can take him with us

He'll be the pleasure
of the palace girls   Bring him

alive if you can but if you
have to kill him I should still like his skin

stretched over a cushion of straw
it would make such a pretty seat

Rama and
Lakshmana stared at the wonder

glowing in the shadows like
the rabbit etched in the moon

Rama   said Lakshmana
That deer can't be real

They watched the quick darts
of its flame-like tongue

flashes of lightning in a cloud
So what if it isn't   Lakshmana

for centuries we've claimed
the beasts of the forest as ours   And

if it is Maricha
in disguise   I'll have killed it anyway

He deserves to die   we simply can't allow
the rakshasas to be in our midst

Saying this Rama set off
in pursuit   but just as he had resolved

to do so   the deer had disappeared   Following
the sounds of crushed twigs

and leaves   sighting the animal
in flares of light   leaping

to rival the sun   now close   now
far   now visible   now not   now a leg

now a diamond-studded tip
of horn   now a band of tail   Driven

half-insane Rama hurled
himself after it into

the woods   Then   spotting it in a shady
nook of the meadow unaware   he

drew his bow with the triple curve
and shot a flaming arrow that glared

snake-like and found
its mark   the deer leapt

in the air   took two steps then
tripped   then regaining its

feet   bleeding   stumbled
dragged itself away   Rama

showered more arrows and one
of them pierced

the neck   The animal
grew still   Immense pain

Maricha was beginning to feel his own
body coming back   his massive size

his two long fangs   the
glistening gold

of earrings and necklace but
before this could become

apparent   Rama felt an eerie
         moment of recognition

when the dying deer screamed
         Sita! Lakshmana!

What will Sita say about this?
Lakshmana   what's he going to do?

Then the sense of recognition gave way
         to a sickening fear   then rippling spasms

left   eye twitching   the deer
         had spoken those words in Rama's

own voice   Unable to shake or make
         sense of or forget or even just put

his mind off what this meant
         Rama killed a second deer

and carrying the meat hurriedly
retraced his steps to Janasthana

Nasik

That old town
with its network of temples
the main water tank
wide enough for the different
sects to share
and the boys that trawled
the pool-floor for coins

Each spot you brushed
with your story—
or left some hook of the real—
a tiny industry bloomed
I touched them all
on hands and knees
and in touching woke my name too
in the ancient fading
population visitor logs

Ravana

If I'd known
a woman such as she
would come to cross

my path then
spurning all
other awards I'd

have begged
only her
from Shiva

Ravana

Dressed simply but not without elegance, holding ritual staff and parasol:

radiating gloom   like an asteroid with designs on a star
like night's curved shadow that swims across the Earth
like the darkness of our Sun in its deepest explosions
like the planet Budhan about to take hold of Rohini
like Saturn advancing on Chitra
like the forest and cities and far ridges of infinity
  each planetary body with its moons   each moon that governs
        a foregone set of inhabitants
like the afterglow of a gamma ray burst
like the coma of gas that covers the nucleus of a comet
like comets   dirty snowballs   signing the skies with their anger
like the coronal holes stirring in solar wind
like clouds obscuring double stars of dwarf galaxies
like the Doppler reading suddenly shifted into the blue
    like the black sphere of the event
like the flare in a field of view
like the imaginary mind on the galactic plane
    already hollow
like haloes and brown disks with spiral arms
  like Jupiter's bloodshot eye
    like a supernova in its galactic host
 like the warm-blooded animal's infrared glow
        like the ionized air
like the untold spheres of the Kuiper belt
like the light curve of an astral orb diminishing in relation to time
like molecular clouds stanching all light behind them
like the protoplanet revealed in the eclipse
like our own moon in its uncountable rilles
    like the Jovian body
        with its back to the Sun

What Ravana Said

Sita   the forest is no place
for a lady   Let me take you
back to my palace

I want to hold you
I want to take care of you

What Sita Said

Ravana   you have
no more right to me
than does
an outcaste to
the household plates
or hearth's fire

Sita and Raavan Rajguru

Nasik

What is it pins
    the meeting of their eyes?

There at that innocuous traffic intersection
    (*"imagine this was all jungle"*)

where the Lakshman Rekha crossed:
    Ravana with nine heads missing

"Raavan Rajguru" to be precise:
    elegant and humble Brahmin with a parasol

      the skin a bright red-orange
    the moustache curled and well tended

      and the most
      striking thing

    his casual expression as
    he stands in the cage

of his shrine—"*not a shrine
but a memorial*" our guide insists—

just a few feet forever exiled
      from Sita

    and Sita half-hidden
      in the late afternoon shade

still holding in her arms
    the meal she had served

to the stranger but now
under heavier bolt

in the cage of her own shrine
—*"not a shrine"* our guide
insists *"a memorial"*—

just a few insurmountable
feet from him

What is it pins
the meeting of their eyes?

the long howl of her abduction
I press your feet with my head

Rama to the Mountain, Its Reply

How soon will you forget me if I die?
...I swear, If I forget you, let everything die.
—Jeet Thayil, "Premonition"

And in a rage he swore
    he'd kill the Earth
suffocate her waters and air
black out the sun & planets & stars

for the animals had been mute to him
    they'd looked to the Godavari to speak

and the river too was terrified of Ravana's reprisal
    and the mountains despairingly
        returned his question
          as answer:

कच्चित् क्षिति भृताम् नाथ दृष्टा सर्वाग सुंदरीम् ‖ ३-६४-२९
रामा रम्ये वनोद् देशे मया विरहिता त्वया ।

kaccit kṣiti bhṛtām nātha dṛṣṭā sarvāmga sumdarīm ‖ 3-64-29
rāmā ramye vanod deśe mayā virahitā tvayā ।

somehow   earth-supporting lord
  seen the one
lovely in all her limbs?
In the beauty   the beauty of the woodlands
                        I lost her

somehow   earth-supporting lord
    seen the one
lovely in all her limbs
Rama, in the beauty of the woodlands
                      you lost her

Gone

What What's that sound I hear no it's not the tinkling of anklets it's the cooing of doves O ruined it ruined everything kadamba tree bilva whose fruit I hold caress in my hands o kakuba tree her thighs O where is she Kill you Kill all of you tiger tell me haven't you seen my love you coward I'll rip your entrails out wreck this miserable earth we're standing on deer o gentle deer come here no come here don't run away tell me don't you know where they've taken her my love I'm so empty I'll kill myself I'll kill you Lakshmana here feel my arrow feel my knife bleed bleed as I bleed how would you like to bleed over there O bees around the tilaka O asoka tree of grief O river can't you flow a little slower slow down you must have seen her go you must have why I'll choke you I'll set this whole forest on fire I'll pummel this planet to dust Does nothing answer Why does nothing speak O palmyra palm forget your fruits my love has nowhere to go nothing to do O lovely O death O ash-smeared face come for me O blister of arm and hands O bee O Sita in her sexy yellow silks O cloud O endless pit O my throbbing arm my left eye why does it twitch like that O come for me let all the people die let all the animals die let everything die let it burn let it burn O the koel

      mocks me with its morning song

Theological Reading

yadi mām āśrama gatam vaidehī na abhibhāṣate |
punaḥ prahasitā sītā vinaśiṣyāmi lakṣmaṇa || 3-58-10

यदि माम् आश्रम गतम् वैदेही न अभिभाषते |
पुन: प्रहसिता सीता विनशिष्यामि लक्ष्मण || ३-५८-१०

If I'm not back soon at the ashram with Sita and us giggling about
  some dumb thing   I'll breathe my last   Lakshmana

    rosham aahaarayat tiivram

   evokes an uncanny anger

    shokam aaharayet tiivram

   evokes an uncanny sorrow

    shokam aaharayet tiivram

"Hence, Rama really wept for Seetha and, in fact, gods really weep
even for us, madly and sadly, but we do not care or wish to care"

Winter

Winter
    the wished-for season

  the waters too cold   the light cut

      by wind

no more sleeping in the open

                    the sun-disk   red
            against the snow

        the moon
a mirror
        blinded by sighs

    Yojanas   from here
their heads   grow out
their knees   father's
feet find   blessing

Jatayu the Vulture

Jatayu   you who
darkened the earth
with your great
spiky-fingered
wing-shadow
cruising the gully in
the vastness of your arms
longish legs
dangling   relaxed   under whose
landing heft the boughs would sag   companion
in the skies   secret family member whom I'd not known
but for your long-ago friendship with my father
Now I sing your elegy my throat goes dry you lying there
blue body like a storm cloud
chest white as milk white as snow your back
and your grand choker of white feathers
your wings still in layers
like a suit of armor
Now you're dead no one remains to eat
the dead   Your great sheltering wings apart you're naked
smaller your great force like
a forest fire snuffed Jatayu
I never knew
you and you
are gone you
are withered
smoke   the snow
of ashes   the white
rock face you
are the great
Jatayu
vanished be-
-hind the ling-
-ering after image on
the pyre
the slowly closing
gap of your
sky this song

BOOK TWO

Dreams & Nightmares

...a region of their existence for which the term "the unconscious" would only be a harmless euphemism...
—Jean Améry, translated by John D. Barlow

...I think I could bear it.

I cannot think I could bear it.

—Robert Duncan

...for fire cannot be trusted; it not only offends gods, but also destroys people, grains, cattle, gold, raw materials and such. Also the acquisition of a fort with its property all destroyed is a source of further loss...

—Kautilya, translated by R. Shamasastry

You've come to me unarmed that's
    good is that a bottle of wine
  between us   too bad   I've a
  headache: neck-knot

constant as those blossoms cut only
        from   dusk's
    ventriloqual meadow

i. Kishkinda

To Crimson

kṛmi rāga peristome   (Kishkindakanda 23.13)

Kermes is a genus of scale insects in the order Hemiptera . . . (Wikipedia)

One commentary: "red, the colour of an indragopa"

Is there not yet
a word for blood?

Must your crushed skeleton
            preserve it?

How far did you come
to vend to me

the vivid of that rouge
What will made you   and made

a husked crawler of you
nibbling through the lexicons

krmi to crimson to qirmiz
crimson qirmiz to krmi

What hands arrived you
under embroidered lock

not as colony but shade
that all mortal eyes

could be blessed under
the glancing blade

You are wet soil
oil to light the fingers   the cloak

that kings ought to wear
as also the song

of secret import
offered at best price

to the rare curled fear
that finds it   that wants it

most   Now bring me my canvas
bring me your stanza

the sun's light strikes   You are
the warrior's last

as it leaves him   but never from
the urge to forget   always

for the little flags
curling up the stem

To Amar Chitra Katha

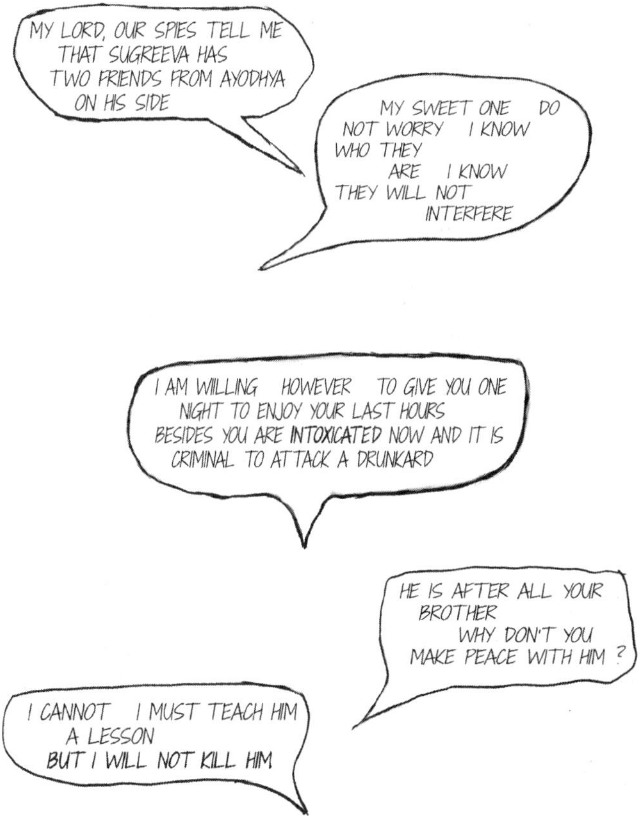

We remember   we remember the figures   the outfits
           the arrows tipping from quiver

                 the bolts of tied cloth
           the sudden implied touch

        between king and concubine   What
        secret thoughts I had   Amar Chitra Katha   reading you

           in public in the complete absence
           of shame   in the reason

to finally like parents   And the names
        of series to come: we kept them

        like lanterns in the world   Disappear   disappear
                 I do   in a panel

     White birds at the corner
and Rama the blueness of his

           body that must come
from you and you

        alone   And indeed with the truth remade
        chewed to balm the rawer instincts   what worked

           on us still was sharp
           flying lines of action

              quick blade strokes against
        the wideness of blue or pale yellow—

           and splatter where
           the arrow had breached

           a chest   And going West
        with the glow in upper panel

I thought even recognized
melancholy wisps of cloud

taken from the Pahari Masters
    also the tight setup

(crosshatching) in the vistas of the Phantom
    the interiors of Modesty Blaise   There were hidden

    puzzles   hastening accuracies
            even along your veneer

            of perpetual moral instruction—
    and there was that cover that haunted me most:

            the Great Vali about
        to be assassinated   by our God

O RAMA WHAT RIGHT DID YOU HAVE TO KILL ME - I WHO HAD FULL FAITH IN YOUR VIRTUE AND WISDOM? I HAVE DONE YOU NO HARM
I KNOW YOU CAME TO SUGREEVA FOR HELP IF YOU HAD ONLY ASKED ME ONCE I WOULD HAVE CAPTURED RAVANA AND BROUGHT HIM TO YOU
VALI, IT IS THE **DUTY** OF THE KING TO METE OUT JUSTICE... YOU HAVE WRONGED YOUR BROTHER WHOM YOU SHOULD HAVE CHERISHED AS YOUR SON YOU **DESERVE** TO **DIE**

The Arrow

Great hero   Vali   splayed in a mandala of gore
      reposed   as if under crimson-dyed sheets
cruor and dirt congealed

                              Bull among simians
Sugriva   *got what he wanted*
a single arrow saved him   *now*
        he has nothing to fear
      and Vali
that shaft sticking out your chest
makes it hard for me   to embrace you   to ease your return
                        to the five elements
      saying this Nila drew the arrow
from Vali's torn breast

                        snake harbouring poison
                              pulled from mountain crevice

                        and sharpened bone of
                                the arrowhead
                        splitting the sun's rays
                              western peak at dusk

                        and the clouds
                              darkened shrouds
                        brushed the earth's face
                              in their passing

                        then like a newly sprouted spring
where the departed arrow
                        had hooked to the bone
      gently at first   with sudden bursts of force
came hard   hemoglobinous sprays   into
                                coppery ochre
                        of green mountain soil
                        Vali's blood   no longer just his own
      and the whole   of the coming war

whispered   into the wound
But what's the use   when an evil act   finds its means
Vali   whom thousands   of Simians depended on
    Vali   securely   held in the arms of death

Then Tara like a star   dropped from heavens
  went to her husband   took his lips
                                        smudging   wiping off of him
that thick slime   of war-mud   moistened
  by her own sobs   crushed pollen
      on the stiffening bark
    of his skin   *the long hostility*
is at an end   *this dastardly act*
has ruined us

                                        said she
                                        to Angada

(still a boy   he had
not quite learnt to weep)

                                Come my son
                                yellow-eyed child
                                Salute your royal father
                snuffed out   like the risen sun
        in dark and sudden circumstances
                Come   bury your father   the hero
            so that the earth
            may send him
    to the next   country without languages

Thus was a great mortal buried in the soil
            and by this act   laid that arrow in his arms
        to accompany him   sacrificed beast
    the decades-long dispute   between brothers

The Arrow

Mist comes as knowledge
  Who are the Simians

 Do they fight over
their lovers as we do?

 Have they known fire
Does their blood run to

   the forehead
         as does ours
  Do they find cause

to regret the censuring hand
 When Vaidehi is not seen
She becomes the weeping curve

of hills   wheels that have left
 their traces   trees bare

    and hanging in shame
 breeze that carried

    the whiff of flame
 and particles of snow

    the slow
  unburdening boughs

   tightly holding creepers
  (Drunk maidens
     of the palace)

Who are the Simians
Are their cities like ours

their courts as unforgiving?
Do they love wine

as we do   O dew that whitens
the grass-tips

Shadow fringes dart
in peripheral sight

a shaking in the branches

The folks that live up here
kingdoms in the lamp-lit caves

where killing a liquor-slowed warrior
is like slaughtering a grown

child in the womb...

Ruinous as the house is ruinous
under the bridge

2.

The rains are coming

The Pampa blooms
the Pampa does not bloom

If I were writing in Sanskrit
I'd open with landscapes

of ravishable beauty
rain hard lashing in sheets

the ground unquenched and electrified
the flora in long careening lists—

sala tamasa champaka
ankola ashoka asvatema   biribilva
chūrnaka champaka karnikara
chava
gajapushpi kakhubka
kurabakha kutashalmali
nagavrksha
paaribhadhraka priyagu
pumnaga shimsapa
tanda   syayesha
tinisa uddhaalaka
vanjula
vasanthi

—many trees lost or obscure to us
if ever they were real

Wordcraft remains
a mocking curlicued salt

All else decays
and the "language of the gods"

—as understood by the human—
diminished by this
very act   fire hidden under ash

wicked man beneath
the self-appointed saint

But landscape landscape   landscape with
animals with peacocks & hornbills

a tiger cub or   a pet leopard
kept at the hut

The leaves warping in or foliate
  fragrant or repellant

the snakes tucked in boughs
or cooling off in pools

    the bears wrestling the burlier Simians
    the rocks of many hues

        No city is intact without
                a forest

      and every true forest
      must encompass   the city: true

                3.

    "Hanuman with the authority
        of Sugriva"

          Emissary
      Simian but at heart

          like a boy
        not quite right for

the message   five toes to tail
        to groin to head

  World as seen from the perch
    of Hanuman's shoulders

    (only when he understands)
    at day's end it is the radiance

        that follows the sun

Sugriva looks away
when Rama arrives

Only this matters:
they've both lost rights

to a wife (your wife is my
wife is your wife is my wife is...)

"The past is a foreign country" etc.
   Do they do things
               differently there?

Growl Sugriva growl
Scream Sugriva scream

Carry by your voice to
unmoored lands—

Rishyamuka's peak
river as boundary   Beyond

only a garland of
champaka blossoms

will tell you from
your elder brother   who is tossing around

boulders and snapping trunks
just to calm the hell down

◆

"Rama pressed
the Simian king's hand"

Someone broke off large
trunks of sāl & they sat

Rama kicked the skeletons
of monsters past

with his toe
sukham ānantaryam

(next in sequence)
Ramanuja's commentary:

"whether contemptible or not
I'll do as you wish"

(*garhitam agarhitam
tavābhimatam karisyami eva*)

One more time
the arrow in the back

and it's not nature's law
that has been violated

here   even if Vali makes a
case for that

with his blood searing
the surprised soil:

(*Rama   you're nothing but a pit
hidden in the overgrown grass —*

*only five among the five-clawed creatures
can be eaten by brahmins and kshatriyas —*

*the hedgehog   the porcupine
the lizard   the rabbit   the turtle*)

(*rhinoceri later substituted in this list
that seemed so clear*)

Vali his mouth gone dry
　　falls silent

"The problem of Rama's colour"
"fine colour and brightness"

　　"bright as gold"
"the gold is taken in two

different states to apply
　　to two different

men: one dark   the other
　　yellow" (the "maxim of the
people with umbrellas")

Rama's response disappointing
　　in our era at least—

　　kāryakārana
　　"process"
　"cause and effect"

—then the fire-bonding ceremony
　　of Rama and Sugriva

4.

And we could have moved on

but for the persistent question of
　　Vali's corpse in the field

　　or always   missing
in the thatched disguise of the pyre

Great hero
sluiced in a star of gore

sleeping under crimson sheets
cruor-caked

great bull   Got what he
wanted now   Sugriva

that shaft sticking out your chest
makes it hard for me to embrace you

(Saying this Nila in mercy tore away the arrow
from the breast that harboured it)

= poison snake in the crevice
sharpened   bone   tip

Western   peak   at d   usk

Where the newly departed arrowhead
hooked on a cartilage

sprout a spring
gentle at first

then hemoglobinous bursts

into the copper
of that mountain soil

with the whole of the warcoming
whispered into the wound

Vali's wife Tara dropped
as if from the heavens

went to her husband   Took his lips
  crushed as pollen

on the stiffening bark

        Hanuman suggests   Angada (the son)
Tara weighs the hundred sins but

"this long hostility
          is at an end"

(the boy hadn't learnt to weep)

        her lap
        masākārtho dhūmah—

  "the smoke for the sake
of the mosquitoes"

        shunya desha jigisayā

  "with the desire for/
    by reason of/
conquering an
    empty land"

harivāgurayā : "monkey snare"

  (Tilaka: "because shaped
like a snare the city itself

  is a monkey trap")

  nispartrayitam:

  "make leafless"

or

"pierce through with an arrow"

Sample Direction: East

Spoken by Sugriva to the search parties

Go soldiers go find Sita
You have a month before I kill you

Go   not just below or skyward but howling out
from the mouths of rivers—the Yamuna
                    that comes from Mt. Kalindi

the Saraswati and others
          now rivening golden

paths underground: the Shona   the Mahi
                    the Kaalamahi...

and don't forget Brahmanada
Videha   Maalava   Kashi   Kosala

          Magadh   or provinces like
          Pudra   Anga   Koshakara

(but wait   "koshakara"
     in the dictionary

is also a silkworm   or one who makes
     scabbards   or a lexicographer...?)   Anyway   if you're

          still drawing a blank
keep going   ever more cautiously on   on

to the lands without horizon
     the tract of the sky desert
               —stark dwellings among silver mines—

          and on through stretches of more
          nothingness to the wards

of people with ears that flap down
and cover their bodies like cloaks

or indeed   where people with lips
	for ears eat with them

Then by such luck make
	your way downriver

to the sectors of the superfast
	or the realms of the superslow

the governments of the three-membered
not to mention the single-footed

the circuits of those whose genitals
turn out to be bigger than their bodies   of those who

headless   talk through chests
and on to the territories of faces etched

on no more than a single living limb—
	arm or leg—and

of humans who consist solely of skull
	with a brahmin's topknot and a single eye

Then the zones of the long-pricked tricksters
	with bones in hand

and those of the sad upside-down monsters
	who poop in the air

and nations where plants grow noses
Regions of famous gold-digging ants

horses with mouths of iron and
areas of many other creatures   unpleasant

but also powerful
Societies of casual cannibalism:

(of course   we all are to some extent my soldiers)
and nooks of gorgeous kiratas with

towering locks   glistening skin
island dwellers   raw fish connoisseurs and

as for the well-known tigermen—bottom-
or top-half tiger—hidden in

the waters   be wary of them
Soldiers   don't leave

anywhere unsearched   do it as
only you can do

mount the mountains
hopscotch or boat-job your way

right to those peripheral reaches of the Jambu Dvipa
And there at the oceans' far coast you'll come to

the blood-red Lohita and the groves
of the silk-cotton tree

after which the place might have been named
But if you still haven't found Sita   well

it's better   get back to the journey
shrinking from the very passage

till you hit the dominions of the ones that live
by hanging downward

and just ahead of that   those who
are burnt to cinders every day

but wake up fine and whole
as the night falls on the water and

falls on the ink
that is the incorruptible

abstract essence of water
After that when the final gold-ored ranges are seen

follow the fields of triple-branched palms
to the last peak   the wellspring

of the moon and the rising sun
and   and   and if our Sita has still not been witnessed

—pardon my heart warriors   brave souls—
you must must keep on

to the starless constituencies even further
where no one and nothing
sticks to a name

Un Trou

The Simian squads fanned out
across and beyond the villages of the Vindhyas

searching for Sita   or some trace of where
or by whom she might have been taken

Entering   exhausting the forests
day by day

regrouping each night in growing despair
leavened only by intoxicants

and the gloam of companionship   they strayed
into a more arid zone of rocks and boulders—

barren   denuded
red or orange craggy foothills

scraggly trees
with whitened leaves or rattling seedpods

It was a land that had once been lush
scourged by the blind anger of a Brahmin

grieving the loss of a son
Now he too

had died but his legacy of
drought remained

Weathered in the harsh noons and dirty winds
thoughts of Sita scrambled

by a more literal thirst   they
scaled the bare rock faces

scrambled to shade
                    where it could be found

          Sniffing furiously
          for signs of water

                    grew weak
                    and slowly crazy

                    By and by   in such tortured
faltering exploration   one day

                    going round a hill
                              glimpsed

                    green foliage entwining
                    into the rock   that

          dūrgarkshabila: first just
                    a hint of night   in the coils

          of a creeper grove   but
          further guarded   as if by

                    demonic curtains
                    of shade

          There   bees circled in
a honey haze   fragrance flung

                    from flowers brightly
                    red or purple

          superfluous strewn or
          hanging heavy

                    from stems
                              Suddenly

                    explosions of wing
          kraunchas   swan   cranes   crows

          shooting from that grove
     pink geese dripping dew

               and crimson pollen
               Dizzy and bewildered

     those alpha apes aroused
          by such wet thoughts

               those Simians   teeth
          grinding   hastened toward

                    the wonder
               with their strength

          renewing   Hanuman sent
     a tentative first foot in the hole

     deeper and deeper disappeared
                    his leg

               Evidently there was
          a drop in there   an opening out

               a cave   a cavern   Tree roots
               twisted hungrily into it

                    the foot-grass
               a deep deep green

     Like the obscene zone of the Daityas
               looking   hearing all the world's creatures

               echoing from inside
               and too those

who had simply arrived at this same threshold
Hard to see   but harder

in every way
to leave

Nor faintest trust
of sun or moon

Anyway   In   Sliding down
Fall to a glassy

mossy knoll somewhere
dark so dark you doubted

you were there
Cave water's unmistakable scent

made you move
through the passage at first

like wind unhindered but
when the press

of limb to stone
became all you'd known

under such curtained atrament
skin   hairs erect

knotting arm to arm
eight miles or more

clinging close crawling
dry throat

judgment addled
where was it   that water

Deep in the cave
they saw a light

ददृशुः   काञ्चनान्   वृक्षान्   दीप्तवैश्वानरप्रभान्
dadṛśuḥ kāñcanān vṛkṣān dīptavaiśvānaraprabhān

सालांस्तालांस्तमालांश्च पुंनागान्   वञ्जुलान्   धवान्
sālāṃs tālāṃs tamālāṃś ca puṃnāgān vañjulān dhavān

चम्पकान्   नागवृक्षांश्च   कर्णिकारांश्च   पुष्पितान्
campakān nāgavṛkṣāṃś ca karṇikārāṃś ca puṣpitān

तरुणादित्यसंकाशान्   वैदूर्यमयवेदिकान्
taruṇādityasaṃkāśān vaidūryamayavedikān

Young and tender   the sun at dawn
Cat's eye studded   in silver seats

Sealed in light from   that cat's eye blue
Flocks of birds over hidden ponds

Overgrown trees   with gold leaf bark
Glittering like   the sun at dawn

Hidden ponds flashing bronzing fish
Recurring mirror   of your desire

Airplanes and chariots   with fat gold wheels
Now you need my body   so we can be free

Softly we fall in   the silver dust seas
The planets they spin   in the minds of gods

For in this new dimness so bright
it needle-pierced the eyes produced astringent

whines   noises in the ear drugged
the proximate senses

the image of a carpet   was a carpet
the image of a lotus-blue silk shawl

was a blue silk shawl in caress of the hairs of your skin
the image of gold amphoras   plates of bell metal

heaps of the finest aloe sandalwood figurines
wine reposed in silver bowls   the sweetest tartest

fermented honeys caviar   silk cushions filled
with swan feathers   juiciest roots shoals of rippled fruit

in palanquins   deerskins   all instantly
the very things themselves

Though sucked
by their own smothered

cravings   our valiant alpha-apes
were a long while unable

even to move   gaping in
the dazzling growing

crowded terror of it
Was this paradise   with

its gods still in hiding   or
had the poor Simian soldiers

stumbled into the bylanes
of death itself?

A woman appears
mendicant in deer buck skin

hair in tattered locks
her taut and stringy body

breath pulsing through rib bones
born of penance   Doomed at the centre

collected within   feeding the light
that follows her

Synonyms: beaming

Swayamprabha <------ self [radiant/bright, luminous

brilliant, effulgent, gleaming,

lustrous, radiant, refulgent,

glittering, ~~glorious~~, glowing,

incandescent, lambent, lucent,

Hey, no worries, of course. Yes, i'm doing better today.

The dictionary won't give tons of information on how to understand the name, but it does give something, and the parts are clear. Put in svayamprabhA for the specific name enry (altho i don't think the MBh apsaras is the right woman), and put in svayamprabha (short a) to get the more general meaning: self-shining, or inherently-luminous, etc.

prabhA is a noun meaning 'brilliance, shininess', and svayam is an adjective or adverb meaning '(by) one's self or spontaneous(ly).

Shiny Yogini
where have we landed?

Tell us   tell us who
you are

—I am Swayamprabha   Maya
was my mentor   who had this place built

       to the exact specifications
of his dreams and the dreams

     of others   with the heedful
application of all

of Usana's arts and sciences   Now
I mind it purely by

       sound thought
  —Yogini

     be straight
are we dead?

—O pitiful Simians this is
neither the place

     of death nor that
of life nor

     of anything
        in between:

       it simply is
      poor Simians

       Not easy to leave
but if you so choose

        I can help

How to know
what it meant

to decide to
leave if they

still didn't know what
it had meant

to enter?
Each

thought like dew
collecting on the inseam

of a lick of stone   A place
for the eyes that

sapphire cave though
often dark

in secrets   Anything called
to mind could be

enjoyed there among serene
lakes so completely echoing

the ceiling they seemed
to rise up in points

to meet it   The tunnels unfolded in
spirals—were you going up

or down?—and alternating
phases of blue & pink

& black light—
fruit groves   pleasure coves

nested nooks miniature rock holes
dissolve & reform around

  your fingers   They gorged
themselves   got fat—

   apples   bananas   almonds
winged termites   honey brewed thick

  as gruel delicate as aperitif
   button mushrooms fragrant

    thyme and cannabis
  wild potatoes   a mouse

                 or a baby boar
they'd catch   They groomed or made love

to each other on warming floors   they
  slept   they slept   To know this

              vacancy at
    any given instant

           seemed already
    a cognizance

    of the long past
Half second   A second

Or a hundred? A million?
We Simians

    have never been
  much good

at measuring time   Visions
  in plain sight

a riff of Sita's yellow sari
dancing in the wind

hooked on a branch   *Silk*
bruised your cheek   How

come my love
how come? But boredom

always the boredom   And
oddly   as its aftertaste

in this prison beyond
seasons: guilt   Somewhere

out there was still
Sita   just a skeleton perhaps

Rama   a galaxy of anguish
Sugriva   a tall

petulant   ruthless
gilded executioner's sword

His threats   once spoken   had
somehow followed them

even here
into time's hollow   If

there was any hope
of finding her

they ought
to get back

Turned a corner
and there she was

Swayamprabha
guide us

—If you so much
as peep your eyes open
before it's done . . .

Lids shut
the dark of the outside

and the dark of the inside
were one and the same

Clutching limb to limb
they were transported

into a fine clear sun-kissed
blossom-floating windy day

on a green foothill of the Vindhyas
the ocean's rolling beat and rattle audible

from down and beyond where met
nearing the horizon

crusty white lines of surf
The end of the world?

And Sita?

The shoreless ocean
the ocean without limit

the ocean as limit
abode of Varuna

roaring and wild
with angry billows

While they'd been
busy ransacking the mountain

of Maya's design
King Sugriva's ultimatum

of one month had
slipped away   He'd be

on their trail
It was spring

Nothing could make them happy
Not the scent of wildflowers

mango and guava trees
drooping down

and covered with climbers   not
the pooling light

rousing winds   This very beauty
planted fear in the Simians' hearts

—(Tara) Let's go back in the bila
that amazing cave   We were fools to leave

—(Chorus of Simians) Yes
yes   back in the bila   back in the bila

—(Nila) Idiots! Do you think
Lakshmana won't find us there?

—(Chorus) Yes   yes   oh no! He'll
find us there   find us there

—(Tara) But at least going back
will give us a chance

save us from execution

—(Chorus) Yes   o yes   going back
going back will give us a chance

—(Angada) Enough! Sugriva will always
have dominion over us

in the land of the alive
Angada sank to the grass   sobbing

For we have opened door upon door
come out from that darkness

only to settle in this new here
that too will never be fully

illumined
And there is but one

way to walk beyond
that tyrant's reach:

we'll fast to the death
on those sands below

Immune to the arguments of Tara
and the judicious Hanuman

Angada   slowly followed by most
of his army—who could

so easily see the sense
in his words—made his way

down the hill
to the jeweled beach

They began to prepare themselves
    for the long days

            of the fast
            Seated

        calmly on gathered nests
        of kusha grass   faces

        turned East   the blades
        of that grass-nest

        on which they sat
    like tapering fingers

            pointing South   Talking
            talking into

            the night until
            the strength to speak

            began to falter   Dwelling
    on the long event-chain

                that had somehow
                    stranded them here on

            the continent's tip
            this final shore

    telling the story of Rama's exile

        Dasaratha's death
    the carnage in Janasthana

    the abduction of Sita —
        that jewel of Videha —

and the killing of Jatayu
the killing of Vali

Rama's wrath
the wrath of Sugriva

that sea of
sorrows   unrelenting in

its waves
the storm that

swallowed all and brought us
to this final resolve

Then the emptiness of
the words themselves

the translucent shells
of their souls

To ascend
truly   you had to be

gradual in the drain
of colour   in the precise

sequence of
disavowal   first no meat

then no nuts   grains or pulses
then no fruit no veg and no juice and

nothing sweet or salty
or sour then last

only water
sapped from the air

and drawn
with the breath

from hole to hole
Taste of wood

unrelenting   Those
Simians seated

like mountains
inner caverns

roaring in despair
Glowed like the honey—

cream of
a second sea   that army prone

against the waves
                    The sun's

glitter thrown
like sparks of fire

the great serpents
roiling in the hell-

depths below   And
the sea married to the sky

and the sky so completely
in the sea and

the sea-like sky and
the sky-like sea:

the king of the rivers
the mouth of the universe

and those star-rushed waves
thick with multitude

suspended like lisps
in between

At first the nights
were restless   restless

to the wake of sun
By the second rise

their vision sharper
hearing clearer

Each mote hung in the air
as if waiting

to be seen
By the fourth

the limbs
slack

the soldiers
on their

backs or sides
and the stomach

a discarded begging
bowl

The clarity
once come now

departed
And not long till

the first lines of ants
investigating the craggy

feet   the caves of ears
and noses   the first

fly on a forehead
leaning back as if

to better read
the fate written

there   O come End
did you not

always reside
in me   casting your sleep

in every cell
and membrane? Do you

not prowl like
an innocuous stranger

at every father's bed
every kingdom's

border? And the meteor
shall know us

by our purpling smoke
darkened clouds

the shrouds
and going

together we go
alone   And the hillside against

the beach   was for a long while
         a graven feast

Sampati

Wingless   armless   all bone   he clung
like a tree-root to a rock

with his nether claws   What he'd seen
was a man like a dark-purple

storm cloud streaked
by a wisp

of yellow sari
then a face

a woman's   maybe
turning to him while

swept away
In Sampati's parched

mind it had begged only
the pleasant thought

of what those humans
might have tasted like   Yum   Yum

Abandoned aging prince
of the vultures

how long   how long do you go
without a meal?

A little while later caught
a new whiff of promise

from the sea   And
a voice in him also with the smell:

Simian dead Simian
abandoned Simian meat!
That way—

down this side
through this cave

to a view
of the patina'd

sands where
like some gurgling gift

of the gods the
splayed bodies in

the dessicating late
afternoon sun

That sky-rover's
electric atman
leapt at the sight

Late guest to the wedding
ravenous Fate

let this food long ordained for me
be mine

परम्पराणां भक्षिष्ये   *paramparāṇām bhakshishye*
वानराणां मृतं मृतम्   *vānarāṇām mṛtam mṛtam*

death as follows death
one after delectable one
let me
eat them eat them

so said the noble bird
on seeing those once-jumping beasts

couched in little grass plates
carved out in lines on the sand

"Look! Yama the god of death
is also born of the sun—

on the pretext of Sita's disappearance
he's come to eat us up"

But the meal itself
let's not forget

was in turn a mirage
like those flightless millennia spent

on the mountain wait—
once he and brother Jatayu
glancing invincible fresh from Vritra's
defeat   from the conquering
of even the king of the gods when like
champions of the sky they'd taken
the sun as target from
its farther mountain   higher
and higher they
charged toward it
until the cities
arrayed below
were no bigger
than chariot wheels
the forests
like plots of grass
the hills like gravel stones
and in between
threads of rivers
and soon the great mountains too

              no more than
            elephants gathered
         at a pond and as they hurtled
            toward it the sun-star
            encircled in garlands
         of its raybeams   they shone
         at first then withered and broke
              in sweats   tired
            and afraid   a sudden
            doldrums as if cooked
              in rudderless air
      and Sampati's brother fainted and fell
         from that sky and he   Sampati
            tried to shelter Jatayu
      with wings themselves burning and
              when the wings
              were ashes fell
              deep down from
         all news of his brother   It was after
            this came   the eight

            thousand years
              of hunger

         Sampati   could
      it be? Is it Rama's story

   come at last to gather
   you in its arms?

         Could it be
      you'd acquire

         wings again?
      That you'd take   after

         all this while as if first steps
      back into flight   hitching

on thermals above us? As with
  the clarity and strength

  that can somehow seep back
after long illness

   how the unlikely story
     wants to eat

how life feeds on itself
  and keeps on burning

Simians, Plural

ten
thousand trillion
or more arriving
from every direction troops
in phalanxes on the road or
bounding in red blazes through trees
blacking the sky ravaging foliage and in
hamlets or even whole cities coursing through backyards
kitchens bedrooms amphoras lamps knocked to the side pomegranates
bitten clean or abandoned private pools behind country houses little
gardens fields orchards grain piles
     apes Simians whatever you call them
bribed begged cajoled drafted or just wrenched from their honey-drunk orgies
     intimate happy happy mango-smacking
   conscripted presbytin or macaca trachypithecus semnopithecus vigilant
gibbons dignified slow loris three hundred million at least from mt. anjana one
hundred thousand million from mt. kailasa a thousand trillion from across
       the himalayas
ascetic hoolocks   arms in front double the length of their legs langurs
    with fur tawny as a lion's or golden langurs their cream coats in the
    sun capped langurs with bright red pricks   cheeks rhesus
macaques fierce as mars scratching babies along the way teasing scholars grabbing
    women   lion-tailed macaques with dark hair coolly falling from trees to
    cross paths swooping musical calls or manly voices or arch guttural barks
    Simians that know the routes through every neck and hollow of every wood
       Vanaras from the star-kissed mountains or those
red as arsenic from the caves primates big as bears stronger than elephants eight
    hundred million   at least from the tamala groves near the shore fierce cow-
    tailed monkeys light-eyed troops from settlements in pilgrim towns
       sons of gods gandharvas ghouls shapeshifters shoplifters generals
officers jawans
chiefs clerks cooks scribes Simians for hire dharma-bound Simians old friends
    embracing   new brawls sparking ranged in packs or rows or queues or
    gangs or battalions with the smell of their sweat their honey liquor brewing
    their   smoke their grunts and expectant barks the thick

hanging dust raised by their feet the din of their drums their catcalls winding
back into the hazy distance sending electric thrills through the bodies

of Rama & Lakshmana as they stood there
almost anonymous   even ignored except for sideways glances across
the crowd   wrapped in crowd   choking the air   newly conscious

Sugriva's Roar

His greatest asset   his larynx:
Sugriva's unruly roar shook

the shivering birds
out of the sky drained the complexion

from the faces
of fair-skinned high-born ladies

paled the cows and
scattered the deer   scared

the horses   knocked at least the sadder
fruit from trees

boiled the streams cooked the fish cracked
as thunder behind the mountains

and echoed back fiercely in waves   that
Simian-monarch's roar: so terrible

it shook even the susurrating bones
of Sugriva himself

God Praise the Nematodes

God praise the nematodes
and the mammals idling in the garbage
God praise the absence of god
in the water   in the transplanted salt
of the sea

in the figure of rain
obscured by the blackened pane
in the street that runs from me
and runs to me

But is "the street" what we should call it?
More sadak than raasta
It is short   Not bustling never empty
but gently stirring   Or scraping with
the abrasiveness of stone

The Mountain

Lighting on something to launch him across
the seas   Hanuman leaned a giant foot
against Mt. Mahendra

The large boulders
of that unsurpassable mountain
afflicted by our mahatman's fat foot

cracked & roared like musth elephants twin-mouthed
under lion attack
—fine powder clouds
of clay & sand & black silt
jets of water
shot from stone
trills of souls released—

birds broken into that yellow sky

And as the report
flared down the slope
in speech
of timber-snapped shower
rock   pebble   ice
even the deep-
root-entwining trees began
to capitulate

Then all the creatures   were ground
to bone dust   or flung
skywards

In an instant
Hanuman
had shot
up and across the seas

And the mountain
was again a stranger

cut from his cohort

wandering in
time's wilderness

ii. Lanka

From *"Trijata's Dream,"* by Ron Padgett

Translated from the Sundarakanda *of Valmiki's* Ramayana

And again I saw him
        your great god!
                falling frozen in terror
                        and crashing on the earth!
and jumping up—wha?
        ripping rags to shreds fugghhhk! fla
    aggghhh! kiizaaaagh!! ga blaagghhh!
        with waves of chaos swirling from his presence

[...]

And then billions of demons
        in red flowers and red clothes
                        went past
     playing stringed instruments
         and singing
      and drinking and laughing

And I saw the magic city of Lanka
    elephants chariots horses
  city gates and graceful arches
I saw all of you in screaming red
      fall into a hole
        full of shit!

Alliterative Kennings

Rama   riparian   by the rectory abandoned

Serpentine sisterhood in lieu of Sita

Hanuman whose hours go hunting
  whistling through the holes
    like the fatherly wind
        the breath
        too holy to hold

  Ravana the rapturous
    the ravenous
  in his relish to be
the master raptor—the road
  to who one is
  at night or in the bright
  of day resolving

Lakshmana: the last   the letter of
  the law but also
the outlawed logic against
lunatics   Lakshmana
  left to the lemmings

Surpanakha   soothing songs
      of slaughter
  saying to no one
  her cruelty-borne sighs
      Starlet sizzler
    the state seeks to set a price
        on your solitude

Hanuman Among the Satellites

The earth curved athwart
its thin blue reach   Impotence

of evidence   So when Hanuman briefly
understood his powers   changed

from cat-size   grew large
the yellow misleading skies

called to him   the rushing blackness
of the galaxies called to him

and before any thought he was
swishing in air

tail by itself to mimic the comet streaks
bright red butt a lantern

And in the farthest stratosphere
this most innocent of innocents

commingled with
the man-made aerials

their steady spidery
frames   what they said

to the inconsolable flare
of cities below:

Reason is the overrated
husband of anger

Reason is half the knowledge
of heart

And with the perfection of Sanskrit
    in the ape-lips

    came the whispering self-
      assurances that

        wherever   people wear beasts for skin
beasts wear people-skin   Each

        own music
      that milled inside

Lanka

1.

Low in the country lies Lanka
  the city by the shore
Forge and forgery means Lanka
  the city by the shore
 Leave me alone says Lanka implacable

Lanka lark line in the cirrus
  when you burned it was brighter
   for the gold of your minarets

2.

The goddess that guards the city
  is also the city

No password suffices
  but unremembered force

  You might be called
 and you will answer

Was the elephant grass higher than your head
  when you struggled through

surrounded? The walls rose from it
the snipers in their turrets

 The season arrives with scorpions
  but there's still one door
  to let you in

3.

The artifices will not leave us
 Strange pain in the chest is it homesick
The texture of the skin as plastic
    the street with the tailor
        still at his machine

I say to you   do you not want
     the kingdom of it all
with every custom known and unrejected
It is foolish   my friends   the Lankans
    go about their lives
Everything they speak is half a dialect
    the rich at their rooftop soirees
     the poor in the slipstream
      of the temple car
   and the idol in front just shaking
       on her seat

In the new moon
    the sea at spring tide
   padlock the doors
     let the inner sanctum
        field the filth of ash
of Lanka   love that enumerated
     secrets

4.

Safer in the evening than by treacherous day was Lanka
   knowing what you want you found a way in Lanka

    Red streaks across the marble of the moon
    The sea reached the bedroom by its spray in Lanka

Rakshasas all out in their finest gold
torch-lit colours that banished the grey from Lanka

Fancy in its piazzas   lush in its groves
lateness was for the scrofulous strays in Lanka

Only Sita shivered from stubbornness & a broken heart
No longer could she tell the dawn from
the one who prayed in Lanka

Ravana's Rooms (Take One)

And then in midnight sky abutted
    as if to spill its milk
among digressions of white light

  witnessed the Ape in his intellect
           the powers of our moon:

  like a bull in heat   lumen
    among Brahman cows

    trampling the world's sin
    nursing the great oceans

  the ruler of the dark rose even
    as Hanuman looked on

over earth   over mountains   over water
    like a swan in a silver cage

  like the ox with the highest hump
like the rub that always melted bitterness

  in the hearts of young lovers
And sleepy or smiley or soughing in thrall

    those hours were full of wives being
    hugged by their others
      as flowers curled on a tree

    Lap in lap devoted
under endless rows of lamps

  nowhere did he see Sita:
           withdrawn

like a peahen in the forest
    from the dance

With time he stole into Ravana's house
    the biggest of them all by law

He passed a flying chariot
        parked in a hangar

    walked through gardens
    like synchronized textbooks

the casual rare metals   the inner courtyards
        with their delicate fruit

... And as a key comes to fit a lock
he came to Ravana's chambers

        Suddenly underwater there
    in a seabed cave

that felt sort of like home—
    a home long forgotten

        Wolves and winged chariots
    on the walls   the banquet
                        abandoned

    being there then the whiff
of cooked meat   brewed drink

made for the sharpest of breezes
    "Come here" it called

            as kin
        to closest kin

The room itself was mistress to Ravana
the pictures on its carpet

like galactic maps
its stars   their dependents and debris

its planetary systems crammed with inhabitants
its countries and capital cities
glimmering in the dark

Sounded by insects in fevered flight
the perfume tangled in tapestries

last smoke withered from the ends
of incense sticks

the white sacrificial flowers

In short   that hall made you happy
just as a mother appeased the five senses

& the gilded flame of the lamp
stuck in thought

was like a gambler defeated by
greater gamblers

Thought Hanuman: Ravana is the cause
Then

he saw the co-wives and lovers
past the turning of the night

under drink's deep somnolence—
soundless in their ornaments—

that listless huddle
calm as a grove

circled by swans and bees
The rows of teeth

behind lips
the eyes coyly behind lids

Hanuman saw and could scent
those beings of multiple provenance

Those faces closed   like lotuses in the night
opened   like lotuses in the light

those lotus faces sure
by addled bees fixed on

over and over and over
Thus he reasoned

those faces equaled lotuses
in each and all of their qualities

That hall of His was patinated
by wives

like Autumn's cloudless sky by stars
and Ravana   the planet

they contemplated
Some of the lovers were meteors

that had fallen from the skies
with their residue of good works

Those co-wives of the thick
dismantled gardens & scattered gems

smudged tilaks on foreheads
disturbed anklets

afterglow of pearl on chest
creepers trampled underfoot by swans

The chrysoberyl seemed to showcase
     hummingbirds

Red brooches like miniature geese
  embroidered on the scene

  settled on nipples or curves or haunches
    that were like dunes banking

rivers of silken fabric
  with crocodiles at the shore

Tattoos and markings
  scarves and coverings

   flittered under breath
fabric like flag at the throat

And the wives' fermented breath
  tickled Him in his sleeps

While pretending they were each Ravana
    they kissed each other   once more once more

  Thus they brought
delight to their equals

Some made pillows of arms
  & pits & hollows

and in friendship in the heat
  lips fell on shoulders

calves wrangled thighs
limbs wound round

one another and another and another
The co-wives were a threaded necklace

of dragonflies   in the forest
everything had entwined

the trees and the roots and
the bushes and the bears

No longer could end be told
from beginnings

no longer the sweetness from the savour
no longer the body from the bodies it had

known or been apprehended by
no longer loves from appendages and faces merged

the bones and the hair and the
swelling roughnesses

Thus Ravana slept in comfort on
that patchwork of

phosphorescent skin and
the lamps witnessed it all

with unblinking eyes
And of those who held Him tight

who of them had been stolen and who simply
surrendered to their own wishes?

Not one there had been forced
he hoped   not one there not

a lover but   not one there not forced
Innocent Hanuman surmised

it would have been perfect if
Ravana had just left Sita happy with her Rama

as his various co-wives and lovers
evidently were happy with Him

The Rakshasa king was a scented elephant
sleeping in a pond

his arms like fallen trees
ringed by protective silver

Scars slithered across
He'd been gouged by animal horns

King of the Rakshasas
lovers at his feet

he shone like the hiss of a snake
a vein of granite underground

swathed in silk
his face brilliant by earrings

His partners tightly holding
the instruments of their arts

The dancers whose arms &
legs had unraveled

the singer whose wordless note
saturated the breathable air

And sleep held and even embalmed
the moment

the concubines clutching the veena's
neck and gourd

or draped on a drum   the mridangam
They embraced their instruments as

another might a husband
    or a child

  Then   Hanuman   who had by now concluded
        that Sita   not yielding to

his search   had definitely died   saw
    one surely equal to her in beauty

    Clapped his hands   dinged the wall
  kissed his tail in agony   almost spilled himself

After some time   collecting together
    the great poor Simian

smoothed his coat
    by the exercise of logic

"I was that"
"Was I that?"
"That was I?"
"That I ..."

  and a sadness rose in him
from the places where no word

    had been made for it
and soured   turned to anger

bright in the safe memory of the day
        And leaving those rooms

the body parts of new people
dropped suddenly ajar

All the citizens
were ugly and deformed

all all pustules and warts
enormous mouths and

long ill-shaped eyes
He clenched his way through

head hung   gaze lowered
and the red skies wept

Ravana's Rooms (Take Two)

asks for the   that realm that

hours past the turn of midnight, lea **Room like sea** New broom erupting

in deep drunk sleep **full of creatures**

full of features fats on stitchtshirts branches

परिक्षते अर्ध रात्रे तु पान निद्रा वशम् गतम् |

क्रीहिल्या उपरतम् रात्रौ सुष्वाप बन्धवत् तदा || ५-९-३५ **dim lights sunk in thought** fairways

tributaries **gamblers** opening of tins and smoke

& mains givers of breeze and tranches

harboured in a tree   ssound in

crammed with creatures **mats depict** cat-cuckold thought

slunk **mountain tree river lake mansions hid**

in thought **in incense smoke** "DONE HERE."with a consciousness stolen

निद्रा अपहृत चेतस:

peacock soft smells of sex and eat a whole by sleep

porcupine **and red of chow & alcohol** call, intimate aand thin

BUFFALO **that calls intimate as kin** BEEF

catalytic wheezing like a sin one-boned fish

chakora (half-eaten) **"Come here"** — partridge

artless **To our unimpeachable Hanuman** silicate slim

sinless progeny of The Wind RHINOCERI walawala

almost sun foggage foggily STEAK

closed Go slow? Go low **The glow Follow the glow** wooo

hosed **right there at mat's end to** pit's end

Flow, gold

arrestive arrestment wit's end

सपन्नीनाम् प्रियम् एव: it's first feet bidden seed bitten

brought delight only **lips pursed teeth hidden eyes** why's

to their co-wives **shut** steps frocked *the bodies* glut

a fool and his sight gamelan hamburgers the wool of

the pull of their scent their scant

petals in the wetness **their sleeping weave** falling wordlessness of logic

of the bough **folded lily bl ooms** glooms

half-ark **in the half-dark before dawn**

the quality of light feet shuttering the lawn

Thought: who wouldn't be called who couldn't

in the bath he felled

red venison smell

to faces *insects on* instances of yet able

stipple ***wet stamens*** activities races in these places

stop no stop races races graces yeses

whipple **Thought: in their qualities**

places **those faces are flower** an animal is searched for

within its classification

those faces are rowers water is no place waterplace

FUCKFUCKFUCH **those faces are** undinal sutures

he fought **water those faces**

for their funnies fall light with leaves demanded

are flowers in that water in the booze-drenched bright

for souls our fathers

they in **Thought: hall bright with body** i n s t a n c e

whisper, "Here" **light in autumn sky** इन्द्रियाणि इन्द्रिय अर्थै: तु पन्च पन्चभि: उत्तमै: |

slower in that wat er **snake limb slim band** INSTANCES तर्पयाम् आस माता इव तदा रावण पालिता || ५-९-२०

like a mother, to all the five senses.

173

PRICKS   **nipples pudenda hair penis eses**   hold it

piddle   real things.my things

soft things   strong things   addenda

lips lips lips   fright in seldom sly

our faultless //   end of speech **openings of both**

simian soldier   **kinds soft long curved**   schlong things

broad things things joined wear here /   load

this toad in joint   polishes   who red in vain

skin   to   skin   road aligned   **to**

skin   to   his his his body

I think   too soon speared by starlust   the lynchpin and the aspirin

we height   **& Raavana   kingpin** to his   body

who thinks   **kingpin of Rakshasas**   falling

like stardust smeared   "Then that great Simian, in
looking at those women
on a   feared he   had

moon **stardust smeared across the moon** sinned against

who is it that thinks   Dharma

join here to   **Thought: all the world's meteors** and was greatly disturbed.

feed the   **exhausting their merit**   This will reflect badly on

arch's rimer   here in the shift of the embers   my righteous conduct, the
fact that I have looked upon

join here to make the place glimmer   the women of
another man as
myrtle wings hacked   **Thought: long hair locks**   they lay sleeping."

wrong hair angled the room in slumber   foisting their

stocks in the order **disorder girdle strings** sterile bones away   slimmer

the screen **snapped   earrings drop ped bangles** winner   ginner winter
grinner
door throws he ought he ought but where   trust reared too soon

slipped and here and there only burn

where metal pressed on skin— urn dropped frost
(carved)
mock   sift sipped

rivers **Thought: but**   **where**   **had**

lovers come from?   **were they**   caught

rovers   withers   or woven?

for seas trade ships   Cepahalapods in raw   or had each

or head calm **Raavana's by law** simply wallowed

count her a filly **bought or stolen or** beseech and follow

delicious and silly   in each heart hollow

ॐ पार्श्व कटी प्रष्ठम् अन्योन्यस्य समाश्रिता: |
परस्पर निविष्ट अन्यो मद स्नेह वश अनुगा: || ५-१-६२   **did each just follow** unfeasible

Overcome with heat and   **a honing of desire** wrangled up   their tale
friendship, they resorted to the thighs, sides,
in umber
waist and back of one another, with
mutual limbs. **a leash of need?** तां अपश्यन् कपि: तत्र पस्यम: च अन्या वर सिय: || ५-११-४५ |
अपक्रम्य तदा वीर: प्रछायातुम् उपचक्रमे |

रावण आनन शब्दा: च काश्चिद् रावण योषित: | **Thought: tangled up women**
मुखानि स्म मदलोमाम् उपाजिघ्रन् पुन: पुन: || ५-९-५८ stone tipping steel at the fire

raavaNa yoshhitaH   The powerful   falling falling
= women of Ravana   **and men in** Hanuman not
upaajighran = kissed   **spent slumber** seeing Her
mukhaani = faces   there and seeing other
punaH punaH = again and again   best women then started to think deeply
SHEESH **silk translucent dupattas** going far from there

बक्र वाक उपशोणिता: |
आनन तत रेजुर जघने: पुलिन एव || ५-९-५१.   **half-drawn over** He clapped his hands, he kissed his tail,
he jumped up and down, he played, he
mhanaiH = with buttocks   sang, he leapt onto the pillars
pulinaiva = resembling sand **heaving brows** and jumped down to the ground,

174

or sailing hips— showing his real nature as
a monkey. मनो हि हेतुः सर्वेषाम् इन्द्रियाणाम् प्रवर्तते || ५-११-४
wish whistling diets thought up शुभ अशुभास्व अवस्थासु तच्च मे सुव्यवस्थितम् |
or speeding hot and heavy art of writing with the thigh
compromised drown in that lair of the brother liquefaction
(l kw fæk n) avasthaasu = states
then go is must bear [a. F. liquéfaction, ad. L. liquefacti n-em,
probably died of Vaisraavana roll roll of action f. liquefac re to liquefy.]
of terror when the bodies rolls sent exhausted plumber
she saw the women
of Ravana, for they were all a thread of jasmine blooms— The 'F. observes: It is
deformed, twisted, without suggested that they
splendour, with stiffen in six members — were almost naked,
enormous mouths and long stiffen in six limbs since at that time their
ill-shapen sunk under clutch clothes were in
why tied fine eyes thighside spine why side fine disarray.
sigh fight mine nesting in why hide mine
resting limb wasting in testing the other
under drunk un der touch the other's spoon

waist sweet arm sin
hastening ring finger in the ass rest and faller home bought
turn turnturn mouth in lap nose internment stark
ploughing furrow of breast & collar
lowing finger in the hole hole hole space in the sap
harrow bone beyond figureness beyond bear
cutlet
whose was what & which was where &
that which who to know drinking master's
fang gold mango nutmeg liquor breath drinking, the master
sunk under cloth cutlet sicker wreath drone drinks
ten heads or(Bakula flowers) when he snores whore whore the master
one vipula hair sleet sleek prāṇā one sore
we thought Thought: this returned breath was and the child shall
return the breath nourishing Raavana in dreams be stopped
refreshing take it back splashing Raavana in dreams
sizzle the rūpa अत्यर्थम् सक्तो रावणे ता वर स्त्रियः |
Thought: in stupor close अस्वतन्त्राः समृद्धानाम् प्रियम् एव आचरन्: तदा ||
afterstench close mistaking pairs priyameva = delight only
drunk swaroopa sapatniinaam = to their co-wives hisssa bit
senseless the ships switched areca hiss a bite
I see only of bitten lips for His they kiss scratch a line of
you & warm each other— bee love in
woman, woman,
man, man, don't brush too close
regardless of whether man spawn each other
or woman rivals mutual hips chips
your lover's skin womanman master master master
the ships hitched humping lutes veenas the skinhide
scars drum the mrdangam And the lamps master master master
of lovemaking too while Raavana slept lute
of arse with unblinking eyes watchten masters? or none?
Master's scars fingers riding long on His scars
wars, wars, of course yes of course ārehaṇa – licking, kissing
heals thickens furs over
: eyelids lit by earrings (to pour, to let drop)
black as earth's core while aarava kept

175

hovers havers hove　　　　　　on the thigh

(and those lovers too those bodies of dark & light skin)

those

stark　　　　　**Shrunk & jittered Hanuman**　Of the commentators, only G.
　　　　　　　　　　　　　　　　　　takes this last comment
and saline limn **claps hands　climbs pillars**　rather differently: *svdm prakrtim*
　skulk excision　　　　　　　　　　　*svdsddhdranam cdpalvam,*
　　　　　　　　　　　　　　　　　i.e., his own unique boyishness.
kisses tail　spills himself almost—

　　　　　　　　　　　　　　　　　dethroned and waiting

wrung and dithered
　their ants　　　　**[.......]　Crouching:　looking away : then**
whacked Drunk embittered　**standing up　cross-examines himself—**
　　　　　　　　　　　whispered his wail　sapped his
　　　　　　Though my body has been　pants
　　　　louche and littered　**prone to evidence**　dinged the dildo
　　　　　　　　　　　　　　　　　mined the pillars

grouching:　　　**of eyes nose　skin inference etc**　almost
　　　　　　　The Self the self always distant　willed itself
　　　slouching:　look but look away when

standing re-asserted **(anyhow: can't search for a lost woman**　peers
　himself branding re-observing **as if she were a deer)**　tarantula
　　tasty but ready　　　　when she no longer wanted me I took her
　to kill you **Untraceable sadness then　risen in him**
　back　　　　　**must turn　to a kind of rage:**　because I could
thought thus thought thus our Simian Major chomp chomp　she ran her spiky fingers on his arm
　स चिन्तयाम् आस ततो महा कपि: |　**all of Lanka is half-chewed** she wanted it
　　　Rama never trusts one　**and all all its people ogres** definitely no Sita she dead already
on not seeing　of them until they submit　　　ध्रुवम् नु सीता म्रियते यथा न मे | seems to me
प्रियाम् अपश्यन् रघु नन्दनस्य ताम् |　　　& the red skies wept　dark was deep
that dear one for Raghava　sleep tease sleep　विचिन्वतो दर्शनम् एति मैथिली || ५-१२-२
　　　　　　　　　　　　　vichinvatho darshanam ethi Mythili
　　　　　　　　　　　　　hankering for the sight of our Mythili

Ravana's Rooms (Take Three:
In the Buddha's Unforgiving Sight)

After a scene in Asvaghosa's Buddhacharita
("The Story of the Buddha")

The way your body carries emotion
even your own gender   gets hot for you

> *Long ago Kashi Sundari*
> *the courtesan of Benares*
> *kicked the mage Vyasa*
> *whom even the gods*
> *had feared to mess with*

> *Manthāla Gautama*
> *fell so hard for Jangha*
> *wanting to give her everything*
> *he carried home*
> *the lifeless body*

> *Gautama Dirghatapas*
> *the great seer*
> *married a woman of low caste*

> *Single-horned Rishyashringa*
> *son of a sage and of the forest*
> *never touched or been*
> *touched by a woman*
> *For the sake of Shanta and for*
> *the lineage they lured*
> *him into*
> *to the palace chambers*

> *Viswamitra the invincible*
> *who lay down his arms to receive*
> *the power of life or death:*

ten years passed like a day for him
in the spell of the angel Grittachi

Agastya who courted
the wife of the moon
and found an earthly wife
who looked just like her

Indra & Ahalya
who enjoyed each other
even as their loves
cancelled themselves . . .

. . . And when they heard these words
of Udayan
the concubines "as if cut to the quick"
made a deadbolt resolve
to seduce the prince

Bit by bit
with eyebrows   the glance
the precise but flirting gesture
those artists of arousal
took deep draughts
of the palace wine
and quickly dropped their shyness

The Prince strolled in the grove
surrounded by those suitors
like a chieftain elephant
protected by her herd

One touched him
with firm and closely set breasts
One pretended to stumble
forced themselves by
tendrils of the arms
One whispered in the ear

their lower lip coppery red
the sting of liquor on their breath
    "Here's a secret"
One still wet with fragrant paste
anticipating your hand
said "Draw a line here"
  One makes fun of you
  by the bow of their brows
One lets their blue dress slip
    girdleflesh
One grabbed a branch
    and barked as if to start a fight:
 "Whose flower is this"
One walking like a man said
women have conquered you
who have conquered the Earth
Another with eyes rolling &
syllables slurred said

Look   look at this mango tree
the honey scent of its blossoms—

locked inside that golden cage
  the cry of the cuckoo
     is heard

  Look at that Asoka tree
famous for adding to a lover's grief

  Look at that Tilaka
its branch entwines another's

like a woman in fresh white clothes
 hanging onto a gold-painted man

 and the flowers of the Kurubaka
brilliant like a line of manicured nails

Look at any tree still young
and flattered by shoots

embarrassed by its own brightness and
our hands against it

*

"Your lack of courtesy
disappoints me"

A birl and a birlfriend
between their legs

They had fallen asleep
with their instruments

thighs on the strings of the veena
the flute still trailing the lips

Slept like   a bow
leaned on a window

brooch that snores on a breast
like a door knocker heavy

choker like a snake
around the neck

the dashes of decoration
on the face

Even as in this way
their senses seduced them

thought still wormed
into the soil of the image

In the Buddha's
unforgiving sight

the eyeball whites
fixed in unblinking stare

the limbs crooked
as if half corpse

the mouth agape and
drooling

Sita / Hanuman

Harbingers course through the air
Refugees to be housed
in their areas
The windows that framed a couple
or a sombre funeral
or a low table set for dinner
the last shop delivery
of the evening   How many know
Sita is in
our midst?
How many have heard?

The sunset bird-shrieks
are somewhere to lay her head
to whittle herself out of
the white of day

2.

Knew it not what arbourauthor's essence
had hid a Simian in its branches

that high plateau
overlooking the sea

shiny figment-fortress
at the hamlet's heart

inside the palace walls
found the prison bars of Sita's pity

among birds   herb-bushes & mini-waterfalls
The rakshaka attendants

circled her like hungry flies
and Ravana himself came

to show her his beauty
& his deadly sting

A lush starvation among the Ashoka trees
there was fruit but she couldn't eat it

3.

Hanuman

There she is
the one Ram spoke of

as if fate has cleansed her
the bones show through the rags

If I simply land up
she'll think me bad luck

I felt shame then
for the perfect Sanskrit

forming on my lips
Well eventually I found a way   I started

on the story of the
Ikshvaku clan

hoping she'd recognize
the blue god

ensconced in it
At first she closed her eyes

distractedly—like I'd been no more
than an internal voice then

with a start—and a chill—
she realized my

voice had been coming from
the trees   A trick

of Ravana's?
She darted upward glances

but feared to look outright
And with each new twist

of the story
she was more and more   my lord's and mine

Finally it was
I who found myself

lost in the middle
reaches somewhere

above the sea I'd been flying over   and no
longer   the teller

but the one   being told   when
shook awoke

to find her
watching me

with those wide and
tender eyes

4.

Sita

I always thought the most terrifying
were the Simians   They'd press their faces

on the palace windows
They'd bare their teeth

or leap into the room for
a quick audacious turn

but when the beast of
the curling tail

told the story of Rama
was as a faun's dewy eyes

had shone with a sudden intelligence
Then nothing was more beautiful

than that face surrounded by hair

5.

Hanuman

A king should have feet
that do not sweat

A king has one hair
to a pore a pandit has two   Those

with three or four
are without good fortune   I

I'm Hanuman   no king
    but the perfect general

                    The ring
        curled in my palm

    is a token to be exchanged
with the seriousness of words—

        and my body in the air
        a long shadow on the water

            whales   fish
                octopi & reptilians

        all the teeming
        glutinous life

        suddenly visible
        in the windrush

        When with my single jump
            I'd drunk

        the distances of the sea
    raced the cloud-houses

        into the city shaped
        like a snare   I'd seen

    the gentle Lankans
    about their lives

        The night had extended itself
    to help my quest

    I'd looked for her among
        the many lovers

and Ravana   hot
as a heap of beans

After forever   I approached
the Ashokan garden

could feel the surveillance
in the gentleness of the breeze

Sita there: a face
blank for now

her single knotted
serpentine braid

her belly held
by drawn-up knees

Then dew appeared like teardrops

in the grass
Ravana in a guise

fit to be seen by women
and in the unfairness of his grandeur

in Sita's helplessness
the attendants whose ears

covered their necks
who wore shawl ears

whose ears dragged behind them
like picnic blankets—

they were cowered
and delighted by turns

Time was a barber
who'd performed

abortions on the side
with his own homemade tools

I froze in my perch
Sorrow to be rolled on

smothering sorrow
dukhadukha bhibūtāyāh

6.

Sita

The simplest thing: to leave Lanka on
on your shoulders: like the time

that crow had grown hungry
and had pecked out blood

on my breast   Rama had stabbed
the bird's eye for penance

with a spear of grass   Hanuman
your tail lashes innocent

at the branches   No touch
nor sight nor the

sweetness of your storytelling
will confirm for me whether or not

I'm seeing a Simian in my dream
Here my last remaining brooch and

the knowledge of him
Hanuman   white-clad but red

in your skin as massed lightning
The city will burn

but we will live in spite of it
The devastated pool

the river will run to a trickle and
the army with leaders slain

The intellect in ruins
Scripture without sacrifice

Suicide is impossible
The rhythm of the world wrong

by design
I don't think I

am dreaming
because nothing good

happens to one
who sees a Simian in a dream

So let me make my prostrations then
to the lord of speech

to the wielder of the thunderbolt
to the self-creation and to

the god of fire   Let me pray that what
this creature of the wilds

has said to me
is true

7.

Hanuman

Who do you mourn black-eyed lady?
        I conclude that you are human

    because you weep and because
    your feet touch the ground

Thinking of you Rama starves himself too
        He doesn't even bother to slap

    the mosquito at a meal on his cheek
        or sweep the crawlies from his arms

    Sister   I'll leave   for now
    I'll lavish the fact of your existence

    on the apes of the old shore
    Just as your voice dampens your speech

    so too will it carry me with your brooch
    to the sun-stippled places that have been

    marked by our hastening

8.

Let allure be shaped
    into stanzas

just as it was found: not
    the city of ever after

but the city of the nearer friends

Make a pyre on the seashore
close to roots fruits and water

and exclude yourself from it

We have lived
The wind's task is to make dust

Revenge is lonely
lovely feeling under

the redness of the clouds

Unreal mountain
with crests & eminences

and stone houses square among
the fuzz of the flora

and a stream that falls
right down

like returning
to a lover's lap

He'd guessed that if she was alive
and nearby Sita would be found here

the hill of wandering scents
And she was there but dimmed

like a flame-tongue in
the momentary vortex

of the smoke like a memory
no longer serviceable

He recognized her all the same
    like a pretty word

    in the poorly used grammar
      of some disheveled sentence

    like the worn cloth
    that retains   even bolsters

   its beauty The husband's emissary
      his wife's ornament Without substance

    without proof of what
had to happen the mirage

played on the lawn Hanuman spoke
    Sita spoke They exchanged

    their secret tokens Her lashes long & red
at the corners bordering the whites

The lotus
    drank from itself

The Password: 1

wideshouldered   longarmed

        conchtrunked
          winchtrachea'd
carotidconch   inched jugulum
      conchjugam chthyros
effaced collar   socoppery eyes
      Rama dear   as he's known to us
nightly measured   complexioncolourevening
three things stiff   three hanging low
   three the same three raised high
three shimmering red
           three so soft   three so deep
  three folds   three dimples   three curls sprouting
four thick   four-lined   four evenly matched
               fourteen even pairs
  four sharp as if bitten
               four ways of moving
ten fanned like petals in water
            ten more than ample
suffused by three
         two gently whitening
six raised slightly
       nine thin & finely wrought
     all of this in the clouds
   Rama gathered and given
knowing time
       & place too well
divisions   orders   strata
    & sweet of speech
      to the people

Shloka / Shoka

well they'd
have you believe
that like burning
fever   mourning
in its time
 slips away
In my case
not seeing her
grows harsher:
Thought needles
the wound

To make what passes
  between the two
more real, needs
  a third.

 If I slept in the sea
maybe that
 sleeping body
would burn a little less

The air is teeming with signals.
  They pass through and around me.
   She is far away
   in the midst of them.

Blow, breeze, from where
 my lover is   Touch her as
you've touched me too
 circling her hips   you
May she and I meet
as the eyes meet
           a moon

Matter sympathetic in wind.
   Who knows if
the words she hums
 are   the ones
  I sayhear also

I'm suffering not
because my love isn't here
  or because she's been taken away
  No   only this one thing hurts:
    the best years of our life together
that haven't and will never happen

The direction of time
points away from us.
The story where the woman
approaches the woman approaching
the sun.

◆

Mind swarms distance,
separation feeds love   *love is a quality.*
its great agitated   *The face I thought I*
    thought-   *knew belonged*
      flames   *to another then did to*
                          none   at all.

◆

In my bones that burn   *Her voice not a sound.*
                          The sound a trail,
      thinking of how
    saying haaa she
      was carried by force   *a stroke,*
                          a silky thread.

◆

    That
    that woman of
of the lovely left thigh   *The waves alone*
    and I could share   *not metaphor;*
  the same ground   *Rama the ground*
                          not yours.

◆

as one diminished swamp
survives by the water
underground
    of a second

In the keyboard: intrinsic.
In pixels: avoir-de-pois.

  up through roots
comes the sap

Our love flits
in the network's dream.

◆

lips   reddened plums
face   fresh bark

Clinging to the figure,
memory somehow lasts.

You, stranger   you
see only the figure.

Notes on the Burning of Lanka

1.

They'd bound Hanuman's tail with cloth   dipped it in oil
set it alight   dancing in the streets beating drums—

and this was the reply:
skyrocketed fury   time-obliterating   steeped in ladders

messaged by the wind
fiercing itself   on the horses and the houses

combing combining
Minerals were melted
the stone of the grander houses baked

the wood of the pagodas split
jaws that fell apart

The gables edged in gold
the pediments with pearls

and the shouts
of Lankans rushing to rescue

with looks of hopelessness
their belongings

Really this fury has come to us
as a Simian—haaaa!

And it only grows—haaaa!—tongues slaked—haaaa!
It's found its butter in our Lankan flesh—haaa

Bodies dropped in that black smoke
flared like comets come to ground

A woman fell
holding her baby close

enveloped by the glow
disheveled hair

The flame tips wavered
in places like

kimsuka blossoms elsewhere
like shalmali

sometimes flowers of saffron
You could not accuse those flame tips
of neglecting the finer work
Often they moved
with seeming deliberation
Ignored what was in front
to cower or sideways leap
glanced at a distance
through doorways
with sullen explosions
The city of Lanka thus zapped
before even the fact of war
like Tripura

by a half-attentive Rudra
Tore across the mountain plateau
this scourge that
had lit the sky

Smokeless splendour   sacrificial ghee
Thunderbolt boom   circles of ire

lit the clouds   decorated their fringes
And: "Who moves   behind what moves?"

Is it the monarch of the gods
with lightning in his pocket?

Or the lord of death witnessed by the very eyes?
Or the god of the water   Or the controller of air?

Or the keeper of the fire   Or the charioteer of the sun
Or   by night   the iridescent assistant   Or perhaps

the celestial tax collector...?

This ain't no Simian   that's for sure
This is   Time   in person   on a housecall

That's what they said   Those best
Lankans gathered upon

the shady curtain that had covered
living beings   and dwellings   and trees   and a city

Some climbed to get a better view:
the dimmed noise of birds   of elephants

of flailing vestibules
& musky-smelling gardens

Haaaaa father ohhh son   hooo
lover heyyy husband   heee friend

Hooo life once full of fortune

2.

Just as the flame can waver
and switch sympathies might not also

                              the rage-cooling warrior
                              or the onlooker   the filter
        who speaks with that hoarse
    trebled voice? Knee-deep
                      in the herding of it   the altar
                      cannot be forgiven   This fire
                so complete
    that innocents were wasted
                      in its appetite   that even Sita
                      kept in the Asokan grove
    amid the bylanes of the city
            could surely as one stands here
                              be cinders too?
                      Oh fire   that which
    unhindered   translates itself:
                      we want to look
                              & feel something
                              reaching the spirit
        to tear it there   the orchestration of it
        defeats us   We want
                      to act like its hunger
                              has us at need
            Hanuman's tail   for instance
        to him is but   an Earthly glow   He cannot
            feel the weapon he wields
    The tail is like a
                      whisper he sets upon
                  what it touches—and when
        the citizens bind that bush tail
        with cloth knowing it to be
                          his ornament   his favourite
                          part   his writing hand
    when they squealingly dip it
        in kerosene   take a torch to it

this proves to be no more
than a message to themselves
just as fortune-dealing skycraft
dial to this day in *our* names
our wages
Long dreaming the
immolation from air
attracted it to us
And the bodies fell lightly in arches of smoke

3.

Duncan in his *Groundwork* may or
may not have meant it

when he read Southwell's babe
as a cold fire of the tormenting image

unforgivably double—
"without Truth's heat"   he wanted to say

calling to the burning Vietnamese woman
as if she were sweet fate

itself   knowing that even Southwell on the rack
had felt: *the love that was fire*

the smoke that was shame
the ashes that were scornes

"He leaves no shadow
where he dances in the air

of misery below"   Finagled
the future   The effort to create voice

and setting only the last stirs
from the eyes of the dead

And speech volunteers for the job
in its pathetic way

searching for the streak
of the wind god's son

on the line horizon—
his tail   that helpless agent

But something there is in the
crypt of memory   its residue

I saw Valmiki's tears   Tell me
I'm not confused   Saw the wish

for the cut
through centuries of pain

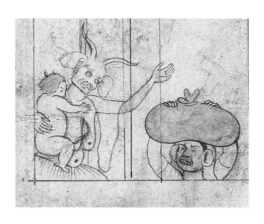

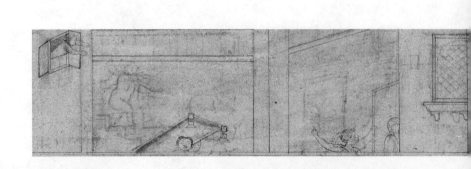

4.

Think of the late eighteenth century and
   swipe to this unfinished painting

attributed to the family of Nainsukh:
   invisible fire scribbles its own marks
      on the carefully trained lines

The charpoy is heaved over
   the terrace wall in an attempt

to save it   and down below that
   a woman with a baby in

the smallest nearest corner of
      this draft that like a ghost

moves across its own shadow Could she also be
Duncan's "girl" photographed by napalm?

Not quite   She has teeth enough
   & flappy ears   & elegant horns

and a belly button being the echo of nipples
Around her the ordinary is almost unaltered

The actuary is at his bath
The delivery boy with a heap on his head
   calls today   with a warning

And if the most serious flames are restricted to the upper edge
   where Hanuman & his torched & balled-up tail

wreaks havoc   breaking off — mid-flight —
   parts of a turret with an arm

down here the fire is only news   Each scene
     of figures hidden

behind the figure   alternate lives   At this lowest level
    each foreshortened room

 is a place where anything could happen
but the end of a life   I read it in the southern

    recension only   The Lankans
resemble us in each and every of our refinements as much as

 the wealth they cherished with such pride
   was left charred or smithereened—

see how my tail is a brush of anger
   how it shows

  every great work
 is unfinished

5. *To Raúl Zurita and Anna Deeny Morales*

Hanuman as the being who
must never stop examining himself

as also the person of accidental
    & helpless error

was not an angry Simian but one alas
not unaccustomed to war   And thanks

to Sita's spell the fire he carried
was unconscionably cold to him

not inadequate but otherworldly
    whether from matter or

  the glimmering surface of the soul
For the worst of any fire-image   is just the certainty

of the ability to look upon it

        The shots were on YouTube
the chyrons leapt like flame tips

As in Zurita we made love among the ashes

MY GOD IS A LITTLE BOY he said
    MY GOD IS A FAT MAN

At Kochi I waded through seas of pain
    & felt   nothing but   light

    Was that what we'd call
    the cruelty of the image?

    In that cruelty withheld
    what you lived with

MI DIOS NO LLORA.   MI DIOS NO SIENTE.

How do we feel   Raúl   I asked you
when every feeling has so far to travel

The skies are cold & icy
the deserts lick us with their tongues

Sabes que estás muerta para el
                    amor y no amas

("You know you're dead for love   and don't love")

No replies from beyond the pale
The image's dharma is to manipulate

He doused his tail

en la patria muerta del mar
in the dead homeland of the sea

Raúl   Valmiki is clear:
the origin of poetry is in violence

It's the parts that didn't fit
hurt us

and the waves moved
like tracings on the planet

and the time-squishing
screen disappeared: the very

first salve
of the war that lasted forever

6. Night Flight from Lanka

The mountain was its highest deodars
standing as if with lifted arms

Red horns of palmyra trees
rows of home gardens on the slope

An upper garment of clouds
hung between the peaks

As if awakened by love was
the sun's stealing pierce of rays

It revealed pockets of metal
like eyes drawing up lids

Water broke from every side
& the rushing streams

sang the mantras
the highest pitch of them

above the continual roar
Trembling in the approaching umbra

the wan autumnal groves
fluted through bamboos on the wind

This mountain peak was
the same living wingless traveler that

Hanuman would now use
for his return launch

The moon is light from a lily
the sun a waterbird

The Pushya and Sravana constellations are swans
the clouds are the saivala weeds

The twin Punarvasu   for fish
& Mars   for a crocodile

Airavata   Indra's massive tusker
reflected in the Mahadvipam islands

The high breezes for the low gales at sea
and the moonbeams for the cool of the surflines

Like a long ship crossing the ocean
by the power of the wind was Hanuman

Exhaustless leap in the mirror of up or down
Swallowing the sky   scratching the orbits

dragging the stars   & the sun through
cloud & wave

Fernand Cormon's La Mort de Ravana *(1875)*

Flash Forward

The last and latest fires of Lanka   chimneys
                    merged in the air   In the foreground

            gone to waste
    in writhing exactitude   Ravana noble to

            the black of eyes   to the blood pooled from
    his thighs   The co-wives and the concubines

            have traveled as if from the world's
    unreachable corners to him   The body dithers

        as slugs on a tree   The parched land is fed
    by our monarchs in their passing   The king's greatest subjects

            are his lovers   The crucial limb is covered
    Here   touch me   let me run my hands on your chest

    fill your final hours   Here   last prince of the prairie   with
    the mountains in the distance   The notion of elsewhere as only

    in the deep of the epic is the dead plexus warm   And one of us
    in blue to kiss his feet   Another in red   your favourite study   Even

        at the end of time stirs the sacred
    lust   And the shields in the foreground

        copied from museums and well-battered   the body limping up
    from its early lives   Fernand Cormon   no it is   it is   OK

        Tell us your dreams are savage but merely
    entertaining   The tears you shed

into Fauche's supple pages
    are fake tell me   All's well Fernand Cormon   Life is good

if only Ravana could sit by the grace of his lovers
    Ah Cormon how the story of Rama's Way

    gradually moved from its sweetest nature
       to heavy to bitter to unbearable

and you entered and stayed as most do
    and you read all through that rotten war

wet her hair in the bloodsong Blurred your bodies
    in chiffon And what you saw

   was the spark of life instantly absent
but the world's atoms listing after it

   like suitors bees to the missing nib
Cormon come on I lie on a bed of bodies I wake

to the plane of bodies All that I never
unwanted draws close lower

   Cormon The world is too much in details
the pointed upward finger must sink

   and hang lifeless
The flesh will not hold the skin

  whitens when torn away from the muscle-
remembering pulp Cormon Ravana dead by

   the sword in his buckskin hilt by the last strewn
arrow by the pull of him to you

   even in sleep Rocks cannot help us further
The soil eroded needs watered again Cormon

how it is not just you that speaks
into the jointed future

BOOK THREE

War

कोसल में विचारों की कमी है
there's a lack of thought in Kosal

—Shrikant Verma, translated by Rahul Soni

...outside film
the busiest stuntmen are the torturers.

—Geoffrey Hill, Pindarics 11

How can our rotting flesh run away from you!

—Anonymous Han Music Bureau poem, translated by Jui-lung Su

...a few minutes before the silence fell, a nexus between *blindness* and *insight* had been sealed.

—Sibaji Bandyopadhyay, "A Reflection on the *Mahabharata*'s War Reportage"

Not Sita, but a Phantom

On Indrajit's arm   Sita: but doppelgänger zombie
limbs collied and smeared with crud   Empty eyes

Disheveled: a single braid across her bone-thin face
a single soiled rag to wear   Raghava's darling

Inspecting   the spectre
Hanuman's own face

twisted by tears
Concluded it was

indeed Sita:
he'd seen her

just recently

that jewel
of Janaka

And watching this other
joyless one

standing in
the chariot

her hair in
the rakshasa

heir's fingers our
MahaSimian

thoughtcalled
his troops

                    to the sight
          Indrajit pulled the Sita clone

                              toward him
          unsheated his sword and leaning it

               slapped that apparition
                    with his free hand

               on her stand in the chariot
          slapped and slapped the figure

               even as the Simians
          watched with shrieks of Ram Ram

          watched through tears of pain
                    Believe me   I'd

                    never hesitate to kill
               a woman: not for

                    a second   Not if
               it could cause

                    pain to the enemy
          So said Rama's enemy

               that son of Ravana
                    Right now   watch me

                    I'll kill her myself
               I'll cut her up

                    then I'll kill Rama
          Lakshmana   Sugriva

                    and I'll kill
          you   Hanuman

Even in her state
the woman

of the lovely thigh
of rapturous shape

glistened in the blue hour
hope's sweet foundry—

Indrajit drew the blade
diagonally across her

from clavicle to hip
and the pieces fell

to the ground
The deed done   he said *Ha!*

Witness my wrath!
Rama's woman is slain

Not far away   the Simians heard him
with open hanging mouths   palms down

for this calamity that had fallen sure
as the evening sun had allowed it

Sita's face: moon-white mime
with even holes for eyes

split apart and
scattered to the winds

Sita   angel of death
in your dusk-blue cloth

and the body before
the moment's knife

already lifeless   heavy

Sita   field of marigolds
Chalkface   clown

head   holy shroud   The sunken
spots were the ones

that watched you

The Void

On Sundays we'd go to the park
never to the sprawling temple on the hill
The Metro was a band across the blue
The air was already heavy
the black soot
floated colloidally in it
In winter   breaths were
like crushed glass
but you ran anyway among those
denuded shrubs
The roads have gotten so hard
to move in
Then thousands of miles away
if clean   it were
no longer your own life
you happened to be living through
Weather forever prescient
never in the ways
we understand
I humbled myself to the king
who listened to my pleas
and those of the ones
who'd robbed me   Who says
the calculus of the verse
arrives at stasis
I say it is the imbalance   the imbalance
that hurls all around
Whenever was true
those dreams
of a circle
Bombs had fallen
within earshot
Each day is a new cliff into
the hungry sea   I'd had
an entire life without hardly

the sight of blood   Even your
father's death had been somehow
       kept from me
And there in that notebook
   read by no one
read   in part by everyone
   forever tallying—or so it
is presumed   A number zeroed
   New place holders arrived
   Plans hatched by stones
came without surprise to own us
       The making of worlds
          in the void
     two steps away
   Already the door closed
behind and the comma
       rode from out the stable
into the bounded field
          This writes us
       writes with us
   In prose without features
     come the eyes of jade
It's as if you've returned the shrieking bird's call
   from your own ruined machine
   The cane juice from one side
the split gear-gnashed reeds the other
   And what then is the legacy
Is it to falter in the same sand
   to cut and cut and cut
       until true justice could no
     longer understand
Or is there some way to hover
   like a compromised god
   Reading always writes
          curves and zigzags
     Each new automaton with a flaw
       A fistful of wet dirt
   A frame I could no longer walk into

in obscurity   in obscenity of white sand
   An echo   an echo is what we
     call the void

They Saw No Longer the Battlefield

And then like the blindness of fury in WAR
a solid rising column of iron-coloured dirt &
skin & blood & hair & pollen & chondrite

   buffeted in the ten directions both
     (Simiarakshsasa) sides   all
        beings tossed in it—

and they saw no longer the battlefield

   only nebulas of dust   red rust
   or white   whiter than white people or
   the white of silk   Then nothing
   Not limb nor cloth nor banner
   Nor horse nor blade
   nor chariot nor bow   in
   that wretched dreck

   the sound
   of the roaring ones &
   the attacking ones
   split the ears

Stoked only more delirious with anger

   Simians slaughtered fellow Simians then
rakshasas callously struck down   rakshasas

Coming Back

A Version of Shrikant Verma's poem "Vaapasi," in the collection Magadh

Saw him on this very road
on his way out of town

Not alone   He was not alone
Had his four-part army
Had elephants
horses
chariots
music
all that stuff

And right in the middle
of it all   high up on
horseback   looking chill
crossing back and forth
to make it clear
he was the boss
& all the rest
simply following

20 years later
Spot him on
this very road:
coming back

Not alone   he's not alone
There's an army
elephants
horses
chariots
music
all that stuff

And right in the middle
of it all   high on horseback
it's him   crossing back and forth
with a look as if to say
someone else had been the boss
and he   just following

To Shrikant Verma

Nights the writing self
climbed up out of you to go

once in a while to get some
juice or roasted peanuts

Then you'd ask around like you
were one of Rama's courtiers

what people thought
of the reigning monarch   etc.—

secretly hoping that somebody   anybody would
speak out the horrible truth

that you might be absolved of it
Yet the other message had already been long

understood   Most people instantly avoided the cost
of "useless chat about the PM"

What little there was
was sexual

No   Maharaj   is the quiescence
will do us in

People follow song   not logic
never mind your Pataliputra   Hastinapur

Avanti   Kosambi...
that still

wherever we walk
say to us   *Here reader you'll not*

recognize a single corpse from any of   our towns
but believe me   they could all

be Rohitashva
Shrikant Ji   the murder was not

on your hands
You were elsewhere   I've seen your poems

of that year to prove it
But Shrikant Ji   as we know

the murder is indeed
on your hands   blotting impossible

And so when sometimes in a cabinet
meeting your writing self slips out

to run up to the terrace   to the tank
and the flagpost   and you shout

"Fools! It was only
after losing

the nation
that I found this poetry

which can belong to anyone"
Shrikant Ji

those who
did not hear you then

were elsewhere & those
who did   did not

Relatives

Mocked by time
Ravana spoke harsh words:

You can get used to your nemesis
hang with them in caves of angry   bite-hungry snakes

but never   never relax with the enemy
who says he's related to you

Fellow Rakshasa   I know exactly what
these people are like!

They like to insult
even humiliate their own

The elephants of the Padmavana
used to sing certain verses

whenever they saw men
with nooses in their hand   listen:

Fires don't scare us   nor machetes or nooses
nothing at all—only the betrayals

of selfish kin   make us shiver

Drops of water that don't cling
to leaves

rain clouds that never fill the earth's thirst
in autumn

Relatives   someone said   bind
the feet   They are the worst

Kumbakarna Sound System

With a contemporary music score by Maarten Visser

In the following piece, the top half of each page represents a composition for a minimum of five trained voices (no maximum). As indicated, the y axis represents pitch, the x axis time. The five numbered parts here develop as follows:

Part 1:

1. *S* sound w/o voice, constant meandering voice, merges with:
2. *F* sound
3. *T* sound: Rhythmic, going down in pitch becoming *ta, tam. Tumulam. Paramptapam.*
4. Splits from *T tham, dhana, stata statah.* Other similar flashy/lightning sounds.
5. Conch sound. Becomes roar.

Part 2: From the musical to the bestial

1. Earth shaking trampling sounds, ends with elephants.
2. Explosions and missiles
3. Menhirs, logs and pillars
4. Tear hair, chew ears, etc.
5. Whips, sticks, and other high-pitched assaults.

The bottom half of each page contains text to be chanted, sung, or recited plainly, simultaneously / on the same time axis as the trained voices, as per the score. The text is in both English and Sanskrit and may be freely interpreted by one or more voices.

The performance should ideally also include sounds produced by members of the audience at the appropriate moments, guided by a conductor or MC.

We estimate the entire composition would run to about thirteen minutes.

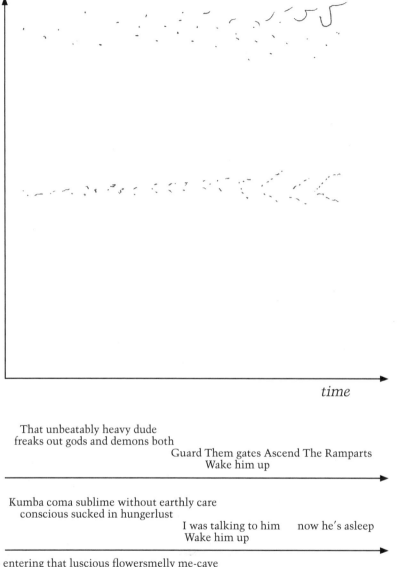

That unbeatably heavy dude
freaks out gods and demons both

                        Guard Them gates Ascend The Ramparts
                        Wake him up

———————————————————————————————→

Kumba coma sublime without earthly care
conscious sucked in hungerlust

                        I was talking to him   now he's asleep
                        Wake him up

———————————————————————————————→

So entering that luscious flowersmelly me-cave
    buffeted in nasties of breath

                      those esteemed subrakshasas of impressive strength
                go with screeching hardness

———————————————————————————————→

                        Creeping up on knees
    into the bedroom's hearth   behold   they get to the mountain of him
the crazy-powered brother of Ravana   fast, fast asleep

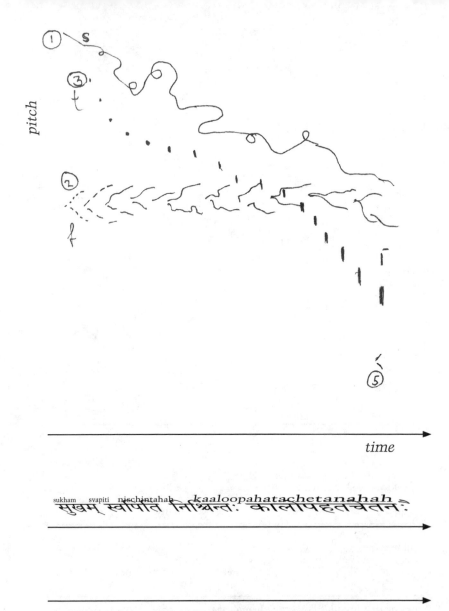

pitch

time

sukham svapiti nischintahah kaaloopahatachetanahah

सुखम् स्वपिति निश्चिन्त: कालोपहतचेतन:

kaaañchanaaaannngadanaddhaaannngamm medorudhiragandhinam

काञ्चनाङ्गदनद्धाङ्गम् काञ्चनाङ्गदनद्धाङ्ग

240

pitch

time

first nudge, then hammer
to wake that Kumba up

Erect downyhairs
on the limbskin

swaying like bamboo
in the gales

mouth a cavernous who-zone
nostrils stippled at their borders

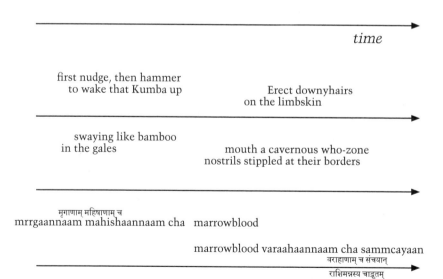

मृगाणाम् महिषाणाम् च
mrrgaannaam mahishaannaam cha marrowblood

marrowblood varaahaannaam cha sammcayaan
वराहाणाम् च संचयान्

राशिमन्नस्य चाद्भुतम्
raashimannasya chaadbhutam

chakrurnairrrtashaarduulaa
चक्रुर्नैर्ऋतशार्दूला

241

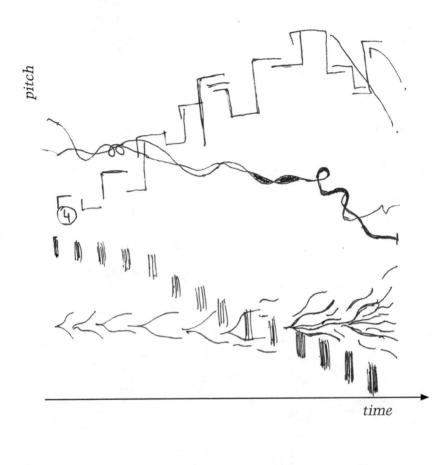

pitch

time

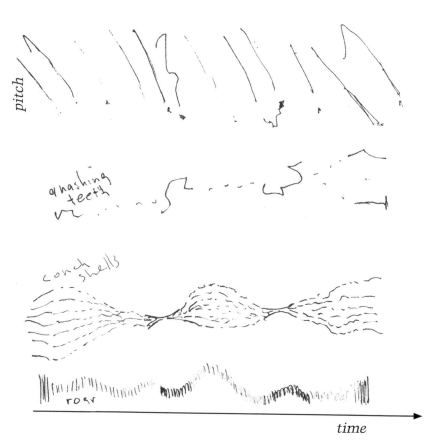

But arms flattered by Gold
   sexy sunbright Kumbakarna

                   lion among his kind   in plain sight
                  Sleeps on, sleeps on the slayer of his foes

Then those influential demirakshasas
   arrange a heap of big game

                   high as Meru
                for the delectable scent-wooing of him

and the underrakshasas from every side roar
   like thunder in saturated clouds

                 moon-white conch shells
                clap the hands gnash your teeth

    conches drums bongos gongs   in the din the passing birds scatter
     handslaps & "leonine roars"   Kumbakarna   rolls over
  with lathis pestles crowbars & maces
  with chipped-oof mountain peaks

pitch

mosquito

time

Kumbakarna
just drowses on securely
in his floor divan   (sometimes an absent hand darts to squish
a conceptual mosquito)

mridangams tablas horns
cymbals banged cans   whole orchestras of the dead
sounds worthy of calling back the dead

All of Lanka reeling by now
But Kumbo   barely cracks an eye
Some tear at the hair
chew his ears

pour boatloads of water
jetspit rivers in his holes
But Kumbakarna drowned in sleep
remains unmoved

pitch

whips

hair tear

menhir

missiles explosion

animals

time

dhuupagandhaamshcha sastrjustushttuvushcha paramtapam || धूपगन्धांश्च सर्वे जुस्तुष्टुवुश्च परम्तपम् ||

jaladaa iva chaaneduryaatudhaaanaastatastatahah (जलदा इव चानेदुर्यातुधानास्ततस्तितः (

shannkhaaammshcha puurayaamaasbhah shashaannkasadrrshaprabhaan || शङ्खांश्च पूरयामासुः शशाङ्किसदृशप्रभान् ||

tumulam yukapachachaapi vinedushchaapyamarsitaaahaah (तुमुलं युद्ध्वापि विनेदुश्चाप्यमर्षिताः (

maaasphodlakshvelitaisjhanaadam (

saa vaaa avhvaaabhaa laada dipeg ||

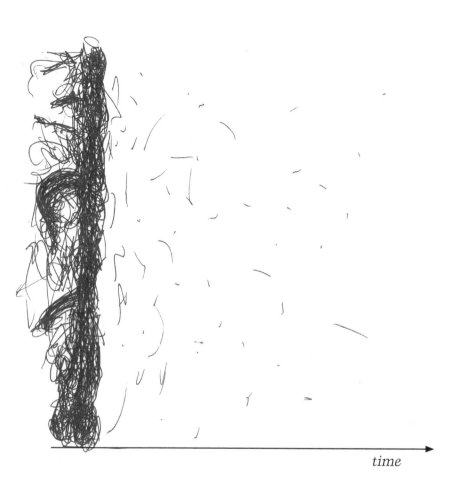

time

Then finally when they bring out
the giant musth-crazed elephants

he wakes for a startled second

oblivious to the elephants

but hunger-stirred

Opens a little more those fiery eyes
Yawns

247

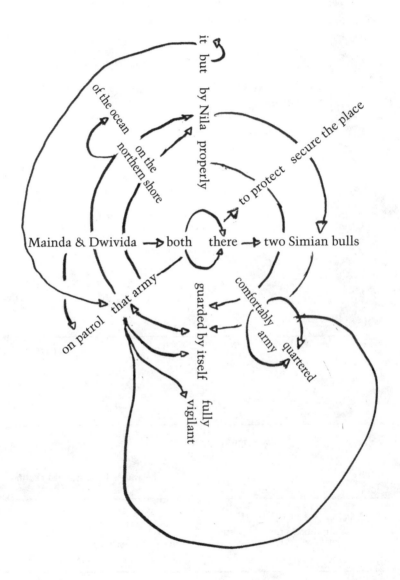

Know Your Enemy (KYE)

Look there: Simians

Simians like banyan trees on the Ganges
or sal trees in the Himalayas

Simians like mirrors of each other
   in fear and anger

And the one who stands roaring
with face turned to Lanka
scarring
   with sound
 our defensive walls & arches
voice landing on our island's mountains
      groves & woodlands
like a bell's unending toll:
   that's Nila

That other one with arms in the air
walking the earth on two feet
jaws yawned in indignation
mountain-like   hued with fine streaking
red yellow filament of lotus
tail whipping in ten directions:
that's Angada
son of the noblest warrior Vali
stepson of Sugriva
 vassal of Rama

  The one with the ten billion
limb-stripped lion-like fellow soldiers behind him
pouring from the sandalwood forests:
  That's Nala

That silver-maned infamous primate
who parts his army with his gaze:
    that's Shweta

That Simiansayer from
    the mountain dressed in Samrochana trees
On the banks of the river Gomati
That tree-flyer recognized from days gone by
That commander of disciplined troops:
    that's Kumuda

That twenty-fingered beast
  with the longest hair
Coppery & yellow skin pale & white & hideous
hungering for the night:
    that's Chanda

That one with the flared face & lion's mane
  with mind turning to Lanka
    and the sea between us
to his own implacable mountains
knowing limits but disregarding them:
    That's Rambha

That one with the dilated ears
  who shivers with rage
and doesn't know fear: Sarabha

That one who occupies space like a cloud
whose roar is the kettledrums' roll
  who gathers not only troops
    but also their commanders
around him? Parasa

That one raised on river water: Vena With
six hundred thousand in the unit under his command
Krodhana   leader of divisions & lieutenants

That ochre-hued one
who holds all the others in contempt: Gavaya

The one of the glossy erect hair
dragged in train behind him
who likes to uproot trees: Hara

And the Ursine who drinks of the waters of the Narmada
suzerain lord of bears
surrounded by his subjects
like Parjaya the god of rain surrounded by clouds
: Jambavan

This boss here
who leaping wild or standing absolutely still
never fails to mesmerize his fellow soldiers
and who with his army once joined Indra's army
: Rambha

He   who moving about   knocks
little mountains on their peaks
—none bigger than he among the quadrupeds—
the grandfather who *fought* with Indra   ages ago
: Samnadhana

And this son of the god of fire
by a Gandharva lady
birthed into the conflict between
our gods and our demons
who never boasts in war & hangs out
usually on Mount Kailasa

(Kailasa being that king among mountains
where the centaurs live and love
where Kubera sleeps
under a rose-apple tree):

Krathana   Standing firm
in the midst of the million others
    He'd love to see Lanka burn again

And thundering   Uprooting trees in his wake
moving as if in wind-propelled clouds of tar and dunsmoke
    down the banks of the Ganga or
blocking elephants from the mountain caves
—dredging the old hate between Simians & Pachyderms—
living on Mt. Usheerabija or Mt. Mandara:
the virile and difficult to resist Pramathi
    leader of a hundred thousand troops
ready to go
                    ready to follow their
general in service to the king Sugriva
    and to Rama

And that one   Kesari   from
the shimmering Mt. Sumeru
a mountain circled by the sun
    and a sun in itself
    trees swaying with bees in
the gold light that yields
        as if its own strains
of bursting fruit and honeys

Note on Large Numbers

1Lakh=100000=1+fivezeroes1Crore=1Lakhx100=10000000=1+sevenzeroes1 Śaṇku=1Crorex 1Lakh=1000000000000 =1+twelve zeroes1Mahāśaṇku=1Śaṇkux 1 Lakh=100000000000000000=1+ s e v e n t e e n z e r o e s 1 V ṛ n d a = 1 M a h ā ś a ṇ k u x 1 L a k h =100000000000000000000000=1+twentytwozeroes1 Mahāvṛnda=1Vṛndax1Lakh=1000000000000000000000000000 0000=1+twentysevenzeroes1Padma=1Mahāvṛndax1Lakh=1000000 000000000000000000000000000000=1+thirtytwozeroes 1Mahāpadma=1Padmax1Lakh=1000000000000000000000000 00000000000000000=1+thirtysevenzeroes1Kharva=1Mahāpadmax1Lakh=10000000000000000000000000000000000000000 00000000000=1+fortytwozeroes1Mahākharva=1Kharvax1Lakh=10 0000000000000000000000000000000000000000000000000 0000000=1+fortysevenzeroes1Samudra=1Mahākharvax1Lakh=100 0000000000000000000000000000000000000000000000000 00000000000=1+fiftytwozeroes1Ogha=1Samudrax1Lakh=1000 0000000000000000000000000000000000000000000000000 000000000000000=1+fiftysevenzeroes1Mahāugha=1Oghax1La kh=1000000000000000000000000000000000000000000000 0 0 0 0 0 0 0 0 0 0 0 0 0 0 0 0 0 0 0 0 0 0 0 0 0 = 1 + s i x t y - t w o z e r o e s

one hundred crore mahāugha one hundred mahāugha one hundred samudra one hundred kharva one thousand mahāpadma one hundred padma one thousand mahāvṛndas one hundred vṛnda one thousand mahāśaṇku one hundred śaṇku and one hundred c   r   o   r   e

No. of Simians waiting to kill you

Some Omens

Dogs ate the ceremonial offerings
Donkeys were born to cows & rats to
                        mongooses
Cats slept with leopards
    pigs with dogs
Kinnaras fucked rakshasas & humans
    Red-footed doves in the air

The time-spirit had shaved his head
        He looked our way
        cast a grudging eye
        on whatever we had

Some Omens

Wood against wood shoots spark
The fire mantra is in the house of fire
but a black smoke swallows
      and smudges it out
Creepy crawlies in the kitchens
Little red ants discerned
      in the sacred offering

No musth oozes
      from the foreheads of elephants
  no trace of milk on the aging cow
Horses though still content with their daily
      supply   yearn fearfully
  Donkeys camels mules   sobbing
  Swarms of crows on the balconies
      of high buildings

My first my second that were as oblations
at the edge of the city: the vast ruins
      that still ruled and gave
        heft to the surrounds

From the *Sukra-niti*

Road-saboteurs   casual slanderers   wall-jumpers
ruiners of water-reservoirs and of houses
ditch-fillers   publishers of the king's
imperfections   trespassers into inner apartments
into bedrooms   into storerooms   trespassers in
the kitchen   wedding- and party- and private
dinner-crashers   those who spit
or pass wind before the king   those who sit
in heroic postures in front of him   those who just
remain seated when he enters the room   those who dress
better than the sovereign   those who approach
him impatiently   those who enter by backdoors
those who come at the wrong hour   those who take naps
in the royal beds   those who lounge on royal seats
those who borrow the monarch's sandals   those who doze off
in front of him   those who sit on seats not offered   those who climb
in view of the king   those who relax when he reclines
those who reach into their pockets for betel or tobacco
and calmly begin to chew   those who talk or speak
without permission   those who insult or defame the monarch
those who appear before him wearing only a single cloth
those who come with oil-rubbed skin or disheveled hair
or shamelessly painted bodies or garlands   those who
shake their clothes about when they walk   who seek
an audience with their heads covered   who wear
hats   those who are skilled in the picking of pockets
those addicted to gambling and drink   those who
study too hard their own noses ears and eyes
those who pick at their teeth   those who dig
at their ears with fingers or implements in
his presence   those who blow their nose
before the king:
these are the "fifty discourtesies"

The Bridge

They trip us up
the ancestors   Don't mean to but

they do   Deepening that coastal
shelf   deepens the sea what

faces us   But Rama'd spoken
harsh to the Depths

they'd rolled & cowered back
receding the tide

& now only the work of bricks and stones
along a natural risen ridge
of the bed

The Simians & the Ursines went to work
in disciplined aggregate

Even the squirrels who
at first had seemed pests

upon the foundation turned
out to have been rolling in

the wet sand of the beach to bring sealant
And despite its force   its lasting power

the bridge was not a work
of mud and stone

It was the thought of
the army on permanent move

and the leap that
turned sights in the vistas

of the foreign-made sky

The island of Lanka merged in
the planet's receding curve

The bridge soared even in the upper corners
where kinnaras and gandharvas lounged

among swirl of spirals   of arches
among v-turned flyovers

In this way the bridge was belief
back to the hold of us

Burlap of sacks   still to come
Sun on a diamond peak just so

Then the call to follow
the advanced shore

Note on "Poem Without Beginning or End"

THIS POEM consists of three separate but interwoven strands. The first strand includes scenes of war from Valmiki's sixth book and other classical texts. The second and third strands deal with killings and torture performed by the Indian state, mostly in the past twenty years or so.

The second strand, subtitled "Martyrs of Dandakaranya" and indicated by sections that begin below a line toward the bottom of the page, draws primarily from several issues of *People's March*, a magazine edited by P. Govindan Kutty from 1999–2012, and then by unidentified editors since 2014. This magazine for and about Maoist insurgents in the forests of central India regularly published obituaries of its fallen members.

The third strand, indicated by sections that begin below a line toward the middle of the page, draws primarily on a report published by the Jammu Kashmir Coalition of Civil Society (JKCCS) and the Association of Parents of Disappeared Persons in May 2019. Ranging in its account from the 1960s to the present, it documents in detail 432 cases of torture in Kashmir.

In working with the sources in the second and third strands, I have cut and excerpted, changed names to initials, and occasionally edited for continuity and flow, but I have not meaningfully added to or altered the language of the original text, wanting the sources to speak for themselves through a distillation of the material.

The second and third strands also use supplemental material from news reports and NGO documentation. See Notes and Sources in the back for a complete list.

Poem Without Beginning or End

Prahasta's night-roving battalions
landed on those luckless Simians

                              (exhausted army
        camp   the northern shore)

      with spears blinking in the firelight
with javelins tall as humans   honed on both sides
              with daggers
          with triple-headed axes
      with metal-helmed   red bamboo lances
              with iron clubs
with blades needle-pointed   broad in the middle
              with hammers
        lathis for beating and breaking
          cut-starred discuses
        wood-handled poison darts
          augmented nails & teeth
              silver scimitars
          frog-mouthed bhindipalas
nooses to tighten on the necks of humans or horses
              "hundred-killers"
        booby-trapped wheeled pillars

      and of course arrows...

        They got every
                single one drowsing there

      Waking to horror

        First things first:
        Prahastha's sword
          slit the neck
        of sleeping Rama

& Traitor Vibhishana was nabbed before
he could slip away

Lakshmana and his Simian commandants
scattered in ten directions
but were coralled and blocked

Hanuman's husky jaw torn
clear off the face at its hinges

Sugriva's attractive shoulders
snapped in two

Jambavan bludgeoned
at the knees

and felled
his torso stripped
like a tree   of branches

Those Simian soldiers obliterated
like clouds in quickening wind
whosoever fled was
harried into the woods
into the sea
the sky

So this is how among troops and allies
your own dark-skinned lord was killed

And   by way of evidence
from Vidyujjihva:

Here   his dusty head
Here   the great bow he carried

Dropped it   Like a lost
football   that lolling skull

O Rama who crossed the ocean for his lover
snuffed here in a cow's hoofprint

◆ ◆ ◆

.... but that was not what happened
            Not   in this wing of the stories
        Rama yes the one elected to win
        Yet in the midst of a war
                        so many others
            the people you met
    fist bumping in other rooms
    hugging in other rooms
    lying in other parking lots
The war of the end of time
    the war of no time
            crumpled like little notes
            next to the arm
    the slashed vein spilt on the table
    The immense height
fate endlessly branching

        & the final entrance—nothing?
            nothing to give
            if the atman
        if the atman could weep—

36 percent of the total power generated
contributing 42 percent Thermal and
14 percent of Hydel power 24
percent of total consumption
450 lakh tonnes of dolomite
reserves 53 lakh tones of bauxite 35 000
million of coal   2336 million iron
    ore   3580 million lime stone
Beyond is a zone that is usually described
  by the government as Maoist "infested"

Hillocks are lovely things for firing ranges

Martyrs of Dandakaranya

Comrade M.. hailed
from a poor backward Caste
peasant family of Mangapeta village
in Karimnagar district   Joined the Party in
1980   Though he did not have much formal
education   in the course of the class struggle
he constantly improved his political
and theoretical level through deep study

After ordering the killing of comrade M.
and seven other comrades in Nallamala forest
Home Minister J.R. "magnanimously" declared
that one member from each family would be
provided a job and a young son be given free education

When reporters asked M.'s 15-year-
old son   K. who had just entered first year
of Intermediate course what he thought he said
he was deeply disturbed that
the very government that killed
his father had come out with such a proposal

Also that he had no ill-will
toward his father even though the latter
had never seen him   Instead he had great regard for his father
and was proud that he had died for the people's cause

Only regret was whether he would at least be able
to see his mother   Com. V. who left him while in the cradle
due to her dedication to revolution

The parents of another Comrade V.—
C. and P. said   though they were sad to hear
of his death they were also proud

to have given birth to such a son
who would lay down his life
for the people's cause

L. a friend of S. from Medak district
said S.'s martyrdom was great in the people's struggle

The irony was that only two names were announced correctly
Finally begin shifting the bodies on 25th night
Panchanama of the corpses
done in Yerragondapalem Bodies taken to Guntur
more than 72 hours after encounter

On the day of the funeral they sealed
the village from all sides   blocked routes
from Peddapali Sultanabad Muttaram Srirampur
imposed section 144 on the roads leading to the village
stopped all vehicles noted their numbers and sent
them back set up video cameras throughout and in Mangapeta

Thousands still managed to enter the village through various means

Guntur and Prakasam districts alone 400 homeguards   then recruited
with a salary of Rs. 3000 per month Another 200
from Adivasis Dalits and backward castes appointed as
special police officers (SPOs) with pay ranging from Rs. 1500–2500

The comrades who died
were taking bath near a stream Three others
who were caught at an appointment place
on June 15   In almost all the incidents
the dead bore ~~torture~~ marks

Half of the martyrs were women

They came by way of tribute
from chieftains to the king
or recruited
in village squares
Payment only a percentage of the spoil
(1/6th to the monarch)
Food   drink   vehicles   domestic animals   metal   jewellery   slaves
break things in a far-off land

Plunder part
of military strategy
Expect to face casualties—

waves of bodies to mire
the enemy plough

And Rama
whose anger was
to be feared

He'd killed fourteen
thousand rakshasas in Janasthana alone
some holding powerful weapons
others caught
in the crossfire

"I'd be the one to kill my brother's son
for Rama
except for the tears that blur my eyes
when I think of it..."

the sea in
disarrayed clicks of the moon

a spine of submarine hills

"the serried ranks of clouds"
the great sages
wheeling round the pole star
left to right

the ocean where fish
were the javelins and battering rams

Rama the Perplexed

stones bleached white
by breakers

He shouted "Allah!" which irked his torturers
        who asked him to say
    "Ram Ram"   or they would shoot him   when he refused
        he was beaten so mercilessly
    that other officers rushed in from outside
and "rescued" him   All the three brothers were

powder   After this   he was put naked into a sleeping bag
        in which five to ten large rats
     were also placed   The rat bites left his entire
     body bruised   but he was never taken to a

The day he was taken out A. and the other detainees
        all assembled in the jail yard
                him The ~~torture~~ continued
             till 03:00 am after which
        he was put in a dark room   He was
     bleeding through his rectum   Shifted
  to Sadder Thana the next day for two

                    kept naked and forced to drink water
  before being given electric shocks   ~~Beaten~~
  with a steel rod and lost consciousness
           when hit on his head by the

This was done in presence of Superintendent M.L.S.
     Interestingly   no questions were asked
        or no information sought from him

   Frequently called to the camps after that
           forced to collect garbage
        prune branches   do laundry   sweep

Comrade V. was an MA MPhil
student of Central University Hyderabad
   This only son of a poor dalit family
   had played an important role
in building the movement in Hyderabad city

   Comrade P. had studied BEd and hailed
   from a poor family of Vargal village
   of Medak district   Up to
      the time of his martyrdom
   he was working in Anantapur district

Comrade "University B." born
in a middle-class Dalit family
in Chirala town of Prakasam district

Comrade S. an ordinary person
with ordinary feelings fears doubts desires
weaknesses uncertainties

On May 10, 1999 Upper Dumri
village of Gumla district of Bihar
there was no option
other than to accept martyrdom

His body though was not allowed
to fall into enemy hands He was laid to rest
with full party honours

Comrade P. from a middle-class business family
of Shahadra area in Delhi Small-built boy
whose friends were amused at his lack of "athletic skills"
consciously developed himself and went ahead
to assume the leadership of military affairs
of the armed peasant movement of Bihar

Another Comrade P. one
of the rising local stars
in the Dandakaranya revolutionary
movement Born in a poor peasant family
as J.V. There is a lengthy
reference to him in the Marathi novel by Vilas Manohar
(*Eka Naxalvadi-chi Ghosht*)
and at the time of his death a long obituary
in a Nagpur daily
Today a song in Gondi

Com. M. a tribal girl
from Ahiri-Etapalli area   First active in KAMS
and then joined the squad in 1991 where
she learnt to read and write

Com. S. (M.N.)   28
also an early recruit   When sent
to distant Balaghat she quickly picked up
the local language

Com. R. was from
an upper-middle-class
background   After finishing his diploma
in civil engineering he joined
the telecom department

All these heroic martyrs of DK have lived
exemplary lives   Their blood has fertilised the soil
of the developing guerrilla zone
in Dandakaranya

On January 10, 2000
Comrades R. and S.
were arrested at Perungadu village Both
brutally   by the STF
(Special Task Force) and "Q" Branch

R. was blindfolded and
shot dead from point-blank
range   in front of S.

◆ ◆ ◆

On December 26   two buses were burnt
(after the passengers were asked to alight)
in Dharmapuri protest against
the dastardly killing
of the three CC members of CPI (ML)[PW]

A 3000 strong force was mobilised
in addition to the STF   Six special teams were formed
to comb the villages

Let the enemy not forget
North Bastar last year
a huge nest of spies
discovered and annihilated

There above a gateway
stood the enemy   Rakshasa king
white whisks
triumphant parasol

with scarlet paste smeared
and ornaments on the arms
dark like a cloud sporting gold

Long chest scars
partly hidden by a cloak red
as rabbit's blood

Even as the other Simians and humans watched
his rival   king Sugriva   sprang to attention
and in sudden swift fury
bounced from mountain to gate
Paused for a moment   Long-gasped
Then rushed Ravana
knocking off the sovereign's crown

Leapt away but couldn't resist turning back

Seeing the Simian ruler coming
toward him a second time

Ravana said   Yes   come   Come here "Su-...   griva..."
I'll break your pretty neck

He reached and flung the Simian monarch
like a toy   Sugriva got back up
moving in the curving arc of a cow's urine &
in & out & in & out &
feinting sideways then retrograde spin
dodging blows   darting
stabbing   chest bumps

In this ancient way at first they fought
but changed it suddenly
those skilled ones:

the two of them   the Simian king & the uber-Rakshasa
stopped the fist blows
and hand slaps
and elbow jabs
and finger pokes and soon
just tore at the mutual guts
holding tight
PARASPARAM *svedavidigdhagātrau*
each to the other परस्परं स्वेदविदिग्धगात्रौ | ichor-smeared
PARASPARAM *śoṇitaraktadehau* |
each to the other परस्परम् शोणितरक्तदेहौ | holding fast like
PARASPARAM *śliṣṭaniruddhaceṣṭau* |
each to the other परस्पर श्लिष्टनिरुद्धचेष्टौ | śalmali and kimsuka trees
PARASPARAM *śālmalikimśukāviva* | |
परस्परं शाल्मलिकिंशुकाविव ||

tau CAKRATURYUDDHAMASAHYARÛPAM | तौ चक्रतुर्युद्धमसह्यरूपं |

Barehanded bitchslapping
they fell from the roof
down between the city's
outer walls and its moat
landed rolling and bruised

lay for a long moment   breathing heavily then
the two of them   circled circled
two of them   wildcats over meat
two   round and round
Sugriva   tackled his opponent at the knees
the two of them   fell to the ground
two   revolutions in the dirt

parāvṛttamapāvṛttamapadrutamavaplutam
परावृत्तमपावृत्तमपद्रुतमवप्लुतम्

(Sugriva escapes)
(and goes on . . .)

According to Mohammad Anwar Ashai
prominent civil society member
there were many interrogation cells
operating during the 1960s
which were used as
chambers   These include
Bagh-e-Mehtab sub-jail
Red interrogation centre
Gupkar Road Srinagar
White interrogation centre
Tulsi Bagh Srinagar

Various district
level sub-jails
Humhama (Joint Interrogation Centre)
Badami Bagh (Headquarters
of 15 Corps Indian Army)   Islamia College
became well known

"Forget today   we Kashmiris
would often offer tea or lunch

to Indian Armed forces
during crackdowns during the '90s"
says Z., resident of Batamaloo

"When you see 8–10 drunk
armed men entering your bedroom
and realise their
intentions   your whole world
becomes dark at that moment"

"Look again" said the army colonel
in a tone that betrayed suppressed excitement

It was a head   the disembodied face
nailed onto a tree

"The boys got it as a gift for the brigade"

◆ ◆ ◆

A.G.'s head and chest
trampled over and he was

from his home   asking him to show
them the short route
to the nearby village of Nambal
But only a few steps
blindfolded
taken to the camp where

some scarring in his windpipe

H. states that he was in a *tonga*
(horse cart) going
from his village to Sopore town

And when he went to a private
doctor named A.Q.
for treatment   the Army
picked the doctor up as well

June 20, 2008   That day a powerful
IED blast by militants at
Narbal crossing   On pretext
of investigation he was arrested
along with many others

That
evening   Army personnel accompanied
by *Numberdar* (revenue head) of the village
came to his home   took him

nearby *mohalla*   where he led

the military officials to
the medical store where his
son used to work   His son's absence led to his

father picked up yet again

◆ ◆ ◆

The Indian army said
it had "not manhandled any civilians as alleged"

"no injuries or casualties
due to countermeasures
undertaken by the army"

"No specific allegations of this nature
have been brought to our notice Likely
to have been motivated
by inimical elements"

◆ ◆ ◆

An informer was brought
asked to identify people from those
assembled   20 to 25 people
                              He was
              blindfolded and taken
to the Indoor Stadium in a gypsy vehicle

and cut
off his two injured
fingers with a razor   During this
fell unconscious   Two

condition   put him into a jeep
took him to Shariefabad Camp outskirts of
sprayed petrol over his
legs threatened
to light them on fire   They
him in order to recover his

personnel of the Central Reserve
Police Force (CRPF) while
trying to save his
12-year-old brother
Died July 14

Five of the dead were women comrades
Some papers reported that the exchange
of fire took place from 9:30am
8:30pm   Bodies were brought down
from the hills in the night   Some were burnt hastily

Comrade V. hailed
from Mogilicharla village   Worked hard
to make the Rythu Coolie Sangham (RCS)
a grand success   Although he was the only son

to his parents   never showed any special sentiment
   toward his family

   Comrade S. hailed from Pydipalli village
      Drawn toward revolutionary politics
      while doing his science degree course
   at the CKM college   Name was selected
   for inclusion in the district committee
   but became a martyr before the co-option

   Comrade S. hailed from a rich peasant
family in Kothapalli   Was influenced by the revolutionary activity
         in the surrounding villages
   while studying in the tenth standard
      Had to fight with her parents
   even to pursue her college education

      Com. M. (22 years) born
in a poor peasant family in Balepalyam village
      Opposed the activities of the splinter
         pseudo-ML goonda gang
   of Suresh (a stooge of landlord P.R.)

      Comrade B.
   was a native of Rayachoti town
   of Cuddapah district
      His father was an army person
From his childhood   he did exercises
   participated in sports and built his body   When
he was studying in Rayachoti   he fought
   several times the goonda gangs of that town
      when they indulged in atrocities
on small bunkers and tea hotel owners   Though
   he got a railway police job   he rejected it
      and joined the party

He was naturally a daring person   Participated
   in the annihilation of informer U.H.

in Rayachoti   Smashed goonda S.S.R.
who attacked the workers of Madanapalli
spinning mill   Participated in the annihilation
of a people's enemy and bad gentry
in Kalahasti   Exposed before the public
the traitor N. who was involved
in covert operations
at the behest of Superintendent U.C.

Besides   Com. B. carried many comrades
who were seriously ill during journeys in the forest
Very simple in his dress   Though he
was doing recky work   in the city he regularly
studied the newspapers   Also learnt car driving
and made enormous effort to learn Hindi and English
which were necessary for city life and actions

Comrade K. was a native of Srirampur town
of Adilabad district   Came from a poor workers'
family   Studied up to the 10th   Participated
in smashing several informers   Remembered
all the bus route numbers   all the vehicle numbers
of VIPs   pilots   escort vehicles

Daring   class hatred   initiative
having general political knowledge
coming to correct estimations
—were the special characteristics of this comrade

Com. P. studied only up to the 3rd
standard but after coming into the party
learnt much   He was a good actor   Played student
and women roles in the street plays
performed by the squad

Com. S. was a native of Inol
village   Father was a carpenter   Though
he seemed to be a lean

and thin person   was firm
in all actions   Always put
much effort on studying   Always
put his study in a question-answer form
written in his notebook

The police ~~tortured~~ them the whole night but
they revealed nothing to the enemy

warriors handsome in helmet
handguard   oxhide buckler
On the   command
banging the moon-white faces of drums
with golden staves
howls of conches
soldier-mouthed
billowed cheeks
dark-bodied

Rakshasa battalions rushed
to fill the field
with the force of a swollen ocean

Then from the Simian side
a responding clamour
suffocating air
& not to mention   the screams
of elephants   the neighing
of steeds   the rattle of chariot wheels
& the heavy shaking tread of the foot soldiers

Victory to King Ravana!
Victory to King Sugriva!

Tore into each other
maces spears   hooks & axes
limbs & strips of skin flying
through the air

◆ ◆ ◆

Who kills an envoy
goes to hell with all his ministers

On the rakshaka sovereign's command
  Shuka the spy became a bird

flying low over the long sea he reached
  the shore and hovering over

    white and shimmering
    addressed the ape king

    before he could even
      finish

     (The Simians are wild my lord
      they cannot be restrained
      they tore my wings
    even scratched at my face
      for the spite of it)

Body thrown
in an orchard
belonging to a Pandit at
Rawalpora

to Bomai Camp
to Watlab Camp
detained for 22
days   Major S.

stick inside G.
N.M.'s mouth
breaking teeth The armed forces
lit a haystack on fire
threw his father in it

◆ ◆ ◆

Tied the men to one another
put the dead bodies of their companions on their
backs so that they would carry them down

the hill to the camp   Army would kick them from behind   which
                    caused them to tumble down
    the hill   sustain injuries   This continued for some
                        distance   until they reached
            the camp on the foothills

This time no   in fact he was given food
                    regularly

◆ ◆ ◆

            The camp's condition   All kinds
        of instruments which frightened the victim
                being only a child that he was
        At that time stone pelting was going on and
            he was forced to give names
        There was another boy who was much younger
                still had several FIRs

        At this moment something happened
                outside the school that caused
            commotion   Towel was
                taken out of his mouth
        and he was pushed into a vehicle

◆ ◆ ◆

            Burned his beard
            and face to the point

        The uncle of M.D.
        saved him   as the victim had helped
        his nephew secure a permanent job
            in a Government department

        The victim replied his watch
            mobile and Rs. 1300
                with the wallet

10–15 days   received his
things back from Wusan Camp
After 2003   wasn't
harassed anymore

name of village
should not be published

killkilllikekilleiekilllkilekilllkkil
kkkklleeliikllkkilllkikelikrleilkilei

war its own faulty contract
the slaughter in the light began

the more you tried
the less it yielded

anyonyam samara jaghnus
tasmims tamasi daruna
struck the other down in that dreadful dark

"Come here and hit me. Try and hit me if you can."
But it's someone else that strikes
and a third still
who looks to be the one saying "Oh yes I will."
And a fourth an altogether another
"Don't you worry I'm coming for you. Just wait."

twisted the neck
yanked the skull from
socket

"You an ape?"   "Rakshasa?"
"Cut the fucker to pieces."

kicking and hacking
even after   mere seconds later
the poor deserter 'd dropped
to the ground unconscious

They had studied day and night
the enemy's movements his
checking places his network
his security arrangements They
attended several VIP programmes
under cover   Used
the communication network Learnt
to drive a motor bike and auto
in the crowded city streets   Several times
they had been close to arrest
but escaped the checking barons

with creative talk   Though city life corrupts the youth
        with bad cultural habits
these comrades never fell for those   even if
   they had plenty of money in their pockets

                All these comrades
           had different skills and abilities
        in different spheres   Studied
         the weak points of the enemy
       in the Umesh Chandra and Madhava
           Reddy actions   succeeded
            in giving severe blows
          Burning with class hatred
       they entered the enemy's den
       with calmness and confidence
     that are pre-requisites for such actions

                 Smashed
            a cruel IGP in the heart
        of Hyderabad city   Annihilated
   a former AP Home Minister in a mine blast

      And that enemy even feared
         to enter the room
   directly after their murder   Opened
       the door hurling grenades
          with automatic fire

F. (wife of H.M.)
registered a case against the boys
claiming they had stolen INR 5000 and a few film
CDs from her house   Lied due
to a land dispute
On the first day   Sub Inspector Hyder Ali
asked the boys about their
involvement in the robbery   which
they denied   Later taken into the   room
and   one by one

Fees of the lawyer   besides managing transportation
charges and staying away from

J.B.   middle-aged woman   lost four sons
and her husband   Provided with INR 100 000
as compensation by the government

that money
She was   sadistically until
promised to give them

the whole money   She
      dunked
   in water mixed
   with chilli powder Later was
   made to lie on floor and current
passed through her toes   ears
& hands till unconscious   The same

   From that day till now
   having heavy periods   lost control
on urination   insomniac spasms in her
   hands and feet   ulcers in her stomach

                  After two or three days
   some Ikhwanis with Army men told
would ~~rape~~ if she refused proposal
      Other option pay them INR 30,000
   Stuck to his decision and did nothing and

      His left shoulder is in
      continuous pain

                  ◆ ◆ ◆

   Recognized him as
S.B. of Brain Nishat who
   was cousin of J.'s grandfather
   The family surprised to see
   their own relative collaborating

They were about to ~~torture~~ them when
grandfather and grandmother yelled "*Ho Sona
   Ye Kuho Koruth* (Oh Sona!
   What have you done?)"

                  ◆ ◆ ◆

INR 100,000 be paid to the widow

On advice of a doctor has to use a waist belt
while walking or doing any work

A "nocturnal knock"

◆ ◆ ◆

"I do not ~~beat~~ anyone or
~~torture~~ anyone   *Khaali mai*
insaani gosht khata hoon (I only
eat human flesh)"
And with this
started biting the flesh
of the victim's shoulders

◆ ◆ ◆

When reporting   he was
always forced to do
laborious work in the camp
such as cutting grass clean
drains and bathrooms
and breaking coal

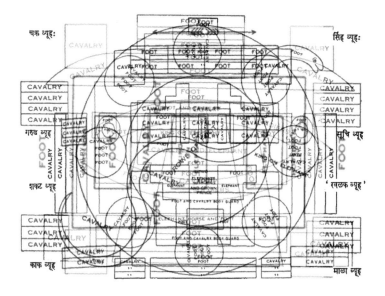

Whatever the detailed
preparatory array
you couldn't understand anything
Couldn't believe anything
Enemies coalesced
Appraisals
spies
intelligence gathering

So much planning
snapping of bones
vomiting of blood
gut-strewn fields

The slides had to be switched
Much of it   unremembered

Negotiations the way
to prevent war
But in negotiations
one shows one's strength

To depict a bleeding from the stomach
was pornography

To put a decapitated head on a page
was to make a clean break of it

In order to cover their tracks
regarding the murder of the three
central committee members

an ordinary peasant   S.L.
(whom the police called Arun) was picked up
and shot dead and his body thrown
with the three CCMs   Now clear
the conspiracy was hatched by
the top echelons
of the AP police   Pounced

on him and tied his hands
at the back with a towel
and took him to the jeep
waiting near the Gandhi statue

B.W. appeared with his real name
  Showed his presence in combat uniform
    from dense forests and lush green
    orchards in the south   Issued
  video messages on different occasions
  saying Kashmiri Pundits were part and parcel
  of Kashmiri culture and wherever they wanted
to live they could live   Martyred at Bumdoora village
  in Kokernag area on July 8, 2016   More than
    one million people gathered

A. killed in an encounter   had
  a stone pelting case against him
    from 2010   His father
  would accompany him
to the court   Twice detained
    by the police for a day
Once for wearing his hair long
and once for staring at
a Special Operations Group personnel

Two rows of tombstones
line the Martyrs Graveyard
in Karimabad   In front   white marble slabs
bearing dates from the 1990s   Behind them
gleaming black stones   2015, 2016

the Simians reeled through the
teeming beauty of that forest
their very thruway quashed it

rushing woodland   bees   gallinules   natyuhas
        streams   cuckoos   lapwings   koyastibhakas
                     ospreys   herons

Absent of humans

("the deep heaving of elephants
agitated the ambient air")

Readying for the fight
the faces of the enemy horses
rubbing against each other
the flagcloth likewise

Subjugal   they understood too well
this that they had been taken into
Moved as if with a desperate
unshakeable knowledge in their eyes
And a solemn allegiance to
the social worlds that
had given birth to them

Porus's elephant who
though severely wounded   carried his master to safety
The immortal Balius and Xanthus weeping
for the corpse of Patroclus—

the horses handsome in
breastband & trellised croupière
the rich paisley on their saddlecloths
the elephants painted & shawled in gold

the long rituals of consecration
bathed for war—

or all of us who
as wretched watchers or
killers or both   however
peripheral

One night the explosion
closer than usual
projectile blazing through the dark
The worst triggered

by a misreading of the trivial
The other's thought that seemed
so transparent   passed in
a long room or on
a white street
grew shaded   as if   sudden cloud
Second later a grinning
young man was face down
unconscious on a curb

Com. N. was born in a village
in Krishna district to a middle peasant
family   Due to deteriorating financial conditions
    his further studies were supported
by a maternal uncle   He had a good height
a pleasing personality an affectionate behaviour
 and a microscopic analytical methodology

Com. S. was born into
a lower middle class peasant family
in village Periyari   Jehanabad district

Even during his college days he could
not develop a keen interest in his studies
For two decades he worked
among the poor masses of the Magadh

Another Com. S. was the beloved son
of a landless poor peasant family that had
migrated to the coal fields for a living   In jail
he wrote and edited the magazine of poems
entitled "The Voice of the Shackled Poet"
(*Bandee Kavi Gontuka*)

From the time of reconnaissance
to the seizure of ammunition
to the elimination of the enemy
he played an active role in the raid
on the Darakonda APSP   He killed
the sentry He finished off another policeman
to take control of the camp

Let us pledge to continue
and thereby fulfil the dreams
of our great martyrs

Arrows on the thoroughfares of the sky

rurushishni
arrowheads of antelope horn   copper   iron   bronze

aaraa mukha   *kshurapra*   *gopuccha*
awl-arrowheads   razor-barbed arrowheads crescent-heads cowtail heads
                                                    ardha-chandra
           bhalla   *vatsa-danta*
needle-heads   broadheads   calf-tooth heads
 soochee mukha
                   kaakaa-tunda
ear-shaped heads   crow's beak heads   fireheads

 karnika arrowheads like earrings
                        or the leaves of the *karaveera*

            The shaft of the arrow etched
        with the archer's name
      & the ends of the bow that held it
            thin and tapered like
      the brows of a handsome woman

        Arrows feathered for speed
          poison-smeared arrows
            oiled shafts
          fire-sharpened arrow tips

        Arrows fastened in pairs
          bone arrows
        & bows joined from
          bamboo or horn or metal
        bowstrings of cowhide
          or sinew or murva grass

        Arrows carrying fire
        Arrows for combat &
          arrows for long-distance execution

arrows like lions   tigers   kankas   crows   vultures   kites
jackals   wolves   fire-headed serpents
arrows like blazing fire   the sun   the moon   the half-moon
the comet   the planets   & the stars
Arrows to pierce   cut   or rend
& guillotining arrows

& from chariots & from the backs of elephants
helpers poured
"pitch   burning oil   hot sand   fire-heated
iron balls   poison sludge
snakes (psych. weapon?)   coal"

rain of arrows
curtain of shadows
curtain of shadows
rain of arrows
rain
The archer's glove stinging
The bowstring's thud
Seconds later
like thunder
when the half-moon blade in flight

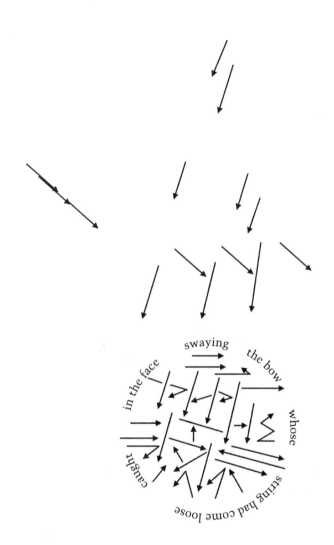

swaying

the bow

in the face

whose

caught

string had come loose

One of the army men untied
her trousers   pulled them down
She was warned
of not disclosing it to anyone
Came to know about her
husband's death from some
local   Later   she also found
that her jewellery two
transistors worth thousands
of rupees   and 30,000 cash
had also been looted from her house

          many
      nights in the watermill
From there J.
      taken to Badami Bagh
Cantonment   Srinagar where poorly
  ventilated underground room
  30 other people   All blindfolded
      naked

After treatment his right hand
has become functional again

K.A.D.
Male / Student
Parentage: G.R.D.
Residence: Seer Hamdan   Anantnag (Islamabad)
Age: 15
Affiliation: Civilian
Alleged Perpetrators/Agency: Not Known
Case Information

K. studying in 9th class
beaten while working
In a paddy field
September 7, 2001   Armed forces
into   field without
warning started hitting him
with the butts of their guns
later a stick inserted
into   Cried
for help   ultimately it was
because of intervention
of village head G.
H.G. his sister and
neighbours that
spared by the forces

Case 209

K.A.S.
Male/Student
Parentage: A.H.S.
Residence: Dadha Mohalla Shalimar Srinagar
Age: 16
Affiliation: Civilian
Alleged Perpetrators/Agency:

1. Station House Officer (SHO) Anzar Khan   Police Station Nishat   Jammu
&
Kashmir Police
Case Information

October 27, 2016 10 am
K. fetched milk and biscuits came back
home   After spending around
half an hour at home went out again   *Muharram*
procession was to be carried out
in the afternoon   so rush of people
since morning   Family assumed
he might have gone
to a nearby shrine situated in
his native village

His absence at lunch did not worry his family much

When 4 pm   went out to look for him   "a painful night"

Next morning brother told by a local that
Police Station H. arrested
4 boys blindfolded with their own shirts

The mother enquired "Who poisoned you?"
He replied "Policemen   some in uniform and
some in civvies"

Mourners with tear smoke
shells and pellets   People performing *gusl*
(ablution) of K.'s body also injured   One
of the maternal uncles

On the second day evening ~~beaten~~
first and then both of his hands and legs
tied to a rope   fixed to the roof
Facing the floor   they called
this position *jahaaz* (aeroplane)

(O when will my shafts dart toward
Rama like bees to intoxicating tree)

The jawans with shields at the front
  the archers behind them
chariots with generals and officers
  also carrying the armory
chariots followed by wheelguards

        the "heel catchers" targeted as mop up
           if they don't disperse quickly

    trailing a further retinue
    of footmen   including slaves (vishtih)
     who carried machines   backup weapons
      instruments and provisions

    And following at a distance
       campmakers:
    "panegyrists   priests   traders
    prostitutes and women of rank"

    also road repairers
     bullocks carrying
    supplies carpenters

    "as soon as the army reached the camp
    the prostitutes pitched their tents
    spread their beds   made themselves
    more attractive by putting on new clothes
     and   like old residents with
     offerings of water and betel leaf
      began to receive strangers"

      (Magha)

The crown prince of the rakshasas
sacrificed the black sheep
according to their customs
tomaras instead of kaasaa leaves
to ring the hearth
the twigs of the vibheetika
for kindling
Their draping cloth red
their ladles made of iron

This was a new kind of ~~torture~~ method
that N. had not
experienced before

After three months A.
transferred to PAPA 1

and beaten simultaneously
A jailor named M.K.P.
detainees in
another room

village
protested against the killing

Based on this recommended
INR 225, 000
SHRC not mandatory
INR 75, 000 as due

forced to work
as an informer promised
financial security
good job in the army

He severed the sheep at the neck
offered the head to fire
        The tongue of the god summoned there
lashed back at the oblation

        So   flame flares   An excellent sign
        Both sides hoped
            to win

        The warrior
"shoulder rings of rare and curious workmanship"
neck struck with red flowers
            and weapons adorned with
        creepers & pink &
        teasing blossoms

            Then those drums with moon-white faces bashed
    by gilded drumsticks   crashed
    the ear   screeks and yowls and caterwauls
                as if from some
            subterranean menagerie   alight
            conch like distorted PA system   tuneless
        and the percussion pure din
that churned your stomach
                smeared   the beat   that always came
                    unwelcome
                kettledrums   big gonged wardrums
                    and rows & rows of infantry

                    in the half hope that
                if they could merge their bodies in it

        by fleshless sound alone   the enemy
            would be vanquished

Ah sound
like black smoke
inside it
you might forget who you were
and who you were

No turning
the one who lost his nerve   lost

"You determine to go forward"

A shuddering seized
hairs alert
soul in the hands
Slaughter that herd of sheep
as if they were enemy soldiers

Half-moon-headed beheading arrows

armours decimated ground forces
battered each other with corpses

Blood seeped from great slain warriors
as resin from trees

The monstrous rulers are nothing but Rakshasas
　　when their interests are hit　Touch
　　　even one paisa and
　　　they are ready to kill

　　The police have a reputation
　　　of partying with sweets
　over the dead bodies of comrades

　　　The comrades are the cream
　　　of this society and the new

one being born   As in life
so also in death their memory lives on
like the sweet scent of the lotus
radiating joy to those in their vicinity

In his pocket there was a letter to his loved one
saying that he cannot marry anyone
who is not totally with the movement

◆ ◆ ◆

"We sowed tomato in the village
But the plants died   We were not
there to look after the plants   The police
stole even our utensils"

"They took away my husband's body like that of a pig"

"Who told you that the police came?"

"The militia was on the sentry   They told us"

"How are we to live   The police are chasing us"

"The party must tell us   What could we do
The party has weapons   That is a sure
protection for us"

"*Paddikothor Mekakun othor Korkukun othor Mirri vaathom*"
"They took our pigs They took our goats They took our hens
We escaped and came here"

"What shall we do now?"

"*Dongalorukun howkakal*"
"*We shall kill the thieves*"

They picked up a man but he escaped

They are the forest dwellers   They are like
the herb and the shrub in the forest   The water

and the sky are theirs   The sun and the moon
belong to them   That is why they are making war

on the thieves who are coming to loot their land   That is why
they are developing war   That is why they are teaching war

The begaar system of
forced military labour was
prevalent in the Dogra rule
(1846 to 1947)   G.M.D. Sufi
in his book   writes
"The people were dragged
out of their homes and forced
to carry military provisions
to distant places like
Gilgit and Ladakh . . ."

Q.G. (S.G.Q. Head
Constable   Special Staff)
referred to as the "Chief
Interrogator" particularly
notorious

Apart from the members of the "Peace Brigade"
who were paid an official salary
the Bakshi regime was
also notorious for the employment

of another class of party
workers   called Goggas
who were personally loyal
to Bakshi himself   rewarded by
government contracts
timber and fishing licenses etc.

October 1, 1992 a BSF patrol returning from
a crackdown in the village of
Bakhikar   in Handwara district
came under attack by militant forces

One member of the patrol killed   Following the ambush
BSF forces   through the nearby village

        Perplexity   the default
        All I know of
        is what I've read
        and what's been bred

           into the enemy army
    as the moth courting death
        goes to flame
               this will not
               end too quickly
   like   broken stone

    water   from   a   ravening

    for   fight   t error   that got   at
you

        arrow   overbite

            shining

      noose   was a shark   the troops

        serpents   of Death

And sometimes taken fright the horses
   yanked their transports not only
     into quicksands but even
    right into the river itself

The storm raged through the night
made the ground mushy and slippery
The chariots kept getting stuck
in the many sloughs and chuck-holes   Those vehicles

proved almost immovable
for being so heavy

Days later
soldiers hurled from their seats again when
rushing into action those cars
jolted and broke on skidding ground
(Megasthenes)

"The Hindu sepoys will throw
away their lives... The sequel
to this history will show
instances of whole bodies of troops
rushing forward to certain death"
(Elphinstone)

Comrade K. was born into a rich peasant family
   in Navabpet in Karimnagar district   Since 1985
working as a full time activist   Married Comrade
   M. (J.) while at home

She had cordial relations with the neighbours
   She maintained the cover so well
   that nobody had an iota of doubt
that this nurse with a frail body and serene face
   could be a Naxalite

Com. S. born in an ordinary family
Right from her childhood used to herd cattle   Got
   interested in revolutionary politics but
   by that time had a small child   Left
        a six-month-old baby
   with family members and joined the squads

There was nobody in that area who
   did not know her: that was the way
   she mingled with the people   She never
expressed the desire to be with her child
   and always said It is only a better society
that will allow true relationships to prosper   In two
police firings on Upper Plot and Nallamala squads
fought bravely with the enemy   In a greyhound
police attack on the squad near Sangidigundala
   in January 2006   martyred along
        with eight others

                    Just two days earlier
        bitten by a snake so in
   a weak condition when the attack came

   Com. L. born in a Dalit family
   in Madduru village of Pamulapadu mandal
   of Kurnool district   Came from a poor family
and background of extreme exploitation
of the landlords of her village   Parents
educated her   Her questioning nature led
   to revolutionary politics while she
   was studying   Began working in
   a women's organization   An
excellent singer   When she sang about
the agony of mothers of martyrs
people wept   The YSR government
wanted to end the talks process
   as soon as possible   So

it caught Com. L.
　　　~~tortured~~ her to death
　　January 8, 2005

　　　Comrade B. belonged
　　to a Chenchu village
　in the Nallamala forest   Opposed
　marriage and the Party educated her
took her into the squads Melodious voice
and quick in learning songs   Learned to read
　　　and write after joining
　　the PLGA   Hardworking soldier
　　　Did not hesitate to leave
　　the forest area when assigned
　　　by Party leadership
　　　Caught while traveling
　and killed after severe
on March 1, 2007, just a week
before International Women's Day

　　Com. S. lost her mother
　　when still a child
　　　The doting father
　　gave her the love
　　　and affection of both
　He could send her to school
till 7th standard   Participated actively
　　in the village revolutionary
　　　women's organization
　　gradually prepared herself

                                                                    scatter
                                                    scatter
                                                              scatter
seeing it fly suddenly up at him   fevered
in a blink Mahodara struck a massive a fevered   scatter   scatter
nearly unstoppable boulder with his weapons   of vultures
                                                      of vultures   scatter

shattered thousand to a thousand pieces of vultures
and the rock bits bounced off the earth   scatter

... well the sight of that rock he'd thrown getting
   smashed just made S. go nuts he
jerked a sāl tree from the ground
      roots and all
   flung it at the rakshasa
but Mahodara   the nightmare of enemy cities
   shredded the trunk with his arrows
lacerating S.'s triceps
               in their fanning path

going completely apeshit now S snatched a bloodied mace
            that had just been lying around
   and brandished it at his foe

               He was slightly tipsy
               having knocked back
            a thousand odd pots of hooch
         it reinforced his natural exhuberance

         a whirling of armies'
   riveragigitatation   immeasurable din

      with great arrow floods Prahasta
      washed away rows and rows of enemies
         in that inconceivable war
      heaped mountains of Simirakshas corpses
         growing on fat of that earth

smoothed by congealed blood
with black tributaries

—like the red Palash flowers that cover
the meadows in spring

On 9 July, 2018, he rushed home
to find an active tear gas cannister
in his living room   "The shell was fired
through the window into the room where
my parents usually offer
their prayers" he wrote on Facebook

◆ ◆ ◆

Female doctor in Handwara who
confirmed that the women
had been "severely molested" but that

because they were not virgins
it was not possible to confirm
whether

The doctor conducted semen tests
and examined the seven women separately

The presence of sperm can
only be detected within 48 hours
    of ejaculation

    October 12 N. 20 and her sister A. 18
    Z. 11 abrasions and bruises
        Semen test positive
    S. 60 no marks of injury elsewhere

        There was knocking at the door
        three soldiers entered asked
    "Where are the womenfolk?"

    One kept guard on the door

"We have orders from our officers to ~~rape~~ you"

    "You can shoot me but don't ~~rape~~ me"

        There about half an hour

        Their brother went to the door
    and said   "The army has come to search our house"

        Covered my eyes and mouth
    with cloths and told us to lie down

        Struck 10-year-old sister-in-law
    with a rifle butt   sent her out of the room

    "We have orders what can we do?"

    Only one came into her room   He told me   "I have to search you"

        I told him women
            are not searched
    but he said   "I have orders"

S.B. stated that three soldiers   When
       she protested that she
    was an old woman one of them
       kicked her in the chest
    and she fell   Then he put one hand
       over her mouth

    the army unit normally stationed
       in Chak Saidapora   "Conducted
    search operations in the village
       on specific information
that some militants were hiding there"

Stated that the search was carried out
"from 0010 hours to 0145 hours during which
       seven houses were searched
    in the presence of an elderly man"

Slain warrior heaps on bank
blood-flood immense water
engulf
deathsea bound
snapped weapons like maha trees
fallen
broken weapon

liver spleen piss thick mud   सेवार
⌐ *Bryophytes* / **Anthocerotophyta**
hornwort
scattered entrails

यकृत्प्लीहमहापङ्कां विनिकीर्णान्त्रशैवलाम्
yakṛt | plīha | maha | paṅkāṃ vinikīrṇa | antra | śaivalām

duckweed?
Lemnaceae
water lens

piss thick

liver spleen   head   moss
gargantua sludge

cleaved the body from the *torsos* fish *and heads of* hair but different
kinds of
tangled guts

भिन्नकायशिरोमीनामङ्गावयवशाड्वलाम्
bhinna | kāya | śiro | mīnām   *aṅga | avayava | śāḍvalām*

of swans   hangout
crammed-in flocks   limbs and member
or of vultures   sway like verdant grass
गृध्रहंसगणाकीर्णां कङ्कसारससेविताम्   of broken
heron   crane   *grdhra | haṃsa | gaṇa | ākīrṇāṃ kaṅka | sārasa | sevitām*

medhaḥ | phena | samākīrṇām
sodden in   मेद:फेनसमाकीर्णामार्तस्तनितनि:स्वनाम्   wounded:
fffoaming bubbling fffat   ārta | stanita | nisvanām   groaning

mMmMMMmmméééééééhdddhdd

jjjjjyyyyyvvvvvpppyyHppHyPHyp
pppPPppphhppphphphhhphééénmuhāāārrrrrʈʈʈTas
vʈʈuuuuuvvvʈsssssssssssss

निःस्वनाम्
niḥsvanām
sound
thunder

hard for cowards to cross
that   stream of limbs and organs

in the season of departing clouds
banks lined with swans cranes geese

tough though the rakshas-
-Simian heroes powered

swift as elephants through
ponds of lotus and pollen

into each other and into it
the bone crunch stomach splatter

the skin-brushed sky dark red
like kumkuma powder smeared

the hunched horizon like some lung
billowing from an opened chest

Com. I. born
into a middle-class Dalit family
in Nalgonda district   Married
a fellow comrade   Learnt
to read and write   She put
a proposal before the party
wanted to work
in an organizational squad   So
shifted back   to South Telangana
During that period she was killed

Comrade K. born in Mettapad village
in Dantewada   Her parents named her
M.P.   The ambush near Torrem village
was her first military action   16 police personnel
killed 17 injured   Whenever some comrades
pressurized her for marriage
in an inappropriate way   she criticized them
in the meetings of the platoon   Whenever
there was an extra luggage
she used to come forward
to lift it   Selected for the assault team
of Daula raid   Fell to enemy bullets
while breaching the entrance

Com R. born in a worker's family
in Kurad village in Kaithal district   He exposed
many a sadhu and held programmes all over the district
Was within the rural masses
when he contracted cerebral malaria   Due to
the lack of availability of quick treatment
it killed him in five days

Comrade S. born in a poor worker's family
in Kasireddypalli   When studying in
the 9th standard came into Party contact
joined in the Radical Youth League
of the village   Arrested August 1994
when putting up posters in Bellampalli town

Comrade J. an only child
Her father a worker
in the RK-5 coal mines   While studying in
5th standard she had been forcibly married off
She wrote many poems on martyrs   Enthused
the people with
revolutionary songs   Encountered
several police firings   Even worked
as squad doctor and served

the village poor people   She was martyred
fighting the enemy up to her last breath

Comrade V. had a great urge
to improve his theoretical level   Born into
the Dalit caste   later adopted
the tribal name of M.
and became popular by that name
among the adivasi masses   Wrote
several songs in Gondi   Killed
while going to answer nature's call
accompanied by his guard
in Maddimalla forest in Karimnagar district

Comrade D. hailed from a Dalit family
suffering utter poverty in Guntur district
Completed his plus two
and joined the Govt. Medical College
Performed the Ragal Jhanda ballet
with the Jan Natya Mandli
all over the state   Martyred
in a six-hour encounter
surrounded by hills
midst Lambada hamlets
in the Nalgonda forest

Com. K.   a squad area committee
member in the PGA   Always preferred
to be an ordinary activist never tried
to show off   Funeral rally turned
into protest rally   with hundreds
as her body
consigned to flames

From wayward and spoiled son
of a Dalit farm labourer
to commander of a local guerilla squad
Com. R.'s was

a saga of transformation   A dab hand
at many things   traversed extensively
    in the Chenchu villages of Nallamala
earned their warmth and got acquainted with their lingo

He was a courier as he had
a thorough knowledge of the winding passes
of the Nallamala forests (Legend has it he could
even traverse those passes blindfolded)
Appearing and disappearing as from thin air

His fellow comrades found
in R.'s kit a letter
written by his brother
expressing how happy he was
on hearing the news
that he would be taking over
the in-charge of an LGS

The shut-umbrella machine
The eloquent tower machine
The machine of glass & fizzled light
The one for moon-manufacture
The fantasy tableaux
The five-cylindered
The one with the wire-bound animals
The poison gas and ear-popping sound machine
The machine of tar layered below genuflective water
The three-leaved machine
The twin-pillared soothsaying machine
The one to change a river's direction
The other that bores a hole in the ground
The one whose top splits off to soar into the sky
The five keys that appear as turrets
The one that gathers
The three-face
The machine that carries another machine inside it
The old hundred-killer
The one that merges in the sky but transports
elephants   camels   chariots on the ground
The one made from metal found
where stars have been sown
The one to look for objects lost
on or under the surface of the sea
The machine of smoke-like-dew or dew-like-smoke
The heat attractor
That device that captures not only the appearance
but also the intentions
of whomever comes near
The one like a bird with beak open
The other like a mridangam with
the volume of approx. 63 bangs
another an inverted earthen pot
The one that gallops like a horse
when set to work by its key

The machine of the three-beaked crow
square in shape and white in colour
that burns trees for their oil
The machine that ferries and releases pigs
The one that makes timber and
the one that makes the hands
that haul the timber
The eight-petaled rain-making machine
The light-filterer The mortar
with sieve-like holes
The one that sets fractured bones
The one that wraps a body in
the bark of the valkala plant and severs the limbs
The one meant for the ~~torture~~ and killing of deserters

At Warpora Camp   ex-militants
forced to crawl along the road
for long distances through the village
   and the villagers forced
   to taunt and spit at them

He remembers the name of one ~~torturer~~
called A. who was working with Military Intelligence

◆ ◆ ◆

Z. was a tailor
Taken to a nearby field

Medical records   "Multiple
   pellets and one plastic
   canister" were removed

CRPF Inspector General Z.H. said
there was "no report or record of this incident"

but would launch an inquiry
if the boy filed a report

His physique was badly affected and
despite being a capable student
had to bid farewell
to his studies

... seeing it fly suddenly up at him
in a blink Mahodara struck the massive
boulder with his weapons

the veena of my guts which is also
the veena of the killing I've caused
my arrows pluck the low notes
there's a middle range in
the cries of the frightened and the cut apart
and the shrill arrowhead
crooked in pinging flight knit
a new and glittering dome

If your sword gets caught
in an enemy buckler

ripe palm fruit
flung by the wind

Comrade S. chose to marry
S. of Messi village
at the young age of 15 when
she had visited that village
for song and dance programmes   She went
further than him in her work
in the village KAMS and gradually
went on to become
the village party
committee member   Her husband became

jealous of her but she tried
to make him understand She was killed
by her husband and the village bad gentry
Messi village North Bastar division
July 2006

Comrade J. born
in a poor Banjara family After she
grew up into a young lady fell in love
with a young man who went singing
from village to village Theirs
was a nomadic life Also learnt
to sing and give chorus Her husband
used to drink and beat her up
Learnt to read and write
with determination During that period
when the squad was conducting a people's court
near Janampet police came
with information

Comrade P. born in a poor Dalit family
in the village Arepalli of Karim nagar district As a child
used to work as daily wage labourer Fought
valiantly injured two policemen laid down
her precious life while defending comrades
against the enemy attack

L.T. born
in Gadder village in the Kasansur range
In 1985 her father became a member of
the peasant mass organization
in Dandakaranya (DK) Both father
and brother were arrested So she quickly
started learning the basics of military science
On November 1, 2005, when the guerrillas
were resting near Manewada village
the special police reached there

Com. V. born in a middle-class family
in Karim nagar district   When she was eight read
all 8 volumes of Mao's writings—not a small feat
for such a young girl from a village
One day the enemy encircled
the squad when it was near Gopalpur
she died in the firing

Comrade P.R.
joined the Gangalur guerrilla squad
earned the people's confidence
By seeing her determination
Party confirmed her membership
Used to do all types of exercises
without any hesitation   If she could not
do properly any item   the next day
would come to the gym
before the roll call   Used to feel
it as a great loss if on any day
she could not go to the gym
Martyred at an early age
in that battle May 19, 2005

◆ ◆ ◆

The police ~~raped~~ three innocent girls   Later
they killed S.M. and G.T.
in close range and the third girl S.
was put in jail with injuries

Com. S. born in a poor Madavi
family in Charwai village   Studied
till 5th standard   Joined the children's
mass organization then
the village militia after she grew up

Another comrade S. born in Amalapuram
of East Godavari district some 30 years back

After she finished her graduation she
was married off   But she could not continue
for long with the beast called her husband

Lit arrows like lasers
streaking through the pitch of that dark
firefly-like feathered arrows
the light that gobbles light
sprung into that night
moths in the black flame

ghore samgrāme loma harṣane
that hair-raising battle

śuśruve
could be heard
visusrureh
flowed

Rival sacrificial fires
ringed by arrows instead
of kusha grass
both in this way the same
Offering oblation

Came down eyes popped at the pupils
tongue spilled from mouth
and splayed on the soil

like a dead fish ashore
or a crumpled washcloth

kālā kancana etc...
black and gold flashing on a mailcoat
as the glow of the medicinal
plants in the mountains

kālā rātri iva bhutānām
time as a kind of dissolving night
its beings its salt

dṛsaya adṛśyāni
invisible visible
visible invisible

Although T. lost
12 years of his life
proving his innocence still comes
across a very positive man

Judgment also recommended
that INR 100,000 should be paid
as compensation in the
ratio of INR 50,000 by SHO M.
F.K. the then SHO
Police Station Darhal

and M.B. in equal shares
and INR 50,000 should be paid by constables
M.S. A.H.P.
and A. in equal shares It also
recommended that
the prosecution of the accused
in FIR number 89/2006
U/S 330 of RPC

of   the interrogators slit G.R.'s throat
with a knife   and then stabbed him in the
back once he fell down   In that state he was taken back to the
   market

not beaten but jumped and drowned in the nallah

   During the proceedings B.A.
   The statements of *Sarpanch Nambardar*

Chowkidar of the village and some
   neighbours of the victim
   were recorded by the
Tehsildar on spot   All of them
in their statements said that BSF personnel

injured the subject after a severe beating
and then killed him by throwing
   him down into the

categorically deposed   her father was beaten
   in her presence
by the BSF personnel

   As the second day
      dawned   he was
         asked for
   his weapon and asked
      to name a few
Taken to Delhi Police Special Cell Lodhi Colony New Delhi

   new techniques were introduced

Even after all of the   when they still
         could not get any confession out of him
            T. was told that
            they would get information
            directly by "testing" his brain

◆ ◆ ◆

When A. replied
that he had not eaten
the Major replied saying *"Le ja bhai
isko mithai khilao"*
"Take him and feed him sweets"
Then the ~~torture~~ began again

◆ ◆ ◆

S. was pursuing his PhD and was
an English lecturer   He
was able to speak fluent English and the army
was continuously accusing him
of teaching the boys all
these new ways of protesting

He was once taken to Room no. 7

Your killer javelin
with the eight bells that
announce it

shall fail its purpose
fall down spent

As we observe the wind that sweeps the forest
only by the chaos caused
one saw   not Rama but
shafts spiking from wounds
limb or chips of limb
on the goodbye from the soul

And *you didn't see him* pulling the arrows
from his quiver testing and
tightening the sinew of the string
shifting weight
and posture drawing to the ear
marking the enemy
hand on bow letting go
No   Only the results
in massed and feathered flight

M.P. was
not associated with any
militant or political outfit
His brother had joined militancy

He could
see a boy lying unconscious in the same room

Finally she gave them 300 rupees and when
A. asked them what for they
were asking this money they said
it was for the food which he had been
provided with last night They kept
his voter ID card with them

No food during these days
except a plain cup of tea
in the morning

The inner parts of his body
had come out due to the

Arrested December 30, 2004
Priya Guest House Darya Gunj
    in police records his arrest was
    wrongly mentioned
February 12, 2005
Gopinath Bazaar   Nagesh Garden

There also to assist his ailing nephew I.H.K.
    (AIIMS)

Priya Guest House Room No. 5
    since 4 days when
    around 9:30 pm
    a knock at his door

One of the police personnel
    mentioned the name of
    D.P.   Deputy Commissioner
of Police (DCP)   Delhi Police Special Cell
    Police Station   Lodhi Colony

A few days after his arrest   the DCP brought
    the sweeper M. into the police station
to sodomize him   M. was a 55-year-old man
    To humiliate him further   they
    brought another person S.
    a clean shaved person who
        was running a tea stall outside
        the police station and forced
        his private part into U.'s mouth

The officer offered him a cigarette
    and ordered for a cup of tea

Aditya Hridayam (Ode to the Core of the Sun)

Victory to those who recite these words
   addressed to the core of the sun
Blessing on blessing that roots out error
   prolongs our impoverished lives

   Crown of first rays
  greeted by devils and gods alike
Worship the light from which light derives
  scours our planet in ruling over it

Essence of a god in those reflected rays:
  protector of creatures and people
creation destruction folded existence
  wealth time death retribution
The moon earthly waters married to it
  mortal creature healing stars
    gods of wind gods
of fire gods of DNA maker
of seasons life-breath &
  house of stored light

Golden seeded daymaker
  Coursing through the sky rainmaker
Rides the seven green horses
  cancels darkness

Maker of thinness
  syringe of life into
the interstellar cosmic egg
  golden foetus

incubator of fire
  heat factory
zamindar of the lunar mansion

                awakener of lazyboneses
                conqueror of frost
                  who pacifies himself
                in the evenings
                  Engineer of coolness also
                    supplier of dew
                    Twelve-step lord

I bow to you behind the eastern mountain
I bow to you behind the western mountain

                O dispatch   O fruit of dispatch

Comrade R. born 1974 in a drought-affected district
   Though no proper food   no chappals
     for her feet only torn clothes
  to wear and no books to read used to go
  to school regularly So poor
    they decided she could not
be married off   migrated to Hyderabad city
   in search of livelihood Walked
  to wherever she could learn new things free of cost:
tailoring typing computer shorthand spoken English etc.
   From childhood faced sexual harassment

by her eldest brother
She used to religiously do puja
to all gods praying that her brother should change

Then joined in degree in a college
came into contact with
a women's organization called Mahila Chetana
Started learning karate   The problem she
faced from her brother was solved with this

Karate instructors were sexually
harassing their girl students
and so the girls were dropping out
She firmly believed
that only women karate coaches
should teach girls
Became a coach and taught
free of cost   Came
from a vegetarian family but
changed her eating habits
after joining the organization

Never fell sick   Started work
as a receptionist in a private nursing home
Sister followed in her footsteps
Parents went to the police
Finally both the sisters had to announce
in the press   they were majors

In Bangalore when state federation
gave a call against the Beauty Contest in 1997
the activists got arrested while
doing rasta rokos   The activists
were dragged by their hair
and beaten black and blue till they bled
She loved to have long hair   But after
the Bangalore arrests   thought her hair
was too handy for the police to grab her

so she cropped it

2003 joined the Maoist party
martyred in a fake encounter
with the mercenary police forces
    July 23, 2006

The surface of the ocean
on which the light
of the great city fell
There a second Lanka burned

From aerial car they could see better
the wide harvest in the field

Armies in waves
who'd gathered or melted the scapes

Then limbs and innards bristling with spikes
armours cloven
bows fallen from knife-sliced hands

Sediments of pus
but soon to be bones rising
in bleached light
then even that   long gnawed
by amnesiac yugas to come

The flame in the mind
when it appears

smokes and splutters
throws out sparks

Before that   they had managed
to hide their guns
somewhere among the stones

Detainees asked the authorities
to allow them to write letters to
their families   Were allowed
but a *sepoy* (Indian soldier)
told them those
letters were never sent

His father had come
thousands of kilometers
just to see him   and was
taken away after
just one sentence exchanged

◆ ◆ ◆

K. mentioned that
during his entire ordeal

he had encountered only
one good person   His name
was Lieutenant Colonel G.L.
    T. stationed at
Badami Bagh Cantonment   Had told
the interviewee he does not know what
    he has done but to him he is
    only a patient and he would
treat him like any other patient

He had kissed Col. T.'s hand
and told him that he was the only
human being in the whole place as

he was beaten up even immediately
    after his operation

◆ ◆ ◆

The bowls used to serve food
    had Punjabi writing on them
    so they thought they could
potentially be in Punjab   However the bowls
were so old that they came from a time
when Punjab and Haryana were
the same state   Soon after that
    started noticing that
Hisar Haryana was engraved
on other bowls   That is how
    they figured out that they
    were in Haryana

◆ ◆ ◆

The victim replied that she
was looking for her father
This infuriated the Dy.SP who
asked her why she was

searching for him   for he had
earned quite a lot and she
could just spend that money
and enjoy her life

She got a serious head injury for which
she was stitched upon
in the 38 Rashtriya Rifles dispensary

Cruelly the day she got released coincided
with the remarriage of her husband

◆ ◆ ◆

Pleaded with the cops
to not remove his trousers
at least as they are also humans
and they should have respect
for human dignity   But the cops did not
listen to him and
removed all his clothes
which made him weep bitterly

Early morning: mostly quiet
   human   animal sludge

  Some laying there with their hams or thighs torn
     begged you to slit their throats
  Others had dug little holes for their heads
    as if to drown themselves in the mud

   A few of the wounded rising
  but quickly slaughtered in their spots
  by stray enemy marauders

               Closeup killing makes me want
                 to throw up   it's effective enough
                look another in the eye
              make the decision to off him
              strike . . . watch him dead

    One Numidian still alive
     with lacerated nose and ears
    stretched beneath a heavy and lifeless
      Roman who lay on top of him—
  for when the Roman's hands had been powerless
    to grasp at his weapon turning from
     rage into madness   he had died
  in the act of tearing at his antagonist
        with his teeth

      (Livy)

Com. R.
from Warangal city Born 1960
His father a founder member
of railway   mazdoor union
participated in the anti-British
movement in the 1940s His eldest
brother B. killed by the police

Com. S. born into
a poor Dalit family in Kolhapur tehsil   Attended classes
conducted in the Nallamala forest   Led several

miltary actions and put a brake
to the enemy's advance
                    In the September 2000 district plenum
        while making self-criticism
                        for his mistakes

        Com. S. young radical student
    of Tekulagudem village in Warangal Dist.
    of the early 1980s   His father was a teacher
        and used to oppose him becoming a
        revolutionary Very popular
            among the people
    with his singing and dancing abilities Wrote
        a number of poems songs short stories
            not only in Telugu but in Gondi as well

        Once Com. S. visits a village means
        men women and children never
    forget him   Leaves his memories alive
    wherever goes   Penetrates into the hearts
            of the people   And after
        hearing about his martyrdom
        many people who knew him
            broke into tears

        Com. R. 19   born
    into a poor peasant family in Yadunathpur   Was
    a student in Nehru College Dehri
        had recently appeared
    for the intermediate exam Used
        to do courier job for the party
    Posthumously given party membership
        by the state-secretariat

        Com. R. from
        a poor peasant background
    from Hussainabad   Had come
        into the squad just 6 days back

Two officers including
one Dy. SP. D.K.R.
and one Inspector A.O.
who were involved in the killing of P.
were killed on the spot   Four others injured

This created a wave of joy
among cadre and the exploited masses
of Bihar   Jharkhand
especially of Koel-Kaimur
and panic among the rulers

Four comrades fell while fighting heroically
after an attempt to attack the notorious
Grey Hounds forces
The bullet ridden bodies were thrown
near the Heritage Food Industries

The beauty of that head in the dust
with its helmet and gleaming ear pendants

he wiped the eyes of his fellow ruler
    with   hands dipped in water

he wiped the conquered monarch's eyes
    with hands dipped in water

he wiped the conquered monarch's eyes
    with hands dipped in water

he wiped the supplicant's eyes
    with hands dipped in water

Two farmers who were
  working in a nearby field
at that time said that they saw
  a boy brought there
by the police in uniform
  and then shot dead

◆ ◆ ◆

He beat S.'s entire body
  with bamboo sticks
and broke both his knees and
  elbows   Several interrogators
  also stretched his legs
apart in opposite directions   which
  caused abrasions
under his thighs   They also
  pulled his arms
behind his back   which
  broke his shoulders

Did not go to a hospital for treatment   instead
    received his treatment at Tailbal
from a traditional bonesetter   Due to this
    he was at least able to walk on his
legs again

Comrade KDR worked as a bonded labourer
in his village and had an inherent class hatred
for the class enemies   Left his daughter
when she was five months old
went underground with
his wife L.   1985

The police as usual sealed off the village
Stopped the people coming from Dharmasagar
Anantasagar Peesara Veledu Kothakonda
Bodagutta Bheemadevarapalli

other places in Warangal and Karimnagar districts
  Shot video film with a view to harass
the people later on   However all these threats
    did not deter the people
who managed to circumvent police pickets
    through ingenious means
    and reached the village
    crossing the rice fields
    unnoticed on foot

    By noon it looked
like an ocean of masses   Slogans of "Ramanna
Amar Rahe! We shall fulfill the dreams
of KDR!" rent the air as thousands marched
  in the streets carrying the body   People
who had never seen KDR during the 24 years
    since he left the village
  came enthusiastically to have
    their first and last
  glimpse of their hero

    The reason why the police
    refused to allow media personnel
to visit the encounter site is obvious   They needed time
  to prepare the encounter site   Hurriedly erected
  five or six tents placed two pistols a revolver
  and a country-made weapon   solar lights
  wireless sets   revolutionary literature
kitchen materials and even cooked food (!)

  at the site   And of course the dead body
    of comrade S. which was brought
    all the way from Bangalore city
    where he had been caught
    the previous day

Across the three-yojana stretch
the trees had become
        trees of heaven
the sterile bore fruit
the unflowering blossomed
the dead slept serene under leaf-fall

"Happiness seeks out a man even if
he has to wait a hundred years"

Made to stare at high voltage lamp	3
Threatened	10
Made to face harsh weather conditions directly	11
Solitary confinement	11
Slits/incisions/cuts made with sharp objects	12
Animals (dogs, rats, piglets, snakes) rubbed with body	15
Chilli/salt/petrol rubbed on wounds/eyes/genitals	15
Kept in dark/underground/poorly ventilated rooms	17
Sleep deprivation	21
House ransacked/looted/blown up/burnt	23
Foreign objects inserted into rectum	23
Water-boarding	24
Forced Starvation/adulterated food/scarce food	29
Verbally abused	31
Forced to drink or eat (unacceptable) things	33
Flesh cut/skinned/Nails plucked out/beard (hair)	35
Trampled over	37
Forced to overdrink (chilli) water	37
Forced labour in detention	43
Blindfolded	48
Legs stretched	56
Body (parts) burnt	70
Dragged/slapped/kicked/punched/glass bottles broken	93
Head dunked in (chilli) water	101
Stress position/hands tied/feet tied/restrained to	105
Hanged upside down/aeroplane	121
Electrocuted in genitals	127
Roller	169
Stripped naked	190
Electrocuted	231
Beaten	326

0   50   100   150   200   250   300   350   400

Number of Victims

                        Some of the army
                officers would see the détenus
            in pain and would throw a painkiller
                or some pills from the
                window   others would   until
            the detainee fainted

        A.R. and his son stripped naked
        in front of each other forced to
            do things to each other

        suo moto cognizance of the case

    Dressed the victim in an army outfit so that
            people would not recognize him

                    ◆ ◆ ◆

        The BSF once tore a portion from his
            thighs with a sharp knife

    He had no FIR registered against him   yet he was picked by Sikh
        Regiment of Rangreth Camp and taken along
            with other boys to a room and

    With a toffee and a pear in his hand
        he went through the by-lanes
        leading to his uncle's house

                    ◆ ◆ ◆

            on the orders of S.M.
            the then local MLA
        of a political party on the
        grounds of some
    political rivalry with the victim

    finally able to trace him at the Gogoland   centre

On the pretext of not possessing the identity card
they took him into a nearby orchard

  a hanging water pot that
had a small hole at its bottom   The water

  broke his four top front teeth
with a smash of the gun butt

     Tied with nylon ropes
asked him to swear upon Dargah Sharief
Ziarat that he didn't possess any   On swearing
he uttered in Kashmiri *myaani Khudaaya*
mai diyizi maefi agar mai kenh khata goi"
"My Lord pardon me if I have done wrong"

   This angered them

the great dirt risen
turamga khema vidhvastam ratha name samuddhatam

"the air breathed at the centre of the column"
        ruroda karna netrāninyudhyatām dharanī rajaḥ

from the hooves of the horses

"was putrid. Dust choked their nostrils"

& the skirling chariot wheels

"eyes irritated lungs gutted"

stoppered the senses
tasmins tamasi duṣpāre in that stubborn dark

"soldiers fainted from the dizziness and suffocation"
krodha mūrcitāḥ damned by anger
    dumbed the troops
    concealed the ability to feel anything

mahāvegā bhakṣayantah swiftly making blotto
vānara rakṣasām Simianrakshasas
kunjarām kunjara the elephants and the elephant riders

    Thousands of Ramas in the field
      and then only one

    Rama a wheel of time
      the spokes and   sparks
      that fly from it

    Turned his back to those
      choruses of arrow

quietly and with closed eyes
like a bull caught in a sudden
                  autumn shower

March 4, 2019
RAIPUR (*New Indian Express*): Dekuna predominantly tribal hamlet Bastar

Known Maoist stronghold south Chhattisgarh
youths dream of serving the nation by joining
    the armed forces   Interacting with young boys and girls
    here gives one the sense
that they have made up their minds
 to defend the nation's frontiers   For them
  being in the armed forces is the only

vocation that comes closest   Dekuna
has as many as 40 youths currently
 serving in the armed forces
After the Pulwama terror strike
which claimed the lives
of paramilitary personnel
    the entire village

"It's because of our soldiers
who defend our borders
that we sleep peacefully"

While the village   mostly
    sends its men   to guard
      the front lines   the women are
          not far   behind

Chariots were disassembled
for transport   Traitors were executed
with sticks and stones or "rolled in a mat
of dry grass and burnt to death"

Allies disappear
as the sun's rays go missing

with the sun

In the ten directions scatter
abandoning their weapons
They don't give a damn about
           saving face
    don't look behind them
       step casually
                    on those who've fallen

Others though unbound
            of the ropes of duty
    just give themselves
       more completely
          to the final slaughter
       killing to survive
       surviving to kill

Good news like the man who
    having swallowed poison
    tastes nectar at the gates

♦ ♦ ♦

The rakshasa race
    eliminated   Ravana's lost all his brothers
(one of them in soul if not in body)
    and every one of his sons
    (as a moral to my nonexistent son)

A real and rearing ocean upon a
symbolic cobra head
The body rolls in its sockets
already in the morning light
I guess he'll live until I die

September 2019

At checkpoints throughout Srinagar
  police politely gave directions
      entry and exit points
  switched several times a day
"They've changed the road
  map of our city   trying to make
      us like strangers
  in our own neighbourhoods"

Satya Pal Malik   said
there had not been
a "single case of killing"
in the previous 10 days

"Some days after
the special status
was removed   the Indian Army came
and handed these photocopies
to us   stuck posters to the walls

"The suspension has led
to the introduction of
the Right to Education
mid-day meals in schools
new central health schemes
central schemes for farmers
Jammu and Kashmir
will see equal development
of Pondicherry   Land prices will go up"

Alive because on his face had
the brightness you never see
on the faces of the dead

"wounded in every part
they tottered like flagstaffs"

Rivers of primate blood
and the rakshasa rivers of blood
with floating hair for moss
and corpses like broken
tendrils of wood

The blankness of a field that waits for
the tilling plough to snag
on a stone—or something
people disappear
The chariot
tipped
the sunken shafts
the abandoned cabin
Our weapons our legacy

Then again elephants stuck and groaning
blood from tusk & foot & ear
& the vulture congregations come to settle
the querulous crowds of jackals

everywhere the strange
animation
of bodies
convulsing from the ground

(*And begin...*)

(Firstpost—July 9, 2018)

On one side of the road
there was a community centre

with small shops and
a common service centre (CSC)

equipped with computers
VSAT micro-ATM and

other paraphernalia   On the other side
was the primary health centre (PHC)

walls with sketches and slogans like "Digital Payment"
At one corner of the PHC   a large LED TV

keenly watching a show on National Geographic channel
"Welcome to Palnar: Digital Village"

Trend Lines Constant

XXXXXXXXXXXX showed us two graphs
   depicting data obtained All the lines
were zig-zag in nature but
within bands and largely horizontal
   no clear trend lines up or down
The lines at the end of 2004
   were in an order of magnitude
   roughly comparable
to 2002   Did not attribute
the spikes to particular policies
at particular times called them
   "ad hoc changes"

Police first picked up R.K.M.
  on suspicion of Maoist attack

  ~~Beat~~ him demanded he identify
his co-conspirators   Out of desperation he named
  colleagues at Keonjhar Integrated
  Rural Development &
Training Institute (KIRDTI)

  "The police hung him from
  the ceiling by his leg   him

so hard that there
was a fracture in his
thigh bone   Actually R.
was ~~beaten~~ so badly
he gave all our names"

"So then we were arrested"

When M. answered
that he did not know D. the atmosphere
in the house suddenly changed   They immediately
instructed M. to come with them   and
assured his parents that
he would be released soon

Two brothers woken up   taken to
an outside area where
nearly a dozen other from
the village had been gathered

"It becomes problematic
for any male to accompany us"

◆ ◆ ◆

When M. was being
taken away   pleaded
with the head of his village

"Please tell them
I am not a militant"

Comrade S. born in Syamagadda village
of Visakha district　Came into Korukonda squad contact
　while still a child　Opposed forced marriage
　at home　Since she had studied
　　up to 5th she could read
　　and read party literature
with a lot of attention and interest　Escaped
during an encounter in Gaddibanda in January 2005
spent three days alone in bushes and finally
met the squad again　Killed brutally by the police
　at Gunukuralla　April 17, 2005

Com. S. 23 born
into a poor adivasi family in Visakha district
Even before her marriage her husband had told her
he would be going off as a full timer
after preparing himself for the task   S.
was not frightened by his decision   Later the couple met
the squad   Expressed their desire
to join   The Party recruited them and kept them
in a den in a town for technical work
Comrade A. born in a poor family
in Bonampally village   joined the squad
in 2001   Sixty policemen surrounded them
and opened fire

Comrade S. joined
the revolutionary movement
as a young girl about six years ago
She had come to understand
that women's liberation is possible
only with the New Democratic Revolution (NDR)

On February 10, 2005 when Bhoom kaal day
was being celebrated all over Maad
S. went into labour and
both she and the baby died

Comrade R. born in a poor family
in Warangal district   grew up
in an atmosphere of revolutionary politics   She used
to work in the village secretly
under the guidance of the squad   Fought
relentlessly against patriarchal
tendencies in the squad   Martyred
in an encounter in 1998 near Kothur

They left   He saw a kerosene bottle
in front of him and thought
of killing himself He broke
the bottle tried to stab himself but
was too scared and couldn't do it Every
    time he tried to   he would
suck his stomach in

The guards came back and stopped him
and then it just got worse

    He was the district commander of
the Al-Jihad militant outfit   Had gone to Pakistan-
administered Kashmir in 1989 came
back in 1990   Caught for the first time by
the 5 Grenadiers at Tappar camp
in Pattan   D.S. the CO
There was a *Maulvi* with the group who
was quite old   had a long beard
and they plucked it all out
and threw it in a pile in front of
  the detainees

Comrade R. belonged
to the village Dorum under Mirtul PS
of Bhiramghad area Was
an active member of Krantikari
Adivasi Mahila Sanghatan (KAMS)
    Participated in all the meetings
rallies and other activities of KAMS
Even during the Jan Jagran -2
repressive campaign she stood
steadfast   She never bowed
before the police and never

When Salwa Judum
started her land house everything
was destroyed   Goondas and the police burnt
    everything   She went to live
with her relatives in village Oorepal   Salwa Judum
goons Special Police Officers and Police caught her
by deception and ~~gangraped~~ her Then they ~~killed~~ her

    with a bullet   Maybe they thought
    that they could stop women from
joining revolutionary movement but hundreds
of women joined the People's War
and proved them wrong

1. 3 bullet injuries
    on right side of chest which
is wound of extreme and exit

No hairs on occipital
        right side of the chest   exits
    on back interscapular region

◆ ◆ ◆

G.A.K. March 1990
16 he crossed the LoC
offered a job in Bangalore
loan assistance by
Indian agencies   However   was very
emotionally attached

mental hospital for six months   instead
of improving   became more

◆ ◆ ◆

Made him wear an Army uniform
because the clothes that he was earlier wearing were torn apart

Comrade M. born
into an ordinary Yadav family
in the village Avulonibaavi of Mahboob Nagar
district   Her father left
and married another woman   when she was a child
Her mother raised her
worked as a daily wage labourer
M. became a member of the first platoon
When she fell ill it
became increasingly difficult for her

to continue in this work   Even while
the Party was thinking of shifting her

    Com. P. born in a village
of Mahaboob   Nagar district   Put class bonds
above family bonds   Married Com. S.
    in 1998 and they vowed to keep
their personal life always subordinate
to Party life   This promise they kept till their death

    Comrade J. 17 born in Bachanpalli village
        to S.R. and L.   She was
    their eldest daughter Studied till
    5th standard Helped out the family by rolling beedis
from a young age   While she was coming back
to meet the squad there was another encounter
    Manigad hills November 22nd   5 p.m.

        Comrade I.
    lost her left leg in the infamous
        police firing in Indravelli
    April 20, 1981

S.
Male/ Labourer Farmer
Residence: Chaklipora Anantnag (Islamabad)

He was   in a way that was new to him

Finally released when his family
came with applications

A rod-like instrument on which it was written
"aan milo sajna" (come and meet my beloved)

Found some receipts of *Darsgah* from his pockets

◆ ◆ ◆

A. the baker said
the soldiers finally left
at dawn
"total freedom"
to deal with rebels

While she was being ~~beaten~~
the soldiers killed their rooster

[the police confiscated:]

"my computer   monitor   keyboard
mouse   speakers   mobile phones
and all old issues of *People's March*"

Officer D.T. 16th Battalion   Border Security Force (BSF)

Took him to the Ganpatyar Temple
(which has since been
converted into a   camp) located
in the old town of Habba Kadal

   bound with ropes

Taken into a room where a magician named S.A.
   K. and a few *sadhus*   some BSF personnel

Someone asked N. for his final wish
Then they cocked their guns and
someone put a knife to his throat
N. began to recite the *Kalimah*

      After that call the officers stopped
                    They changed
      their behaviour toward him
      took him out to feel the sunshine

N. replied that
he felt that he had
been there for 15 years

◆ ◆ ◆

They told him his real name was Aadil and that
he possessed a satellite phone

Then they tied a wire into his penis

using the
same methods over and over

◆ ◆ ◆

Was not allowed to
bath Several layers of dirt
accumulated   Hundreds of lice
would cling
to the fingers
if rubbed through
his hair His

continued for the whole night
At about 2:30 am   SP A.B.
came to the interrogation room
wearing a tracksuit

BOOK FOUR

After

The Hindus wanted an epic, and they sent for Valmiki, who was an untouchable. The Hindus wanted a Constitution, and they sent for me.

—B. R. Ambedkar

Four times
>Wagadu rose.
>A great city, gleaming in the light of day.

Four times
>Wagadu fell.
>And disappeared from human sight.
>>Once through vanity.
>>Once through dishonesty.
>>Once through greed.
>>Once through discord.

Four times
>Wagadu changed her name...

—*Gassire's Lute*, translated/adapted by Alta Jablow

Whatever King Arthur chooses, whether to overlook the betrayal or to prosecute the crime, the choice is not the issue. For, one way or the other, the king must now be sad.

—Gillian Rose, *Love's Work*

Dhvanyaloka 2.1

virtues appear when
readers perceive them
the sun's rays in their kindness
                    make the lotuses lotuses

tadājāyante guṇāyadāte sahṛdayair gṛhyante
ravi-kiraṇānugṛhītāni bhavanti kamalāni kamalāni

All the answers are told
    in the book that comes at the end
and questions heap on it
    like wood to fire

One morning you heard and
heard   And you loved her more
knowing she was going
for her appointment

i

Rama and Sita, Just After the War

"Like friends turning back": trees that had yearned to his leap. Hanuman, the Simian general, was the first to come to Sita at fighting's end. A crimson twilight—blood-soaked cloth—descended. Islands in the middle of oceans, lands bounded by sea. *Sāgarāntaḥ*. The flora in unseasonable bloom. The last of the sun's gold left, counterintuitively, on the waves closest to shore. He bowed to her and asked, "Sister, what shall I do with the many wives and lovers Ravana has left, should I kill them all?"

"No." She replied, "For they have done no wrong." Sita, pared essence: single braid, single torn cloth, eyes that seemed to have no lids, bone-thin body trembling like plantain in the wind. The solitary force of her power. All around, fallen swords were lifeless cobras. Look at her, so long in the house of the rakshasa. Let me abandon all cleverness, scratch at that hardest part of me
that ruins the intellect.

"The creator, I'm sure, must have meant this body for sorrow." Marriage: founded on apartness.

"Foremost of the Simians, I want to see my husband, Rama."

But when Hanuman conveyed her request it was Rama that startled them with the coldness of his reply, he of the simultaneous emotions: Joy, Sadness, Anger.

Looking only at the ground, "Let Sita be bathed, made up, and dressed as befits a proper queen: only then will I greet her."

An asteroid low in the sky
tracked a hot sulphurous wind

blazed somewhere
into the horizon's woods

Lanka, the twice destroyed. Smoke smeared out the moon, all your hankerings. A caravan passed on the slow road. Campsites, the new half-built housing, the guards in the lookout cages. Among chalk-white heaps of bones, glimmers already of the coming regime. Ravana's younger brother, Vibhishana, the successor king. ("He who uproots the foe and does not replace him goes to hell.")

Vibhishana carried Rama's reply—this new and odd requirement—back to waiting Sita.

She said, "But I want Rama to see me as I am now. To know how I've lived."
Her insistence was brief but clear.

The imperatives of state and of public decorum reasserted themselves. The white umbrella sheltered the story. The power of the right arm and the power of speech. The four strengths: arms, mind, expedients, relatives. The four expedients: conciliation, bribery, sowing dissension, punishment. The prince who'd done things deemed necessary, just as in certain grammatical operations one substituted for a root.

Sita relented. Attendants washed her hair and covered her with exquisite clothes and ornaments. Agitated groups of Simians and turned rakshasas and other folk there to get a glimpse. Vibhishana tried to quell and restrain the crowds, to make them throng to her less, to make a clear path for her approach.

But an angry reproach from Rama stung him where he stood:
"Don't touch them!   How dare you harass my subjects!"

jñāsyati
he will recognize

drakṣyati
he will see

His shouting at Vibhishana shocked his closest devotees. It was ominous. Rama said sternly, "There's nothing wrong in showing her to the public."

And when the exiled prince, now about to become king, began by addressing her formally—"*bhadre*"—"my good woman," there was even more the sense of something very wrong.

"I've won you back by smashing my enemy. The hurt and the insult have been avenged. In the heat of war, my valour has been asserted. The goal has been achieved."

She began to cry.

"Your presence hurts me like a lamp on a diseased eye. See the ten directions? Choose any one. You might as well go live with one of my brothers. Maybe Lakshmana or Bharata? Or Shatrughna? Why not try Sugriva, king of the Simians, or Vibhishana, right here in Lanka? Whatever you want—I cannot take you back after all those years in another man's house."

She asked Lakshmana to build her pyre. When lit, hurled herself at it.

But the god of fire hesitated to take full hold of her, and before he could, the gods of death and wealth had arrived on the scene; and the god of the oceans and the thousand-eyed god and the dreadlocked god with a bull on his banner and the god of essence, of creation itself. And thirty gods in all stood before Rama and addressed him, reminded him of his provenance.

And through such auspicious intervention was statecraft rebuked.

Rama answered his heart and took Sita back.

Kingdom and love had been kept equal, both restored. In the house of rules desire also flourished. And in such infinite rule was the lineage preserved.

That's how Valmiki's sixth book ends, the book of war. And it's an end that has made so many people happy for so long we would be tempted to ignore the existence of a seventh.

But there it is. The book of the aftermath, the inevitable reopening of the seams in the impulse to lay matters to rest. There Rama makes a *second* rejection of Sita, one that lasts, that will never be forgotten as long as the Ramayana is told. Rama's actions prepare the way for her turning away from him, her return into the shelter of the Earth who was her mother, her origins in the furrow. A meeting of soil, water, and the plough's metal teeth.

> The shadows fall hard on us
> a kind of rain
> The blood from pools diffuses
> stains the gentle kusha grass   The sacrifice
> brought again and again to the altar
> will never once shirk from its job
>
> Just twice
> in a millennium under truth's archer
> might we enjoy a few straggly years
> of grace and freedom   with the spears
> laid to rest with love and sex
> free to do
> their thing with words
> an instrument of inquiry
> and not a catacomb of fear

Ayodhya

Forgotten cities scattered across
a plain: against the faint
reanimation of those corpses
do we ourselves live   Slowly the fog
spreads thickens our lungs   forges the sight
of middle distances till all
that's left is cloud   Sound will
guide us   in the constancy of its assault
The fan in its fluttering proximity
The vendor calls that echo
    from your childhood into
the dead of noon   No one shall extract
a confession from them   The car
    horns   their cry   To exist
is to bleat and navigate by the bleats
of others   You walked a simple compromise
of winter night   by the nala   the nala
itself   as such   no longer there   and the little shrines
that appear on the corner as if
by a sleight of hand: first the stony
    assertion then the
 accretion of devotees   then the
formal idol arrives   then an
electric light by which
to worship in the dusk   How long
    how long as a
relative of the lone spread   how
many cities   will it consume
in its greed in its anger
    The walk through is a history of loss
The friends that are no longer or perhaps
no longer mine   The circles and lives
and allegiances split by peccadilloes
that might not have been peccadilloes
and turned monsters under the law

The closeness   the intimacy
of the prison   The FIRs
in sequence   The cold stream
The hush inside the colony
under the chowkidhar's stick
The angry main road   accursed
lives of force   The paths half-
constructed   as walkers weave
through the possibilities   You never
understood how pain could wrinkle
the livelong eyes   The cars
  came to you   came to you   headlamps
scooping the body in their wish
to get somewhere   But the first
evening with a few
handfuls of vegetables   Amma in the stark
sleeplessness of her nights
    and how night always falls
        where you walk

Ganga: n Views

1. Not at Gaumukh

13.8 bn years ago was the most recent
total nucleosynthesis among push-crush
cycles and cycles—do the stories they tell

on the other side mirror ours? Nearly 5 bn years ago
our sun and we were born together   together because
 its very heat contained its children and its future

    4 bn years ago our moon after long close hurt
drew away and the days   especially the nights
        grew longer

then the planetesimals brought her
    as ice in harbours of dross
    first a notion faint as crystal

  not counting on the billennia when
  we'd hang our very existence
    on her fall and rise and fall

Yes she'd come from the heavenstars
        filtered by Shiva's
mountainous dreads but equally

  true to say she'd been there long before
the meditating god had even wakened to himself
  and that hailing from stars

    she was never foreign to us
  But she fell and she coiled
  and only in interruption of her

did the first continent form
At 3.5 bn years we got proteins stromatolites
Then photosynthesis   then paleosoils among

the glittering citadels of zircon
  and hard-thrust black rock
  from the core   All that time this

unnamed one was with the promise of shape
    and in its cooling anger still with the craters
      of fallen gift-bearing angels

And gold arrived   and much else
and our canopies of oxygen went up
  and there were a bn and a half more years

of such assault and reabsorption
  such flaw and reformation
the unintentional puzzlement of the continents

Then squidish creatures arrived   then sex
  then arthropods and forests on land
then the reptiles from whom we learnt

so much   then the great Dying that was
  cleansing and closure and
the memory of violence on which

we'll plant our fruit— just think of those volcanoes
  that ravaged the Deccan 4
    mn years ago to found

  our landscape   our song   And each
time on those ashes she fell and revived   our Ganga
  though she'd changed her name and wandered

from East to West or West to East by
　　the tilt of dreamless plates as ancestral Indus
　　or apocryphal Saraswati or sprouts

of Sutlej　Ravi　Chenab　Jhelum　Beas and the Yamuna that hewed
　　east to be recaptured by her　Or remorseless Arun
　　or the Bhagirathi Alaknanda　Dhauligangi

Mandakini　Pindar that fed her　　And the Sarayu
　　that brought her to the lonely shores of a city called
　　Ayodhya among the desperate plaints

of the plains　But way before that it first needed flowers
and the idea of flowers　and grasses and mammals to
eat the grasses and a massing bulk of a plate that split

and hissed and stumbled its way in geological hyperspeed
　　toward a mass　　shivering in molten flows
piling islands on itself and making of wing-clipped mountains

　just so many folds of seam　And among
the very last of those shivers it was　we bipeds arrived
　to love and worship her　both because

　she gave us place　and because she wandered
—knowing wanderment at the heart of what was us—
and because she could be harsh and she had to be appeased

　And we feared and were awed by
the way the sea floor had risen to become our planet's roof—
　the layers of fine-crushed creature bones into

limestone and marble　superheated granite speckled
and silicate at the base　And all manner of spewed rocks
in the sudden charge of guileless air　banded gneiss

or darkened weighty basalt   the rocks that
were made by the crushing of other rocks and
the rocks that fell and those that rose again

and those that in flashes of colour merged
   or cut their way into the sediments
and the gift of the mountain his daughter

   our Ganga mothered by glaciers
      carried by cataracts down
to her very frills where we drank and bathed where

   the stones were   smooth and bright
And from the cliff-holes she sprouted unannounced
   to the permit-hikers that walked along

her canyons and gorges and the nimble-footed
   local wanderers arranged her pebbles
   into cairns or little lay castles as if

   in acknowledgment of her own simple time-passing art
   and theirs   And in the places where her rocks
made spontaneous shelter the nervous

soldiers were assigned to patrol her and teams
   of researchers were beaten back by the climb
and tour groups of elderly European tourists

   were followed by heaving porters   And for
      the mildly glum villagers life moved slightly
   too slowly as did the ruthless pine groves

   foresters had once fallen in love with
and the bhojpatra birch into whose layered
delicate bark   among whose lenticels like

extended and extending dashes we'd etched
   some mortal lines of verse as
     steep stairs cut in a slope

And the paths strayed quick down
   to the booming valley banks   and among
the graded shadows behind the peaks the light

  had never quite learned its horizon and
the naturally occurring lingams and yonis
    lay among the snow-burnished tops

from the hot sun of where you stood
taking in the frothing untrammeled cyan
of her where she had both cut through

  and been given a path her stones
stark white or a deep wooden brown
or black or the calm there-ness

 of grey stacked in improbable postures
And the traces of human existence themselves on
the point of being relics and the bungalow

of the forest officer by the bank and the swish of vertigo
that made you consider what it was you wanted
and the joy of simply lingering as if nothing done

   or thought had much consequence—
And the nature-blogger with his fanciest cameras
and the jets of water that as in Valmiki   shot from stone

  And the fleeing ball of the sun behind
   the sheerness of an afternoon slope and
   the lingering pink afterglow before

it blued and blued and the quick-falling night
with its mysterious unsourced illumination
and every minute something else taken away or

   newly offered and
   the lone bulbs of the checkposts
and the shift soldiers launched at little televisions

   that spoke for and frightened them and
the crude plumbing with its mini-orchestra of hisses and whines
 that was trying to communicate her and marked

the tentative beginnings of infrastructure
And the ditches that formed an inner edge
and the stumbling unlit country roads where passers-by

eyed you with fear And how on the way back you were
   unable to recover the suppressed memory
of the way there And the cow and pony bells in the night

   And how you circled the temple
  in its upper grounds unable to find
    a path down through the dark and how

  to come back down at last
  to the roaring of her in the night
was always   a kind of consolation

2. THE WINTER CLOSING OF THE TEMPLE AT GANGOTRI

The endlessly compassionate Bangladeshi blogger
   was nonchalant and brightly logical and also
concerned with cultural documentation
   and how to photograph the place

When the question of fascination came up he said
"I'm not a Hindu, so not interested in it"

"Try to think of it not as religion" I say
   "but as theatre" He looked

 unconvinced   and how could I blame him—
from us to the inner courtyard to the main sanctum was a seeming
   mobocracy of hustles and any sense of altar or idol
      blocked from our view by the thrusting bodies

of priests or patrons or patrons of patrons The queues at first
            were like last night—mostly the village's
         prominent families albeit with lengthening trains
of less successful relatives but by mid-morning this group

now swelled by many dreadlocked monks set down next to
   their carry-sacks or phalanxes of young couples
or important men hanging back and encircled
or probable secret service   who scowled at you from behind

mirrored sunglasses or the army   some
bored some engaged some sneaking cigarettes
 on the sly from the owner of
      the temple bhojnalaya And those

   devotees that came on buses and
   those in tempos and jeeps and those
with private taxis with harried blustering patriarchs
      at their head   And the loners with

      cellphones or other recording devices
   The night before was tempered intensity
   with little shots of action across the grounds
multiple simultaneous preparations and processions where

I'd first heard the big leading drums
   and an idol in veiled palanquin
doing the round of the sanctum
then down temple steps

past the main archway bell
down to the lower pandal
and then to the bank   Stupid me
in the cold night you'd

forgotten who King Bhagiratha at his own
shrine was so of course you'd think
the first idol out was that of the goddess Ganga
herself   That's why you'd come   because this

temple was hers and the waters that coursed
fiercely over stones outside were she
and the dark lord in the sanctum was her
and so doubled was she also who was always

only one   And that it was
the day after Diwali   a quite convenient
marker to wrap it all up before the chance
of debilitating snows   The pack up

of Gangotri was underway—
the yearly closing of a temple by
which we'd decided to connect inside
outside water bank rock sky   But

how to do this   Chiefly   where
to watch it from   Some had already
taken spots on roofs or on
a massive boulder that loomed

above ground   Seemed
secure   So this was it
then? Waiting all day for some
unspecified event to roll out from the centre def-

initively   waiting with all manner
of restless unfocused as you? Another

day chalked up to sleepwalking
Hinduism? By now there was a full bagpipe regiment

also starting to hang about   polishing their
instruments not even promising to say much
That was when you heard the drums again
and an idol invisible but for

the palanquin it rode down the steps
to the large-rock border and the shore
and the shoulders it traveled on
who in the drums' signal to crush mind

belonged to men wholly in her trance
carrying in sharp but drum-governed shakes
their cargo to a new seat by the river
Meantime the sanctum that asserted importance proceeded

on its own time and sequence and axis
as if unaware of these prescient exits
of gods and spirits down to the bank—
not Ganga herself you understand who had been kept

still in obligation of feeding dressing propitiation but
the other gods and guards of the area present as residents
or as visitors on the backs and car-tops
that brought them   And this time it was bankward drums I followed

not the sanctum's cold hoarding   And in following that other
rivulet   you were outside among the stones   the first in fact
temples that just self-organized   understood the havens
sheds mounds and mini-castles they must make

and the goddess's calm inletting and the swirls
in shaded inlets and the sudden trip into
underground shafts   garrulous or
murderous eddies and all this society still land but one

where the furthest outcast also had stake
there where the indisputably real goddess was...
So simple "Hinduism's" fictions of coherence
good enough to keep donations coming in at the sanctum

and the register ringing in the management office—
good overall for management But the real truth of it
    each tribe each clan each cult
each theoretical position on the question

of the non-self and matter and self
  in matter given or ignored in the spill
    of its own zone Find a place or move
    just keep moving Because more is certainly

on the way The idol of Shesh Nag—
none other than Vishnu's serpent as also
the essence of serpent in us all—was I think
  visiting from its own seat in a shrine

elsewhere on the pilgrim's path—now taken
    to meet the great river to pay respects
on far burst of rock beyond the beach
  where the wet real women danced like its wives

    both utterly free and full
of mourning In time this too was over
and the assigned priest was pulling out
a wad of notes beneath his coat

    to pay off the musicians for the round
Then another came, other processions
and sometimes the separate
    trains met so the idols

might greet and dance with each other
for a spell An idol of Durga

from Yamunotri village
  had been brought

like this to the bank   the drums
stayed on and now the main priest who'd
set up shop on the walkway shivered
    into a strange delirium

and with shaken hair sometimes mirth
sometimes grim power   the goddess Durga
    came into him   And now they were woman
without speech but only grains of rice

and a universal language of hands
  and expression that became oracle
  and kids were brought to her
and couples and unspecified troubles

and she dispensed advice
which could be understood
or else be beyond an understanding to
an acceptance of whatever came next

  and by now I was on a parapet
with my own phone held high to capture it
    as long as the oracle
was still tossing a rice grain in the air

to see how it might fare then
coming as if through translation
  to the supplicant
  by the art of hands alone

  —though strangely
when finally she looked up and
blessed me with her far finger-splayed
  sprinkles of prasad   and gestured right at me

I found it half-interpretable
and froze in fear   as usual of my own inauthenticity
Thinking back now on her fist-releasing gesture—
how it moved out in a wide circle like planet's orbit and all

she may have intended to show was
how the circle described by the camera lens
was also any circle at any darshan's edge and all who
had been there had been bound

by this memory and this recording   Sometimes
a crucial difference between water from here
and water from there   For now I was of the bank
and strictly drinking only the former—

often on my stomach to fill my Bisleri bottle because
the jal collected right at the shore
could be sandy and it didn't hurt to lean
further out onto some rocks at a snatch

of the river's edge where in a soft depression
the water smoothed some large pebbles with
white curtains and thus became
smoothed as well   and delicious

Hurtling toward noon and more and more
of the satellite devotions were completed
By now one could no longer distinguish
the different crowds that mingled

among us whether tourist or
seasonal pilgrim or TV crew   Hundreds
were being fed in batches   Those presumed
secret service guys in mirrored glasses

seemed to be prowling at arches at gates
at promontories In the most inviting room

of the central square   the temple chairman
received distinguished visitors many bringing yearly

contributions but occasionally one barking—in
this last moment before the next spring—that his illustrious
ancestor had been disrespected by the leaning of
the framed photo on the carpeted floor in interface

with the unpleasantness of the secular world
which surely had implications for the worlds
of the spirits as well   All that was going on
not only the high sun and the mist on the waves

and the clarified eddies but the climax was
    now coming and the smartest of the crowds had
already found their places   and those that remained
    the majority of us   like migrants going wherever

we might fit through and see something   And the drums
had started up something fierce and at last it was
    the goddess Ganga's turn to leave her seat
    before the winter closure to mount the palanquin

and veil and be off to her village hibernation
And now the whole of us trying to get a last piece
    with our phones held up or down
    from the roof where I too tried to hang

    for a spell   And the drummers
and the local horns were followed
by the bagpipers of the Garhwal rifles
    by which strangely the nation-state had now

insinuated itself—even as clumps of us with unclear
plans were trying to get into the spare crevices
    of the taxis back along the roads where   the idols
    themselves ambled toward village homes

3. IN BETWEEN

The kind of Garhwali town where only traces
   are left on the motorable road   Tea stall

sporadically populated through the day   Bus stop
  where the jeep taxis pause if they have

a spot   Maybe also a boxy store selling the barest
 of supplies and an old man in formal village clothes

wandering around looking in vain for someone
   to change his 2000-rupee note   But down

a set of stairs and you were at the ashram
  of the famous fighter pilot who in bleak descent

over the mountains   in warfare   had understood the nature of death
   and given it all up   Gigantic statuary sung out the myth

but photographic evidence also gently supported—trim
  and stylish in aviator shades uniform and jauntily positioned

  military cap then the later Baba as pot-bellied half-
balding sadhu stepped from a plane with his wealthiest disciple

  And today: if the nation is a goddess where
  does she even begin? Ministerial stays at the ashram

 with their battalions of staff and security to make
the staff bitter The manager talks with endless

  admiration of Lincoln and Washington—biographies
 absorbed in a marginalized Hindi childhood—

but flares in rage when it comes to speak of *any* Indian politician
   knowing the utter unspoken contempt of that class

for the poor   This is just to say nowhere was spared
   from the heartbreak the fascists gave   even as

   the landscape seemed to remind
   of the paltry scale of lives   Ganga

accessible there from a gorge on
the right cutting deep rift in the rock

   down which one of her streams raced
      to a bridge that crossed

to some other sanctuary's
   private grounds   And with the minister

      done and gone the whole of the stretch was for a day
         mine   with the exception of a couple cows

      a clutch of nervous ponies   and those
         who tended to them   Walking the land

   you could take a higher route along sandy
      banks occasional raised concrete platforms

and other more inexplicably decrepit structures while
      kids from the houses above called

   out of the slowness of the day or you could climb
      the big rocks right on the shore poised

      even without any silt to seal
them as if the drama of imbalance had long

      ended and that   apart from the occasional
      jiggle these massive jagged drop-rocks had now

      "learned" to stack and wedge themselves
      with the firmness of regular foundations   By only

a slightly different logic the pebble-towers
  or circles or shrine-like structures and designs

of the locals   stones as the first and last
  of idols the shivlings of different colours Then further

on this dicey path with sudden trails of garbage and
  plastic packets As if born to your eyes a glacial

waterfall irresistible whether at height of afternoon
  when the clothes could dry on your back

or in the morning cold   And the force
  of that tightly banded Ganga the places where

she went white as a greybeard's hair   the still
    bristling pools she spilled to tattoos

      on her surface the little turns
    and trials or semicircular currents sometimes with

faint rock peering from below with an edge as if
  to write on her from

below   rippling curtains or moon-like
  crescent whites always in the same place or

somewhere indistinguishably close to it   Thus a sameness
  to the carpet of the ever-flower

in the joint-authorship of these rocks and the way colour
  itself as it drained depended on her   And the sky

    in mighty late autumn perfection and the stars too that were
  no strangers to friction   The smear of them as they rushed and rushed

4. KASHI

Lugubrious   the boat on
the lugubrious Ganga

Panorama of the ghats in sequence
the alleys asking their way

to the steps
There's the problem of age—

how soon or how long has it been?
Was the well that

drenched the childless couples
in egg and ritual seed on

the 12th of the month
as old as the Earth-springs

and Earth-caverns themselves? At night
the little balls of dough

that fed the fish
the sullen wish

the perpetual smoke in the air
the diesel's designs on

films of water
Yet someone built this

Some royal invested in
the public good

gave the command
to pave these streets

to grade these steps
into the flood plain

   to haul the bigger stones
     for the step well

Yes indeed   some royal invested in
   the public good

   and a ready generational
   store of slaves   In any case

   twilight of the age
of works now The government

   has no plan   The patrons
we look to are the jewelers

(the well-meaning kids or
   rapacious parents)

   and the mobsters and
the smooth and global hoteliers

  And yet   the silt: after
the monsoon tides the black

  coagulate crept up
the walls of temple & palace &

palace temple In the night the new
statues and the gardens the plastic

   wrapper fires to keep
small huddles warm The tourists

   who are so integral
to this ecology try the dark

from the famous pizzeria
On the ghat itself the last teenagers

at the steps with their glowing blue hands
Soon the city itself drifts

north down some quirky crook
no longer able to be to mean

anything but what it is
the city that moves on the water

*

Deep joint-pulls   the boatman
leans back   rowing as if casually

with one arm   and our boat
spins in circles   into and away from

the shore   Morning fog clung
to surface   Migrating gulls scatter

in wavering v's   In so many homes
the maintenance in full gear

humanscaping the floors And the motor's
limitless scream There is no clear

path to the image but the boatman and the
drawling map he makes across

the river's page   Each ghat that passes
is in fact spanking new in historical time

but densely settled by
imagined millennia   And has

its own bespoke melancholia   The
ghat for Brahmins the ghat for chamars

and the ghat for chamars (the boatman repeats
   in case it had slipped by too quickly)

The ghat for kings-turned-corpse workers
the ghat for corpse workers   for bodies

and for visitors to the Blue Lassi shop
   The ghat of the temple where

the most exquisite fish is served
   as prasad—the secret of the recipe being

salt and something called *Ram-ras*
The ghats of the pigeon callers

who stand on terraces and shout
   and sway the birds in

Slowly he moves   and the words that
speak through him are no longer just

his words   just as   no matter how earthly
the *paani* will be   the *jal* intrinsically

   pure Each statement made by
   the taking away of something

5. KALIGHAT TO KUMARTULLI

   Never thought that's what
a red-light district would look like

utter normalcy and a few well-dressed women
at doorsteps   the police heavy

on all of it following you with anxious
aggressive eyes   their main station a kind

of castle flanked by armored vehicles A strange
   place   but yet so many other oddballs

like you   local or blondly not   sometimes
asking questions otherwise sniffing at

the river's edge   each one of us solo
And my attempts to strictly follow the bank

   the ghats here on the Adi Ganga
a more charming   rooted version

   of Kashi   thwarted by the person
with her pots   looking vulnerable saying

   Raasta nahi hai   And that great temple
   in such ruin and vacancy the slow

      excruciating passage into it and how
   it flushed you out in a money-smeared grab   only somehow

         reechoing the great power
of the true goddesses on the bank   And later

upstream by evening with Gourab
   near where Job Charnok happened

            still a place to sit
      on the steps   park your

   exhausted eyes on the water
Calcutta   Kolkata whatever I salute you!

You let me walk your streets   I salute you!
You let me feel free   I salute you!

You told another story, another possibility
(possibly?) I salute you!

Ila

Parvati goddess of motherly compassion
bless me your child that I might
    give up this penis for
    a vulva   and the hairs on my skin downy
for six alternate months of the year
I've understood what happened now
    in the sacred grove where
the dreadlocked one made himself female
    for your pleasure In the midst
of their divagating plan in that gesture
    where all beings turned to she—
    so also did I who was the proud king
    the trespasser in that grove so also
    every one in my regiment

    No mother   I won't go back
Grant me instead that from now on I'll be
not one but two just as the celestial two
    are one   in the blessed join
    I want to know the other
    then forget then know the first
as the other I'll bear a child
    for Mercury   and on the mountain
    slope where I met you
my soldiers will become wives
to the kimpurushas: the
    "could-be" men

    Parvati: mother Mother force
Let me stay in the cycles of the moon
    and the cycles of forgetting
    as man and as woman
Give me leave from the life of the king
    marked and bound
by the father the altar the white
    umbrella & the iron plough

Ahalya

Should have known by the acknowledgment
  the impostor brought
  —mist still in the fields—
    he was odd
Knew by the acknowledgment
  the impostor brought
    he was odd
And considered often
my husband to whom the act
  was incomprehensible
in the long days when thought
was my only existence or in the years
of grace when my body
    was given back to me
  cold in its own flesh   Or the millennia I've
    strayed beyond death   unable
  to answer a certain question

Wasn't the way I rode him the way he
filled me with his urgency Wasn't
his hair brushed against my shoulder
or the fear when   pressed together
we heard my husband back
    from the stream   One isn't fated
to remember such moments too clearly
    but the soul in my embrace
belonged to me also   and the single mat
we lay on was ours   and that trickster
whose punishment was to receive a thousand eyes
    and a thousand vulvas
was nothing like   the one who'd held me
and whom I had held   into the first
        slanting rays while
      the pockmarked moon
        clung to sky

Shveta

Found a wood
 with the most astonishing plants
and animals but absent of people
 At the heart of it was a lake
and by the lake an abandoned ashram
 Spent the night in that place
  Hours into my sojourn
on dawncusp   just before the blue light
had slipped to red   heard a sound outside
  sensed presences It was
 a celestial visitor
with crown and horse
   and modest entourage
and he hurried to where a body lay
 a beautiful body a fresh high-born corpse
as if just gone pale Saw this
 from the window and then the bushes
as panting sweat broken he tore
at the flesh with implements and
his own teeth   spongy belly first

The companions looked solemnly on
and I watched too Was a long while
before he was sated By then he had
meticulously dined on every scrap from
toe to eyeball and hair   Then
as if in sudden awareness he glanced
 up at his companions Shuffled
 to the water to contemplate
  himself a while before kneeling
   to wash his face
                        Until then no one
had paid me any attention I walked
up to the ragged split corpse and saw
 that the one who ate

and the one who had been eaten
were the same He stood beside
me now   the living double
 and though he was calm
I could see how shame hung
    on his posture
"I am Shveta" he said
"I gave my kingdom
to my sons and came here
to find solitude
and build force
    through tapas

" that is   self-discipline   an elusive goal:
years of it and I came
    to feel invincible
in my virtue But when I
finally crossed beyond the gates
of the eternal world   felt only
   insatiable gnawing hunger
and thirst   Then heard a voice:

'No seed fallen on unnourished ground
can sprout Shveta   in all your years of tapas
 you cared nothing for   and gave
 no alms or comfort to this wood or
whatever lived in   & cared for it Now
   only one thing will satisfy you.'

   "Since then always at this hour I come down
to feed on my own re-immaculated body"

The Nobility of the Rakshasas

Like all the other beings
    (danavas asuras daityas)
  who fell from favor
  when order pretended to arrive
 Like all those returned
  as the ocean did after touching its shores
the rakshasas always pursued
  their own excellence and stasis
They studied the sacred texts
They gave to charity
They performed the prescribed and inscribed rituals
They achieved lives free of sickness
They stood firm in their dharma
And like a lion chased by a sharabha
like an elephant hunted by a lion
  like leopard by tiger
 like a dog by a leopard
 like a cat by a dog
 like a snake by a cat
 like a rat by a snake
so too were the rakshasas subdued
or decimated in battle   Think
of great Kumbakarna the ardours
he undertook with steady mind
 in a quadrangle of fires
while the sun blazed overhead
or when he was soaked to the bone
and balanced on one knee in the rains
 or in winter the whole of him
 held underwater Kumbakarna
on whose behalf Saraswati
the goddess of poetry once spoke

More than anything the rakshasas were our equals
and later friends with the Simians too in

their subjecthood And even Ravana
his earlier career as serial rapist
        known and hated who
    had gone so far as to murder
his own sister's husband   even he
once said   *I was crazy for victory but*
in the blind heat of war I could no longer tell
    my own side from the others
        And Lanka that city built
    by those fleeing from Vishnu that city
 of the endless vistas engineered
    by Vishwakarma   The years
of prosperity it had as a capital   the
        thousands and
    thousands of happy rakshasas
        who thronged to it

Ravana's Earlier Career

Even the gods began to fear
his normlessness   Indra
   nominal king of the devas
Kubera   keeper of celestial wealth
   even the Sun the Wind—
all feared him   And Shiva the one
whom he could not breach   was strangely
   tolerant   From a child greedy
to fulfill his mother's ambition
   to the remorseless
 abductor of women
   who confirmed for
them in their mourning that
not any man was to be trusted   Like
a gash on the earth
from which the lava flows was
   Ravana's earlier career

A different Ravana here   in
Valmiki's last book than that
   sexpot warrior of the long scars in the 5th
swirling in his room of fantasies
mesmerizing those lovers who gave
   themselves to him
Different Ravana   Different source
Native fury   power gone mad
as if to devour its own precedents
and masculine to the core   such that
 in the final era   it took a woman
and none other   to return the inexorable end

Silk Smitha as Surpanakha

The only truly dangerous thing about her
was her nails: like little rapiers   they revealed
her strength   That apart   she grew up
just like any other girl   married a Danava
named Vidyutjiva   Then life
   took a series of turns   Surpanakha
discovered she had both power
and wiles   but everywhere she went
   certain men   were in charge   One evening
coming home   she found her own
brother's sword plunged
in her husband's heart   Ravana
had stormed the house oblivious   She became
a wanderer a dancer   an enchantress   Every
one of the many she loved   she kept   as if
    she were theirs alone
The woods were sanctuary
for human flesh eaters   and
  for innocents   and those
  like her   in between   She lived
  with devotion to the truth
of impulse   In the night   in the water
her dark skin held its own luminosity against
  the banded ripples but   not even
  these icy baths could cool her when
  she burned for the want of a lover

One man in particular   who'd treat her
like a moll   turned out to be
her fatal weakness   and also
  the trigger   of endless war

  Surpanakha   like the sky
writing on storm clouds
  like the flicker in each

of us that is obsession
like the white rapt cloth
of self-sacrifice
like the blood
given by fallen bodies
to the thirst
of an unconquered land

Hanuman vs. Rahu

Baby Hanuman   born monkey
   but really cat-like

with an insatiable explorer's instinct
Always with puzzlement

   is he in the world
One day sets out to pluck

   the white fruit of the Sun
spoiled by his father   the Wind

who keeps him cool   and the Sun also
indulges   agrees to become a plaything

      Then the Northern Eclipse
—limbless as a planet all head all shadow—

who'd already been planning to eat the Sun
         himself that day

complains to Indra   the busiest god   who
      chucks a ready bolt at the ape-child's face

Hence Hanuman   "swollen jaw"
hurt   for the universe's sake

Hanuman   whom we too keep
   closer than any humanoid god

Dandakaranya

Danda's forest
or "the forest of punishment" or

"the godforsaken forest"
so astonishingly beautiful when

you got there   despite predators & epithets
overspread and uninterrupted with shoots

fertile ever as husbands on a first night
Trees arrayed   entangled

strangled or splayed   shallaki badari
bhallataka (the marking-nut) we'll

tell you about today   even groves
of bamboo by the stream—

places within the reach of rivers
or reachable   only *by* rivers

and the remotenesses beyond startled vistas
as the sun emerged as circumference

in the adjoining slopes   The mountains
groaning from years of ancestral bones

themselves a testament
to microhistories of incursion

to the rishis who brought territorial fires
and the soldiers who followed them

to the honey-locust trees one embraced
as punishment   to those that lived

here first in their anger and loss   Even
the remnants of a city taken by the enemy

and turned to kingdoms of rubble   the bridges
destroyed for spite   the moats choked

the removal of protections   of rakshasas
("protectors of the sea")   those

squished in the stone and those who still
lived fierce   in the half memory of it

Then the Ursines and Simians who got honey-drunk
grabbed their gonads   and showed you

their assholes (the "pathways of breath   of wind   of
the gods") and barren patches absent of bees

and caused by an absence of charity ("here, the fruits,
leaves, the flowers & the bough;

here my lifeless body")
The domains of the women and

of the half-men and the always cruel
domains of men   No unspoilt land this   In fact

its earliest records showed the violations
that ruined and tried to govern it: its witless king Danda

born to be punished   His brutal rape
of Araja for instance   a founding myth

But on certain winter nights   also an awareness
of the earth's curvature   how even

rainbows were a kind of proof spawned
in the lens of rain an aperture

Pushpaka Transport

In all the *Ramayana*
the only blameless one

was you: genderless transport: *vimāna*
Like an island unto yourself

with wings   a residence
and battlement on the move

Outshining stars   shearing clouds
with your reciprocal extensions

Self-generated from
a crystal of yourself

and the tiny sensors that fenced you
like sheets of uncut gems

to greet those beamed up to your panel doors
And whether light years were traversed in you

or a mere ocean on the return from Lanka
you did your task   fleet as a thought

I remember the years Ravana left you
parked in the main hangar at Lanka

unlike the sportier models he kept
for abductions and military outings

Pushpaka transport   How fitting the universe was
as it skipped past   your doubled portholes

and the joy of arrival eternal in its deferment
when your arrogant passengers

forgot how to command you
  and lapsed ourselves to stone

ii. On Certain
Illuminated Pages of
Abdul Rahim's Ramayana

یا بلنگ کو سر و موی سپهر و ریش او بغایت دراز و همه علامت او دال بر برزکی و کبودیست

و لبو بنا در بر افکنده به قد و قامتش مانند قله که به سپر بلند و روشنی او چون شعاع آفتاب چهره

او و جنه او چون طلای که در آتش یافته باشد و وقتی کز آتش بر آمده طبق از طلای خالص دوست

پر از اطعام سپهر و پیچ که خوردنی دیو بناست و خرشند کی ان طبق طلا بجان بو که هر کس در الا

ارتش طلال آن خانه بود و آن خانه را از برای خواب او ساخته و مانند غارش مُحجَّن این در مغاک کمین
بود و پستو نماید آن از طلا و بلور و نقش و نگار خاتم هندی آن از زمرد و دُر و مهارهای زرین و محزش
بر دور او بسته بودند

و در میدان خانه از دندان فیل و رصیعهای آن جواهر و لعل تعبیه کرده بودند که به کرن محم زمین خانه
رفته خواب کرده و نا هزار سال پرهیزکان گذشت که ناشنیده ماه خواب میکرد و در هر یک روز بیداری هندی نمی
هنوزده باز لحواب می رفت و او را بعد از خواب کند غرشان و دو بها و اجان و ماران بزرگ

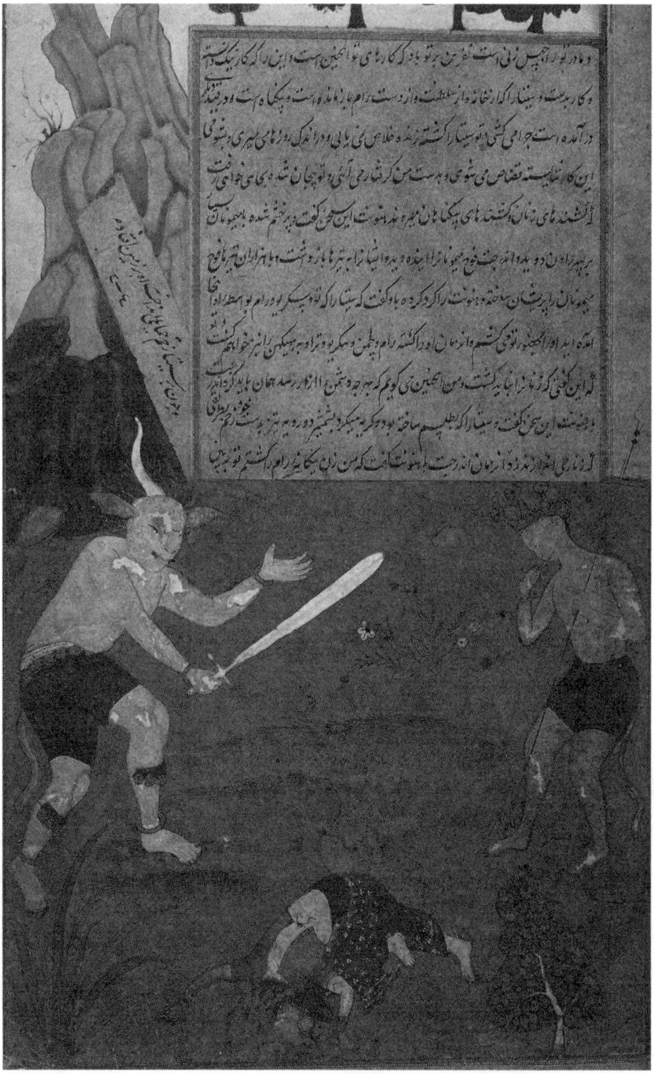

1. Ambarish Sacrifices Suhnashepa

Credited head painter: Nadim

Opulence is three-quarters of the law
The epics were for amusement and awe

before terrors   An inattentive browser sees at first
only the royal circle and the beseechers—

two monarchs actually   One celestial
  one earthly   the former seated

  and the latter who proffers
the sacrifice   It's only an approach

  of the fire in a lonely corner   that reveals
the sacrifice on which this kingdom depends

  No longer a horse   cow   or goat   but Suhnashepa
    the middle child everyone could spare

    whose own father sold him to the king
        for a   wealth of cattle   Who

            will light the pyre
      when the logic of ritual eats

    one of its own? The question frozen
as is painting's uncanny privilege   in the second

before the answer will come   whether through
    redemption   or our darkest hour or

of every hour where somewhere   as I speak
or you listen   someone's killed or torn apart

for the sake of an anxious polis   And we'll have to choose
between the uncertainty of the faces and the painters'

other fair interest—the fineness of the cloth and
the delicacy it drapes on limbs   In the dimmed

    workshops the team must quietly ask this
or indeed not ask it of Abdul Rahim Khan-i-Khanan   poet

general translator polyglot atelier-owner   founder
of the famed library at Behrampore and loving maker

    of books   of this book   And the master painters
Hindu and Muslim   by their names   lost in the brute work

and planning   the positioning of the figures   the dark
blue of the evening sky to which all must tend

2. RISHYASHRINGA 101

Govardhan

    The trees too have their ridges and depressions
        What is form but the asking of a fruit?

Each visitor is wrapped around a wood   The repainted faces
    where they appear are   a chasm   The true faces

a softening   Rishyashringa   unselfconscious in his slender horn
    counts off with his right   even as his left

    can't help but long for her   Out in the upper reaches
the clouds still traipse implacable but closer in the middle

    a river of daytime dark spawns   a black so hazy
    it seems to feed on the colour around it   That's Rahim's

Govardhan   who though he followed a similar scene
   in the emperor's own copy   stopped short of actual touch

   to underwrite instead this power of unseen forest
Returning home after long workshop hours just as

   Rishyashringa's settlement in the city itself had grown old
      and churned   with contentment and regret

3. The Divine Messenger

   Nadim

"The Akbari Persian *Ramayan*, however, differs in its early manuscripts.
I have access to the second and third oldest known surviving manu-
scripts of the translation (held in Doha and DC, respectively), and they
differ from one another at points."
                              —Audrey Truschke, tweet on December 12, 2018

Three Persian *Ramayanas* for Akbar
   but only one of them for Rahim

   later in the hands of a Colonel Hanna
and the "Detroit industrialist" Charles Lang

Freer and if like any true *Ramayana* the text
   diverges at the core   the paintings also coil

away into their own patches of narrative space   as if
sharing the story alone   were too much to bear   The Divine Messenger

who rose from the sacrificial fire   somehow stripped here
   of all royal occasion   alluringly orange but as if

   just stepped in from the brush   in a single black buckskin
with a golden chain-link ceinture   and his bowl of

future progeny   resembling a begging bowl   The king
barefoot   in this domain not his   The wives

one too many   And any chance simply taken
   by the sprawl of a tree signifying with scarlet finches

4. THE LABOURERS

Labourers Build a road to Take Bharata to Rama, *by Shyam Sundar;*
Hundreds Drag the Bow of Janaka, *by Nadim*

  Amazing how much this *Ramayana* loves bystanders
They populate the frame—never crowd it—even in scenes

where kings launch into war or return from exile
        To call these people

  bystanders is itself perverse: each
puts their own work into the picture with

curiosity purpose direction and   a selfless love the leads
can hardly manage   Lines and landscapes stripped to

almost a catalogue of trades but for
   the heavy rapturous wheel of the State its

                projects its forays
            clearing paths for settlement

When was it ever worth   tell me   the unheeded labour
   Our lives extinguishable   and when the time came

        the word the monarch planted led to
            the water's edge

5. Sita Sustained by Celestial Food

Ghulam Ali

In sleep whether seated or languished on a lawn
The rakshasis are at their closest   to being angels   Sita

who must still draw half a veil between Indra and her
nonetheless takes from him the celestial food   those

alms without earthly substance or nourishment
        by which she'll sustain through

    the peace and scents of a grove   There is
a single tree that Hanuman has not yet

appeared in   A jug   for water
or for wine   No culture but for

the work we've put in
to construct it   no calm

    but in the grind of colour juxtaposed
just so   How patience made for the painter

this creature that had and had never
    been   How ours was that

    of the knitting   and
    not   the tearing asunder

6. Kumbakarna's Sleep

Qasim

    Kumbakarna   great beauty
in the humility of the hairless head

in the unblamable kiss   of your sleep
The goddess of speech   cruelty and deceit

hijacked the while   of the boon owed to you
made your award instead   this

lost-to-the-world slumber   Here Qasim cuts away
from that grand house made   for your rest gives you just

a tasseled cushion   a mat   a pillar
to be spanned against   Who knows

what worlds you'll encompass
in the simplicity of this pose?

Galaxies   whether of sex or sound
or the implosions of the digestive system

or war   a distant drum   that hasn't
yet needed   the warmth of your touch

7. HANUMAN'S UNCERTAINTY AMONG THE MAGIC PLANTS

Yusuf Ali

All that green   but only four plants glowed
You were proud to have whittled it down

but no way to proceed further
Hanuman the first   the truest of intellectuals

steadfast and encyclopedic grammarian
you hate   or can't see   your instincts

at the crucial times
Two and two alike

all with their guardian snakes
I never understood

what beauty was
  I was afraid of it

    mistrusted it
even after the decadence

of that gold on paper
doubling as a kind of fire

8. Not Sita, but a Phantom

Qasim

  Not only the nausea of the scene
not just the harshest most meaningless crime

      nowhere the armies arrayed
        the mirages of distance

Not from the height of the chariot   and the sword
  not the ritually certified diagonal cut

  Not Hanuman so close here as to be implicated
And Sita—no not her but   the representation of her

      Not the representation of her
but her limbs twisted like the children of Kushanabu

Not the text filled with choicest curses   Not Indrajit Ravana's
  talented son and a practicing magician   looking here

      like a hardcore thug   despite
        the loveliness of his shinlets

Not the artist who lives in the exploitation of violence and pain
  Not the apprentice who hankers after style

Not the critic whose chin feels slightly displaced
  Never the reader the distracted assassin

 Not Valmiki whose debts are absolved
Not we whose role is in the quelling of the air

 Not the dose by which it is kept unspoken or unrevealed
Not the people of whom it is said would rather have it fed to them

  Not the soul whose price is dignity
Not the individual signature that confirms the collective guilt

  Not the numerous unpainted pages   of the manuscript
all the way from early in Valmiki's 4th to well into the war

   Not the trace of missing images
  in the hearts where they may have been hidden

 Not the history for which the living pages were made
  nor the one into which they were written

   Not the zone for which   life itself
    was a kind of memory

iii

Ram's Arm

After Valmiki and Bhavabhuti

He rested his head on his arm
  long lithe serpentine
An arm like Takshaka's torso
   in the waters of the Ganga
  Arm of golden shoulder rings
   patterned with pearl and gem
     Knew well
the fragrance of aloe & sandal
Glowed like the sun
  with sandal paste
    Handsome arm
that supported Sita's head
  in the conjugal bed
An arm like a bolt drawn across the door
  Arm which burned
   through the foe
 on the killing fields
Arm to gird sea and earth
  Hammer-blow arm that
 had gifted thousands of cows
   and had felt often enough
 the loving pressure of massaging hands

Yes: also the arm that banished Sita
Killed Shambuka with a whoosh of the blade

Shambuka

Among all the things that Rama did as part of his rule, this one, the killing of
Shambuka, I can never forgive. Its cruelties found in the fantasies of the Brahmin
skull only—and Rama's nearly wordless deference an aporia that jigs in the place
of governance so the whole state needs a hard reset through ritual sacrifice
shortly afterwards. "Sure, but please not the holocaust of the rajasuya," his aides
tell him. "Why not another Ashvameda, the horse sacrifice?" A neat little
re-marking of the bounds of royal space, a nice echo of the epic's beginnings.

But before that, Shambuka.

And *cruelty*, as in the assertion of *era* into bland and featureless time. What
is grief but the suppression of anger? A penurious priest walks into Rama's
public chambers with his son's corpse in his arms. Then it's none other than
Narada—he of the well-known fork-tongued celestial commentaries—who sets
the price to be paid for the child's return to life. Not the ills of our own class
being visited upon us, no—but the synchronic existence of another blameless
one: Shambuka, the shudra monk who, in self-attenuation deep in the forest,
has hung upside down for decades and grown quietly strong and beyond earthly
sovereigns and governments. No one knows the real truth of Narada's sly
injunctions/injections. But with the child's corpse somehow preserved in oil,
robot Rama sets out in a trice.

Shambuka, obviously in a state of balance, opens his eyes to greet the king.
If he knows by inner understanding that in the next second Rama will casually
inquire about his caste, and that in the next nanosecond after he's answered will
behead him, then the monk shows no trace at all of that foreboding in the calm-
ness of his expression and his eyes.

Harsh judgment: not on Shambuka but on the ruthlessness of a certain king.
So harsh most later *Ramayanas* would prefer to pretend the incident never
happened.

But a few pockets kept the memory of it, whether as a cautionary lesson to
the underclasses, or in appeasement of them, or in the living proof of the episode
in its continual re-enaction in everyday life—hard to say.

And at least one place where I heard Shambuka was given an altar right next
to Rama, a fort temple from the twelfth or thirteenth century in the martial
branch of the epic's legacy. There, in this place called Ramtek, in eastern Maha-
rasthra, near the Chattisgarh border, a local legend says, "Here is where Rama
killed Shambuka."

At Ramtek

From Nagpur deep into where they say
Shambuka still lies   a hill by which
to watch the invaders   a temple
        and a fort
  the swords and muskets kept close
in locked display cabinets
   by the altar

Monkeys—mostly langurs—run the place
They corner you   steal the lotus for offering
from your hand   then sit down to eat it
      like patient fruit
   petal by petal
              stamen and down
to the quick of the stem
      Tourists dance around their tails
   crowd the sentry towers so

away   the steps to the lookout
   and the well   the road
to the Jain mandir   And further
 into the proud town below where
kids chant from coaching centres
      the Shiv Sena boys
lounge and drowse against each other
   on the floor of their little shed-office
              and the local patriarchs
      too   by the main square
      and its provisions store

         Young lovers speed out
   on mopeds into the woods
Everything reiterates   The teak groves
   are new and sturdy   One small home
 sports a mural of Marx   Che

Ambedkar   Then a family of elderly
mourners brings their urn to the lake
   gathers on the grass for a meal
      of poha afterwards

            Shambuka
      where are you? Was it you
    to the right of Ram   that humble
and nearly untended Shivling there?
Or are you in fact closer to this ring
of Shivling shrines around a lake
that older layer of worship
   in the late evening light
   Madhu the photographer
   catches like a darting cat?

If you're here and not up there
   by Rama's side then you're
   no longer one Shambuka but
a hundred   countless you're long trails
      of paint-daubed stones into
the thickets   the dwelling places
the seats of tapas   And the winter
      fog rolls   rolls down
            the roof of the lake

Valmiki's Students

Great care to fashion the gold to go in place of a banished Sita on the approaching sacrificial night. The finest sculptor's workshops consulted and commissioned. On the first day, the splotchy black horse let loose and followed by an army, greeted and festooned in every hamlet it strutted in—for who would question Rama's universal reign? Chosen for stamina, the horse took several days in finding settlements as far as the hills could see.

And there met Valmiki's students—one dark and one sallow, the first scraggly down over lips and cheeks—on a daily round of alms and street performances. *Rama's Journey* was one of their most requested numbers, which they sang with bristling audacity.

And as they lived by a song in his praise, Valmiki's students had come to despise Rama: in the very act of telling, the gradual deep, the hero's errors, his fatal and minor flaws, the institutions he gave sanction to.

So they confronted the sacrificial horse for the heck of it, even tried to kidnap it, but, by their sheer prowess, the way they sang to meter, light percussion, and lute, the way they drew upon the store of phrases, improvising into and out of, and not least by their credentials as Valmiki's students, they were soon reciting the poem for the king himself in his court.

And Rama was lost in that recitation for days before he understood who the hero was. And as recognition came, searing guilt. And in the worst of it the nerve endings went blind, checked out, only to wake up later in the phantom room of self-wounding.

And days more still before he came to know who these ardent and supremely talented students of Valmiki really were, the grotesque and tender mirror of these bards who hated and were fated to become him, inherit his own throne and weapons.

A Knock on the Door

I may die before my time.
I may live before my time.
—*Gillian Rose*

(In the voice of) TIME:

I don't relish my job   but it had been
given to me to carry the message
to Rama   of his impeding end
and to test Lakshmana besides
  Wearing ragged river-washed
  mendicant's clothes I showed up
   at the palace and was given
an audience   When greetings and
pranams were done   I looked him
straight in the eye and said

"I need to talk to you in
  complete confidence"

   He said "It's in
     my heart too"

"Then anyone who
interrupts us will be killed
without hope of pardon"

   He said "Lakshmana
will be our guard   He'll never
   betray us"

As soon as we were
in private chambers I said
"Rama   my lord I'm Time You've
  been like a father to me for years
but don't remember it   Now it's due
to give up Rama's body
   and return"

He stood silently for a while
absorbing the news   Then said
"I have some last things
  to take care of"

"So be it" I said   And in a single
question without seams I began
to describe to him the stellar
and planetary configurations that
  had impinged upon us

LAKSHMANA:

I heard them in muffled whispers
but even as they apparently discussed
   some essential secret
the old sage Durvasa   harbinger of
imminent mortal power and
(usually)   acrimony   showed up
 asking for the ritual feeding and
 to see Rama immediately

   When I refused him
he threatened to turn all of Ayodhya
and all of its people to ashes

That's when I understood it
   would be a matter
 of only one life: mine

   I interrupted Rama in
  his meeting with Time   And when
Rama couldn't bring himself to kill me
even after Vashista's admonishments
I Lakshmana as always solved the problem

The life of duty is a lean one   The life of duty
   is laughter as it sounds to itself
    Whenever was reason praised
      for its favors?
                By the riverbank
I stilled my thoughts and then
   my body and my breath

Sarayu, from Line to Circle

Rama: your turn now   How long have you
   trained to be this corpse
in the fields of corpses you harvested
by your astras   your sword   your arrows?
But that wasn't the hardest part though:
   The heave of blood through
      the arteries was pain
    and the balm of sleep was pain

 Walk the long river then
wading in   The smallest waves
register   Fish-handed distress
To groove into that rapt
  split   it's the
 water's turn to drink
   and to break the bond

 The people following you
shook   with excitement
               Heaven's
no happier than the Earth   the
gods also frustrate and fail

 Struggle from out your openings
Do they hurt   the lungs? Is it hell
or the simplest forgetfulness?
 Is Vaikuntam close or far?

Let's make a separate universe
   to keep you apart
You'll wink from that sky
  soar through our song
   but as Ravana burns
you'll also drown and drown
  with the tideline licking scalp

Rama: Vaikuntam is the sea
on a perfect afternoon

Collective

Rāmakṣayam: Rama's departure / Rama's destruction

Millions went with him into the Sarayu river
Millions   as each became something else
     on the onward journey

The water broke its banks
    we poured into it   every tribe and
      trade of the city   every sect
and heretic coven   every species spawned
in debt to the sun   Even rocks in the midst
of action   It was so

       our fates would join
     —balance sheet unsettled

iv

railway platform in its mingled and recurrent selves
moving backwards out of the city   saddest the settlements by the tracks
   people half-hanging out of rooms and balconies
buildings precarious   even leaning surrounded by *malba*
—construction and demolition debris—
a small car parked in a nook or a motorcycle leaned on a wall
  crossing the great Yamuna slowed by effluent
a woman and man at work with cloth wound thickly into a seat on their heads
   jhuggi as a kind of farmhouse

Ramnagar

December 11, 2019: tour of Ramlila sites in Benares/
Citizenship Amendment Act passed

Who is left to doubt   the purity of the quest
  Who is left to doubt   the purity of the text
  Who is left to doubt   a little tank is adequate
and practical for Hanuman's leap

 Who looks to where the fields   are burning
 Who knows what that clutch of young men   is up to
 We quizzed the night   & it answered   too honestly
 The land   gone but a single   shook touch   might revive it

In Memoriam Mohammed Akhlaq

2015: Bihsada Village, Dadri, Greater Noida

In the far southeastern corner of Delhi's spread
into a neighbouring state   just
where the white turns green with
  wheat sugarcane rice   Mohammed Akhlaq

  was their local fix-it guy: electrician
ironsmith   plumber   even country gun maker   Wife
a seamstress   They *were* the service economy   as much
as this modest patch could afford where

  the Thakurs owned and worked
or worked their relatives in the fields
Akhlaq: friend to everyone   guy who came and
  did the necessary in your own home

    But he was a smith   descendant of smiths
    who'd traveled with the Hindu armies   and
    in his fifties   quietly prospered   After his son
    became an air force technician in Chennai

he began to refuse jobs even though he knew
the locals too well: the fascist party leader's sons
  had eaten mutton at his home for Eid   Whose
particular anger killed him we still don't know

  nor how much land-grabbing exercise
  And how much impetuous youth?
  How much adventure gone wrong?
  How much in fact the calculations of elders?

  Mohammed Akhlaq was hated
for the slim pickings he'd put together
  Hated for his fridge whose contents were
  tested and retested in labs far and near

But above all   he was Muslim the one they hated
without ever comprehending why   He was
　　　　proud   perhaps too proud of
　　　　his son   And he'd grown pious

　　　and his piety had only served
　　to shame them   frame their
　　confusion That night when the mob—
was it thousands? Or just a half dozen—

had him at its heels   the bitterness
that knew no bounds broke free—
like an arrow bent from the target
or banking *toward* a target   And the hope

　　　was always for the easy win
　　　　　and the result always
　　　the unwished-for horror rained
　　　with omens   differentially but

unsparing of any house in the hamlet
And the true sacrifice at the centre
　　was never a cow but the *very first*
　　the ancestors made—admitted to

even if very rarely spoken of—the cut
　　done at the separate altar
that trapped us like figurines
in our guilt: the sacrifice of a one

who was not us but us   whose blood
when it broke was both distant
　　and sickeningly familiar
　　A one whose very innocence and

trusts in others and in everyday life—
his genial entreaties   his refusal of evil—
galled them as signs of his weakness: his

stupid kindness his lack of worth for

their world and the angry fantasies
  that ranged in it

Nagercoil

for Chandramohan S.

The continuous hoot of the station
  into the retiring room we booked
the day through   departing at evening

But a death had shifted our scheduled meeting
  away from us   so we were loosed
with this view out past the gorgeous

waste of railway land   then fields and
  the last of the mountain ranges
before the sea   Nagercoil   place of the sea

homeland of the dead and of suicide
as also the shore of new encounter   Soon
we head out into the city—or maybe the town—

through the thick knots of the artisanal sectors
into the church where you asked me about God
"I guess I don't believe " I said   Your own answer was

something of a shrug too but we stilled
at the peace of that cathedral and
  the open seats it gave us

  And we sat there or walked out into
god-knows-what-happened land   the certainty
 —knowing our country very well—that wherever we

stood had seen stupidity   cruelty   genocide   slavery
 and the most sordid fake piety   sure as
the merchant district or the solitary mall

we rolled about in   Was that why
you refused to come into that temple
with its own   to me   fascinating enigmas of

usurpation and appropriation   its Jain pillars
  embedded forever with tirthankaras
swallowed up by a Saivite sect   thus fucking up

—I hoped—   their "chronologies" and ours?
"I always hated the propitiation of the deities"
you said "It's like another form of clientilism!"

          You were right of course
          Temple economics was
          an economics of death but

        this time we were in it together
        though headed into a future
        that held out no clue

      And as the sun rose to its throne
     & bore down on us   the mall failed   inexplicably
to feed us   and the dust was in our eyes and in the eyes

of those   nameless so casteless   community-less
    whose gentle paths we crossed
    Found a restaurant   a comfy one

so we could stop to think and maybe eat
    And there and elsewhere   before
      the returning of the key

how well we drafted   my friend my brother
  plans & histories & resolutions
  futures for the well-being of all

and especially the poets and heroes we relished
as if the world's ministrations depended
solely on what we could manage to work out

between us   before this dusk of parting

To Shaheen Bagh, In Absentia

Bas naam rahega Allah ke
Jo ghayab bhi hazir bhi
Jo manzar bhi nazir bhi

Yes the name alone will stay
   the unseen   still here   and
the thing seen being   also the observer

        —Faiz

I wasn't there at Shaheen Bagh
   those winter days
 when thousands gathered

when it seemed all of Delhi
in the brilliance of its inventiveness
in the earnestness of its grit

was there   Is it true the roads
almost belonged to us   that we took in faces
  with such renewed curiosity

and song stuttered forth   in the unbeliever's hands?
   I've known what it means to rub shoulders
in a place like that   when the glance of touch and

the touching glance   slipped like its own
innocent being through the evening's rush
  This melancholy distance of the seen

   and the thereness of the unseen   The way
something will sprout at the most innocuous traffic light—
   an idea   or body   or refurbished/refurbishable item

and soon the corner will come to that and only that
and the goods and minutiae of traffic and crowds
will learn to flow around it   in both impatience

and attentive embrace   I wasn't there at Shaheen Bagh
in those first days of its glory   to see it hold
 this way   clasped to memory   and habit

but whatever happens   the name will stay
  swim to the skies above us
given as token to the witness of paradise

and the real blood   it asked of us

Maitreem Bhajata: A Translation for Padma Narayanan

 maitrīṃ bhajata akhilahṛjjetrīm
ātmavadeva parānapi paśyata |
yuddhaṃ tyajata spardhāṃ tyajata
tyajata pareṣu akramam ākramaṇam ||
jananī pṛthivī kāmadughā(ā)ste
janako devaḥ sakaladayāluḥ |
dāmyata datta dayadhvaṃ janatāḥ
śreyo bhūyāt sakalajanānām ||

  Grow friendship at the heart
  See other souls as you see your own
   Give up war   Give up competition
 Give up the acquisition or occupation by force
   Invent   thrash out & make real
       the three da's:
        damyata   datta   dayadhvam
     —restraint   charity   mercy—
 & prosperity for all the peoples

Ayodhya

So many in that compartment
   dreamed of going there
dreamed their temple to the infant Ram
might one day be finished—though for
    nearly 30 years nothing
 of consequence had been done
which all pretend not to notice

   We'll come after the temple
is built they told me   And in fact
when the stop came I was pretty much
the only one who alighted   Akbarpur two stops
earlier had all the action women
    in burkhas with lovely hyperactive girl children
 darlings in their parents eyes But

when fell to that dusty
    platform at Ayodhya
in the middle of the afternoon   I knew already
the chill of a town that had destroyed
 itself almost brought grander Faizabad
 down with it   Yet Ayodhya had had its glories too
  and not just as a presumed birthplace of Ram

or great Buddhist world city Saket or even the Ayodhya
  that was owed a Korean princess The city had glories
on its very sight magnificent buildings courtyards public works
palaces grand residences   and shrines accessed at each doorway
   Sometimes you even thought you recognized
    those minarets Ayodhya: how it imagined itself
and how it had been before the emergence of the Site

 And how the Site had taken over the way

people of different faiths mingled   and lived   farmed
by the water   And the very first e-rickshaw ride
   from the station to the Naya Ghat
   that showed you this grandeur
   even in chipped dilapidation
   There must surely be a way in   you thought

But there wasn't   It had become
a city of closures   a lesson you learned
   by meeting them   one by one
 in a wanderment of diminishing hope
from the sombre unbuilt lane on which
your hotel stood   to the mosque overflattered
   by police attention   To the lazy Jain garden

on the cliff or the harsher citadel
of Hanuman's hill   all was as if
a blanket of uncaring had
   descended even
                as the poor
city's fame soared in the national
   news   these years

   Those first hours in the hotel
just the force and speed by which
the night arrived   and the fullness
   of shadows that formed
in this city of suspended construction
   city of an age still to etc. and the sense
of desperation crept among its people

   Wasn't sure if I wanted to stay
      but couldn't put it off any longer
   to know where it is the story of Ram goes
This was just one place   with its strange martial legacies
   The akhadas for instance   where innocent boys
   trained to protect the faith   or how so many

sadhus here were gangsters   and gangsters

sadhus That first night   following a "service road" of pure
dust   and rows of unlived-in quarters to
the bank   the long bathing tank gone to sand
The river too receded revealing mud
and the bands of laborers
crossing it on their way home The city's
    bitter survival about it

and a sense of shame so deep   it looked
  like it would cry Was it poverty alone
      could leave such a hell
of resignation? Where was the glory
that had deserted   in the very moment
our kin had taken the prize   ravaged
  the mosque   Triumphant

rubble   heaps to be cleared   things
    broken that will never again
be healed   even rows of half-completed
new housing that   astonishingly people
  seemed to be living in—concrete
  structures hollowed out   awaiting tiles
      and details and pipes

and electricity   The great Ayodhya
waiting with trembling eyes
                              That first night
from a window along the ghat
a tuneless jarring screeching voice
  singing something that must
have been a devotional summed up

the pitch-dark dustbowls of the ghats   both
in the terror depravity despair and in the calm
  of the foreknowledge that will somehow
  forgive faults and for the next three days like

a true creature of the place I too wandered
    without hope   until exhaustion
  claimed me and took my last words away

2.

  The sheer emptiness of that place   like the emptiness
when Bharata returns unknowing of his father's death
  The pandits who began to stir expectantly
at the faintest visitor's step   and those given over
  to a sleep that shunned all visitors A city entirely
of open drains thin almost invisible slivers
    that followed each shelf of the road

The loudspeakers' *Ram-Ram* in endless versions
from bhajan to rock 'n' roll style from lilt to rasp
  The locked doors and the half-locked doors
   through the day in industry-less Ayodhya
    Ayodhya whose only business
was devotees and pilgrims The many roads
    where vehicles were scarce

  And when you entered the security zone to the Site
the corner soldiers just merged into the scenery as per
  the startling Kashmirification of U.P. but
    the first time you noticed them they
were polite—simply asked you to produce your id—
examined it took a picture turned it around
called it in your Hindu indeed South Indian! name

    must have reassured him but always some dots
in my questionable Hindi And what happens when such keys
of the State its awesome destructive power are handed over
to godmen? Mani Ramdas ki Chawani The structure
  like others in the city grand and with several
levels Most of it inaccessible Intimately
  protected by the army mufti or uniformed

and each of their phones   an eye
The aarti vouchsafed by automatic weapons pointed
   at it and at the throng of devotees   and by much much
      videologging   And all of this just
   warm up for the true prize   the truest
      spoils the "re-"captured territory
         that by invisible court order sent

a whole chunk of primetime Ayodhya land
into the sinkhole aka the Site   as it called you in
   and beguiled you   and eluded
   any entrance   until you asked a soldier
   and even then were discouraged
and questioned again for ID   Could it have been my
problematic timing in early December? No! You

   got the sense this was just the everyday   The army
did its thing though also bitter at being ordered to fight
      its own citizens   Soldiers on plastic
chairs or behind bunkers   Many corners
had made "recruits" of all the little girls and boys too
      Everywhere being watched and noted
Finally   the way into the Site   for commoners

   turned out to be the back of a simple shrine
that was almost a ruin   For a moment you thought you
were there   but then the duck under an iron-pole gate—
   all activity in the city   in principle   illicit
No instructions   the right to change all rules
   at notice   and then   at the corner   first
intimations of the meteor-sized wormhole

that the Site had become   You seemed to be with
   a trickle of people at best   and
   where was it we were going? A few
   hanging about or perhaps
lazily dusting the streets   wave us on

Not far but more
and more of it   Outwardly we'd

stepped from the village of Ayodhya
   into another village of Ayodhya
      a little more abandoned but
just as ordinary with the same half-
closed temple fronts   By now the army
along with plainclothesmen mingled
   among you   YouTube videos

   were blurry on this point   You feared to even
      draw your phone for worry
of being fired at   Innumerable little
   altars in doorways seemingly open
for business but none of the growing straggles
      of visitors   encouraged by locals
were going in   (or else how could I have

walked right past Sita's kitchen
   into nothingness?)
Came by various shoo-ings to
another corner but before you could even
   get there   the touts got you   and
why not? Just Rs. 20 for prasad and for
the locker space that was this

market's most important business
   Once I'd been divested of all devices
and sundry contents of my pockets—save ID
and a ten rupee note— my "agent"
   showed me the strange maze-end from which
   I had to emerge and then I became
      a cog in the bottlenecks

Us men single file into some improvised
booth that sometimes felt like a rabbit
   hutch   Felt up   got used to it and to the

514

inside-out of the pockets by the third
    point in   Security had grafted
a whole order of anxiety onto
itself—it checked checked checked

    as if only to underline the fallibility
of the next check   And also with purpose
  to scare you   discourage you   tell you to go home
  and don't come back till your Ram raj
—if it ever—arrives   And go go on to the vortex
      at the heart Tell all your friends
        what the situation

    of the infant god is   After
    the 4th or 5th rubdown and a passage
    through entrances we came to a path
through a yard   completely enclosed by metal
caging: neither could we leave our cage-path
nor could those outside in the yard access
us easily—not the Simians climbing directly above

or the roving soldiers with rifles ready to kill you
    Each guard's mien was to communicate
a sense of inevitable trespass   Every official   with
    the sole possible exception of the priest
    at the distant altar told you to move
on watch out   don't dawdle   The embarrassment
    of this   28 long years after

    the galvanizing mosque-raid   1992
      sucked the life out of this city
and established the Site   So I walked in it and into it
and true to form   noticed virtually nothing
    but the monitored cage
in which I moved   its endless maze-like
twists and turns   Finally the cynosure

a little opening by which a priest
and a soldier stood   where you gave
   your prepaid prasad and even took some
   back if you wanted   As always in Ayodhya
the idol   the sanctum still distant   as if to underscore
the devotee's unimportance   and to say no journey
would ever be worth it   no sacrifice

   blessed   And the infant Ram finally
in a paltry tent some meters from you
Couldn't even see him with your shabby eyes
   And the people ahead   had all
disappeared   the tense-bored lurking of
the soldiers in the park   half watching
   the animals in the cage as they made

sense of their surroundings   In zero time the desire to
linger pushed up against a desire
to no longer stay   and the spirit began
to rush   even as feet dangled   to what seemed
like a cage-free outside   a wall   a railway forest
   seating   a sense of diminuendo   and
still the soldiers poking exhausted pilgrims

on the bench   For the soldiers would not
let us rest in the city of Ayodhya   and neither
   could we bring them rest   Walking back
   from the Site after some more detours
   from the Site that had taken all and
   given nothing to the ghats that closed early
      but where some semblance

of cheer and the everyday was kept alive   And with night
   stealing back in   you could see how the grand
   mansions of Ayodhya were falling apart
      not just the paint but often the cement
         or plaster come off   to show   like

a spreading crystal the raw brick
  below   Every dwelling

was in principle a shrine that carried
more than an installation
        but a flame Bare figures
    squatted round   You passed through
      the neighbourhoods
of different religions   and nothing
gave a clue   but the shaking
of those who spoke to you

3.

It was in Ayodhya I first understood
  the full range of Simian speech
from the mouse-like squeak of the baby
obligingly leaping from my path
  to sometimes like birds a complex
twittering   sometimes like dogs   or even
panthers a low growl   sometimes even

the stereotypical monkey screech   but
barely so   This looked like a smaller-sized
  subgroup   At first I was struck by how
the Simians of Ayodhya   seemed to carry some
of the same shame as the humans   their apparent
acceptance of the order   Then I
suddenly understood why humans

in Ayodhya carried sticks   and the mood
was less charming   The smell of concrete dust was in the air
I should have noticed it   I walked till halted
earth-shifters   indicated I could go
no further   back down a pitch-dark road
with the wall of Ramkatha park to my right
and a great undefined pit to my left

on a road that became the fanciest
(if incomplete) avenue by day   And the early morn
on the ghats still something: the purity with which
a young bodybuilder sang the Hanuman
Chalisa   the way he gave himself over
to it   The mahuas and the sita-ashoks
on the bank   the boat ride so calm

and endless   Was it real security or
simple land grab that had ruined
these chances for beauty and for grace?
   Soon I could not tell
the barely unreached flood bank
from the grey of the river itself
That night among a whole squad

   of elite soldiers   in phalanx
around him   you thought you recognized
that figure in saffron   short squat 40s with a close crop?
   He went as if with stiff robotic movements
jarring impulsive   that sadhu of the Goraknath math
   who terrorized us as a leader of State with
almost inconceivable powers   Quick appearance

   at the aarti then off with his protection
into the night   Still the strain of the hurt caused
by he and his kind   In the morning
the beautiful azaan and then a preacher
   in Hindi with calls for peace and reconciliation
      drew me like a bee to the honey
   of a mosque but actually getting there

was another matter   The whole
neighbourhood was literally walled off
 with wooden log barriers a soldier
encouraged you to climb through
 and when you finally reached

it seemed the very streets   and the people
in shops and houses   for the streets

were empty   were egging you on   But at last
   as you arrived at the small mosque on
a hill   its modesty   rows of neat chappals outside you
were intercepted by the security cordon   a whole tea party
of uniformed soldiers parked behind a tree
They looked like different regiments   You had to wonder
if they were really there to protect the mosque

              Either way they
were not happy   Stupid you producing passport
instead of PAN card (no Aadhar!) as if that
would establish higher credentials   but instead it was
an invitation to extreme scrutiny   each page studied
   like it was a plan   Each stamp
turned upside down and right side up

Then after that you were perpetually in their sights
   on this bored and uneventful anniversary
of a demolition   It seemed all non-Hindu places of
worship had been made off-bounds for you   (and you
didn't dare go near the Site again)   and
at each place   the small-built plainclothes guy
arrived before you   and a soldier took pictures

of your stuff and ID and asked questions
to which the answers were presumably known
because he told you you'd been at the mosque
and your heart grew heavier and heavier
   and your own eyesight began
to hurt you   and when you got to the hotel
   the owner was livid and wanted

new passport photocopies immediately
   for they had called him also
and now that all the security in the city

was watching you   like a deer
in unfamiliar forest   you knew you had
to leave   counted the hours to
train departure   That night the sporadic

firecrackers celebrating what
should have been the recapture
of Ayodhya   And you hated most
of the religions   their stupid
strictures   their love of
politicians and important men
But in truth those days of blankness

also had moments with the brightness
of coexistence among them:
the sweetness of a shopkeeper
or the grace of the Kabir ashram on the edge
of town   where the witty old monks entertained
themselves by reading aloud
the weirdest Jain sagas

A Ramayana on the Delhi Ridge (2)

1.

> Next to where I worked for years
> those memories lost their sheen
> before becoming background

Much of the Enclosure blocked off by fence like a vast embassy   The many phases the many stages of it—some intimately maintained—others effectively walled off to let terror breed   The first time I breathed the Northern "ridge" I had given myself a task to go to Motilal Banarsidass and moreover the light was failing and I couldn't afford to dawdle   I moved through with a sense of wonder and the idea of a *Ramayana* of the enclosure was the vaguest of ideas despite having already been in search   Find the gate breach of high grey wall   At one point I'm curving round on either edge a narrow pavement and though this was not the regular place of the Simians still intimate and intimidating one or two were grooming themselves and their young   That patient fingernail picking of fleas or other insects from a coat   eating the findings   Then a gate and a policeman placed there   Would there be another side to emerge from? Google Maps thought so but the feet's own maps were unsure   Soon found a great many do cut this way of this very evening   returning from work   with brisk and total confidence even a kind of annoyance   as if wading through something

Many answers and many ways to answer   Depends upon what you think the envelope is   The inside echoes the outside and versa   The neighbourhood trees are also planted and tended to   Was I already straying from the main path to a rawer state? Had I already encountered how marked and lived-in it all was with prayer cloths tied on branching arms even in the most forbidden areas and often near the exits a cairn giving scant clues as to its age or a hovel to Hanuman or the goddess leaned against a peepal trunk? But the Enclosure's reputation and a friend's angerterror of it of being chased there   How there had always been the question of men watching us on walks   I recalled my aloneness and fear in the unspecified breaking of the rules   There were two men walking in front   Not to mention the loner   seething with unfocused resentment   in the middle of a task or not   standing just standing just off to the side

This first time was to beat the light   It was more than enough to simply follow the briskest walkers   The lovers and the hangers-around had long thinned

Struck again by how lush this section was when others I had walked had been sparse emaciated   The trees still unknown still unrecognizable   both frightening and alluring   their sinewy entwined torsos   I pressed blithely on as if damned with the simple fact that others had traversed here before me

The next time transport and the Enclosure right next to us in minutes but without entrance and evidenced by high canopies and happy rapacious Simians lining the wall-tops for the dual view   We wandered lazily while M gave a rhapsodic account or perhaps a fantasy of the best college canteens and what they had served   And his odd story of straying into a cavernous house somewhere around here where an old woman lived alone and going in to use the circular loo in the middle where facing multiple doors he was quickly lost   M was thinking about lunch   Chowkidhars kept waving us toward some kind of opening that could have been far or close   Two dogs fucked at a bus stop or perhaps a kind of boss dog came round to accept the instant subjugation of another pressed its penis and shook around a few times almost as if to dourly confirm dominance more than any thought of pleasure   And still we walked   M possibly still on the subject of the most exquisite canteen food   or street dhabas   stopping for some spiced chickpeas then matches and water   Most of the city in little plots had become no entry like this   sometimes in parks the visitors from the basti had actually been murdered by the upper class fearing encroachment   When the *essence* of being upper caste was encroachment

The sun climbed on   we discussed more of the various disasters that had befallen our friends   Finally reached a gate   A state of submergence   and not just to hold hands or spare a kiss   to go off in a corner to drink   or find a private place for a piss or a nook under a bough surrounded by high yellow grass

A midden   I'll never understand the little random piles of plastic bottles perhaps some kind of collection point   some transition never made   Sometimes looks like it's been there for decades and most likely has   This part of the Enclosure seems the most intentional in the sense of kept clean enough but not overmanaged   kept interesting   M in search of some monument   was it a kind of miniature tomb? The guard waved us toward a somewhere and certainly a nice tarred path in   My Krishen book with me for the very first time   only renewed the thought that all possible walks had already been written   Soon in that continuum from controlled path toward liberties—not just the walkers and the interlopers but the trees and creepers too   The thorns to your skin and clothes   Dozens of hangers-on   little spears of flora   Sometimes like a rapier claw that hooked right in and wouldn't let go and sometimes a gentler brush of quills almost as if to be taken as memento

None of this too much for those seeking fear and desire And to arrive again to where a band of Simians similants sibilants surviving cousins hung their sense of ownership indicated by the complete freedom which with the littlest ones were given to wander and play In retrospect it was very much like wandering through someone's yard a big extended family's communal yard One felt a panic what they might do to us since our species was arbitrarily in charge cruelly superior We were the demonic gods that harassed and manipulated all the worlds they tried to live in They who were many here smaller than us but much much stronger M ever resourceful found a battlestick from somewhere but it too was just part of the theatre We abandoned it at some point But the Simians I wanted to say in the absence of a proper interview were happier in this place They seemed more at ease with visitors now crossing in great numbers into the Sunday afternoon Sometimes they didn't even turn to look at us maybe because we carried no obvious food Once by a shrine a Simian saw us and immediately climbed to a vantage point from where it could comfortably study the contents of our bags Nothing to eat alas save for M's spicy channa But mostly coexistence finding our way among many species A lot of the mesquite that had at some point been brought from South America or the Caribbean—the "vilayaati keekar" as they called it here—against which one felt inexplicable resentment as it had taken over in powerful twisty clumps with a symbolism that was surely no fault of the will-less plant itself Or is it that these plants did have a kind of will had desires in the unpredictability of their arms the fine arrangements of their leaves Why not the ficus even the hallowed banyan tree that always began in the harsh embrace of another perhaps to suck the life out of it or at least to make shortcuts? Desire rawest in the aerial roots and the banyans in Calcutta that existed into and out of concrete The ficus among the most beautiful of tree genres whether in cities or out The arid heart is not a natural state but written and overwritten as much as left to its own devices introduced or wandered into by chance Who cares to tell the local from the foreigner vegetation? Tomorrow I will sit with the Krishen and try hard to remember every tree I've met so far

The rapier of the peepal the jamun in the opposite pairs of its leaves the knotty-trunked chamrod the Krishna figs with leaves that were also pitchers The humble fruit of the Ber tree cherry or olive-green at first ripening to yellow or reddish given by the ascetic woman Shabari to Rama *Nothing could equal those fruits when offered with such devotion* The kadamb of the quilted leaves The veins of the leaves of the pilkhan that made loops at the edges The long earring-fruit of the doodhi The trees that flowered in the hottest months as if to assert beauty in the cruelty of the heat   The broad leaves of the teak or the kanak   the twice-feathered leaves of the gulmohar   All your life you'd walked by potential friends   Now they arrested your sight   making each inch and square interesting   The shrines clearly active against the monuments   Let me go closer haunted whether haunted or not

A rotunda where someone pulled out a guitar to practice songs in earnest The two young women who asked *Are you historians? You look like historians*

2.

Next day Metro station   fancy area   streets wide enough   but with gated colonies nowhere as walkable as it seemed on the phone-map   "Biodiversity park"   An old sarkari feel to it   The airline employee quarters   Those properties all now in question   The glum grey "Budget Bauhaus"—got that memorable phrase from Baviskar—though the interiors are surely modern and fancier   Security to the lives lived here   whether as civil servants or employees of the govt high or low or even as servants of those servants   guards or maids with built-in or nearby quarters   And "good" schools like the Chinmaya Vidyalaya   But something else: the foul air easily among the worst in town   Air so heavy it had a tangible whit- ish presence   Dimmed the eyes not just by burning them but by that crushing weight   Ostensibly posh area   sparsely populated   even genteel   with not so many vehicles on the road   Could it be the closeness of the airport   separated just by that swatch of optimistic Enclosure?

Again the unanswerable   For "biodiversity" was surely in many ways a new concoction   whereas the airline colonies I'm guessing were carved out of the 1950s   Maybe the air was a geographical accident   And another possibility: the time of day   the early-winter afternoon light already losing its colour by four 'o'clock   Shortcut through the colony bustling with kids and teenagers coming home   Help and delivery staff leaving for the day   Gatekeepers with an eagle eye for the unfamiliar interloper   the less than confident walk the not-at-home Without ever answering whether the road was public access or not   O litany of bored authorities   That the wanderer be banished

Round I go to the main road and round again through colony space naggingly surprised that no one new has intercepted me   That long dusty white path into the Enclosure straight as a royal path but left and right fenced off   Struggled to see or make out what was being held back   Looked like more emaciated trees planted into a gridded space between that made them unconnected nodes   Was this an attempt now lost abandoned permanently faltered as a government's initiative can like a train paused in the middle of nowhere gathered blessings of dust? At any rate in this section of the Enclosure the mean path is the only one given to you Its caged way uncannily recalls another that enclosure within an enclosure mother of all Enclosures the Site where the sky itself had been sectioned and serrated

Here though trees labeled with their names that simple joy of knowing To jump the fence would be trouble Promise of a guided walk that would happen according to a manager with a house on the premises never at all And the specimens along the road poor stunted or very young by comparison to the pretty naturalist's book

The startle of dusk continued to creep More and more daily walkers alongside They averred a thereness to the route that would take me out although none of them would be using it all would be coming back Didn't want to be alone here in the night inching my lightless way forward but it reddened and a magic was thrown on what I saw Lush and the happy purgatorial surreal As long as this path went somewhere other than a locked entrance I'd be fine They'd have rickshaws there

A while longer Longer than seemed likely for the Enclosure was mind-addlingly huge I came to a whole other alien land scarcely aware of the one I'd embarked from A modest city park with concrete and gardened edges with office goers and unspecified others and even street vendors and a shrine Two lovers suddenly uncoupling to my arrival The many moments like these I'd stolen myself A huge parking lot in the dark The young walked out to meet their Ubers On the other side I discerned some kind of officer's club A buffer a bittersweet traverse before I was again at a main road rushing with commuters

3.

> How long had the war between
> city and forest lasted? It has lasted
> forever even today there were casualties
> Rama: singularity caught in its alabaster

Central Enclosure on the map is one long if massive squished square of green Looks like it's all connected no sense of at all of the walls & forces that actually govern—or try to govern How different it is depends on us But there is a system of management in place   Guards grateful for the salaries but wondering what to do all day   Dandakaranya   Exhorted P to come along knowing the terrain itself would tell us how to read it   From the precarious and unpleasant crossing of that thoroughfare above which the Blue Line snaked and the Hanuman Mandir towered   Politically ignoring it   moving on trying to find an opening   Sometimes the simplest shrines   a little altar or a photograph and wispy incense   Sometimes by age or power or grace or sheer beauty   to discover or perhaps know by family tradition the innumerable   where saints paused or meditated or gave successes   where the bodies of saints merged with the soil Shrines loved trees   needed them for a sense authority and place   Deep inside inhering with the very decaying power   those who dedicated themselves gave succor to the broken and deranged   Trees did not necessarily come first but shrine and peepal grew together   For the Jain the "vaan" itself was shrine   crannies and sustenance for the sounds of all beings   The active Indic idea of the woods as registering solitude sadness marker of territory   The Enclosure had preceded the city the Google photos show patches of green on the other side of Bhimrao Ambedkar Marg   that vast green template snipped here and there Carved up bits   dismembered fallen in chunks among the buildings and the flyovers and the tense traffic crossings   Sure as the giant Hanuman towering at this crossing a small dargah of great aura its square its swatches of fabric and air of welcome and holy peace   and sequins on low doorways   Then to a wide reservoir empty except for very shallow water and NDMC water tank that had been huger in the satellite's eye than it seemed in life: a half circle of intense grey concrete   Some regional park do's and don'ts then down paths not quite promising   Then a kind of intense unnameable structure   Isn't this the stone of the Tughlaks? Upper level vantage on the surround and an inward section with recesses for lamps   Strangely the husk of a modern toilet branded by Delhi Tourism   Those that are there with us are youngsters that look to be escapees from a nearby college   All they know is the place is haunted   In fact it was once a hunting lodge

Traversed the undergrowth   Came to a road seemingly leading out from somewhere but manned for the sole purpose of discouraging visitors   The nonplace they were defending was a huge amphitheatre   a theatre in the forest There it is   sure as you read this   just beyond yonder shrub   But we never saw it   The next day not wanting to be thwarted by dusk I set out as early as I could Knowing now some of the ways the Enclosure had been cut up I thought I could come in on it through the east side   With P I'd tried from the north   Hadn't fully cognized how deep the geographical surgery   Invisible fissures   Jurisdiction even jurisdictions of neglect   packets or passages governed by separate polities   A way in   and a way out   And sometimes a way between   I go to look it up and I'm diverted   as if by a mysterious chute to Facebook   where Uttar Pradesh burns   I needed to pee and when I saw a fellow male of my species hop over the low wall   I guessed   this was a borderline   with eddies of activity   on certain unstated corners   Was there a little cul-de-sac in the bushes? There was   I had discovered this kind of place earlier when   intently following down a path one returning on it said *Are you sure you know where you're going?* (All this in a language I have forgotten)   *There's literally nothing that way but piss and shit*

Indeed he's been relieving himself   And I with odd-seeming politeness stood and waited for him to be done and come back out   for which I earned first a questioning stare then a shrug   And watching my own piss arc into a little depression of the hill I was almost a defender of where I stood

But contrary to what I'd found the earlier day   no dead end or simple cul-de-sac   this was but a narrow irresistible *onward*   The fumes   the acrid waste and refuse   the roars of city though powerfully stifled   Why so afraid of it   Absence of people or a different kind of enforcement   or of noun construction in general   Whether trespassing or not   later when back outside realized yes   Railway land no matter how wild   is precisely supervised   All railway land is subject to prosecution   But railways and their stations are also the public's passage

Walked on a smaller ridge   the ridge duplicated in its parts   Along that edge some lovely specimens   Kachnar for instance   those massive "camel-foot" leaves or the generosity of a chamrod   Then the stark bearing of tracks in the woods   the view onto them from above   the way they were so much a part of this   those iron-orange lines   always spaced the same occasionally hidden but leading in loops and curves to divide the landscape to show a way to cross   The other side that seemed a mirror of us but was not   Soon I was at the platform   Station quiet not quite empty   Carriageless engine chugged back and forth at intervals more than one would think it needed to   Was it a test   a way to keep the station and the ring rail alive? The ring rail that most never took or even knew of and yet was so packed with commuters the one time you rode it   Up top to my right a genteel avenue would begin   And although the tracks turned out to lead nowhere for a human on foot at the far end of the platform a man sat and watched me with disinterested eyes and made no objection perhaps was even half-grateful for the company

On the other side of Sardar Patel Marg an undivided stretch of enclosure with slats and simple diamond eyelet fencing still foreboding   Was the fencing whether wall or wire   hard or soft   meant to keep people out or keep the wild and its creatures in? Good luck with that latter task   Gates appeared too but were padlocked   Finally a bus stop and just behind it   a breach   a slat half-open comfortable enough to slip through   I could only read it as an invitation

4.

The entry had erased itself in my mind by existing purely as portal   The walls that prevented passage I remembered better   But soon enough doubts   All had been slashed and regrown   leveled and raised   reimagined   reterritorialized for hundreds   thousands   of years   Nothing could be native in that sense but the conditions   the caution that all arrives at sand and debris

And suddenly panicked I was bearing by the sun as my phone dwindled in its charge   Sometimes reopened it to peer at the map of where I was   And the sunlight didn't seem to align as it should   And the crow alone flew away to the Buddha Jayanti park   flew right over that choked t-junction   flew over even the elevated Metro in its flight

Who was it that shared this place with me—commuters racing toward a bus stop or a place of work? The groundskeepers surely must have an intimate map in them   a knowledge of regions and problem areas   And what of the vagrants the thugs the druggies   the licit or illicit lovers? They too were wandering in this with me so perhaps in this little stretch of city forest all was in fact known

The woods and shrub thickened   at first imperceptibly   In the satellite image it happened in a south-eastward direction in alignment with the army cantonment   Why don't we zoom in on the photo as far as we can which means still no humans spottable at this resolution   You see now the trees are but canopies no sense of the barrenness of branches below   The orienting phone dimmed further and became unrevivable   I tried to bear north or northeast by the sun tried to keep the fence on my right

The termites to their hills or the burnished red they covered the edge of the path with as if to brighten it   Soon climbing through at hairier places   The trees extended themselves   took nips   I trusted in the remaining hours of daylight even as the shrinking winter sun fast climbed the sky   Sometimes a worshipped tree with red wound round   Who'd even come in all the way to make a prayer except   the obvious answer came to me   to find a place away from others

The light gleamed gave succor   Took pleasure in the quest as once I'd done as a teenager   The night was presumably filled with dacoits   I was older and much more paranoid   Startled by a band of Simians and me startling them too in a settlement without roofs   Their divided lives by the wall   begging and being fed out there hanging out and getting away from it in here   Their own version of home and the world Later on a map I saw this corner of the Enclosure had a name: "Monkey's Forest" If the map was to be trusted it carried over on the *other* side of a main arterial road as well into the Malcha forest

Straying through their territory getting lost and moving in triangles   The walls in the places they joined had no breach whatsoever At one corner I could hear on the other side   the persistent whistle of a traffic cop Tried to hoist myself over   could see the urgent intersection and even a vendor on the pavement but fell back Tried to pile up heavy stones and abandoned massive tile slabs hauling them in painful rolls trying to balance each one on the previous and then to climb on that In shock an overturned boulder revealed a termite nest

Massive diesel generator apparently abandoned to the elements Holes almost large enough to crawl through   A deep ravine-like trench   Had to consider which side of it I wanted to be on   By now long since lost any sense of usable path Wanted to follow the wall for security   But afternoon now so shouldn't the sun be in the opposite quandrant? The bush near the wall become impossible Real path or just a little trench made by a dried-up stream? Heard a stirring may have heard a voice   Then saw a human figure   I was not alone! Before second thoughts had already called out A man or rather just the top half of him emerged   At first he'd not answered at all   but I'd been foolishly persistent Then with a sense of great reluctance with a blank not exactly welcoming look *What* I asked *was the way out?* Unconvincingly he gestured back to where I'd come from Not loquacious at all or even curious I was clearly in interruption of something Persisted and didn't turn back Saw no future in the confusing bramble behind me Soon the same structure from where the man stuck out from a different angle and a second man appeared from beneath the first Had I been witness to the overhead of a blowjob or had this just become my fantasy? They seemed the only others and there had been nothing to say between us

Came to a piped canal bits of infrastructure but nothing climbable Then the little clearing where the red and orange puja cloths had been tied then a little patch that had perhaps been a drinking spot

Made it much later to the boundary a little bit of half-wall to a less thickly forested section Then walked around to find a surprisingly easier way out where trees and saplings were being neatly groomed Here intercepted then questioned for ID Why had I been in the jungle?

Fled in a panic but longed to go back That ever-present light that respite

Something visual about the way the place clutched at you or you clutched at it To be sure I'd encountered just the scrawniest little corner of the Enclosure true to itself as any microcosm unique as any habitat Now on the outside following only the wall it seemed strangely diminished I arrived at the same stretch of the wall I had earlier been inside of with the Simians and saw a beautifully done attached metal dippy and a stone tank they could drink from and banana peels the clearest markers of how they were being fed But even this detail refuses to answer the question of whether the feeding came first or the Simians

And just ahead the Jain Vanasthali Why not sit for hours Many inside were doing just that on idyllic benches among sprinklers hard at work The Jains had a delicate classical taste for nature Was this a matter of density or a lack of something more sinister in the ground cover? In any case the goal for the day lay a little further was Buddha Jayanti Park: where I had heard a shoot of the master's original peepal grew

Took a left where I should have taken a right but a coconut seller turned me back around Wide welcoming parking lot with autos hovering Startlingly well tended with happy trees A little artificial lake and the statue of the Buddha sitting in the middle of it Behind him a scrawny young peepal but indeed one that must have arrived not so long ago as a cutting from Sri Lanka as a clone of the very tree that had traveled millennia from Sarnath

A Ramayana on the Delhi Ridge (1)

Walking the one foot
with the other   you met
a track—the way life moved on it
and in long journey   left trails
Trust if you're going elsewhere
into the next forest and the next
to a grove where   peacocks
the blue males flashed arrows   the trunks
embraced under shades of leaves

Once density was the preserve of wood
Now here   the only places for space to express itself
and at last the birds called   in wiry chorus

So enclosure upon enclosure upon
  I followed the trail—

 Each came up on the previous
like an elephant hidden in a lotus

   Expressways greeted me as I crossed
between   somersaulting the red light at the rapid transit corridor then

   back   an old brick shrine built into the wood
Nannies herded multiple dogs on single hand on straining leashes
   like absent charioteers

Park enough to signify
 —though long subdued—
Rama like a blue snake you
     flit from hollow to hollow

Here in that nook you beheaded the Shudra
Here your touch made the hibiscus bloom
      turned stone to water
Blue tyrant with the heart of a lover
even now we can't say what to make of you
   Slaughtered yourself a billion times
   so we'd know the blood was soil

  Always   a path cut through grass
   becomes a street   attracts a shop
   then we follow the crooked lanes
      dreaming of starting afresh
    What's left from this process
       is presumably these Enclosures
with their scatter of strangest chargings
   only more hidden
    like the kind of disrobing
     that ends with you
   dropping to the scratchy ground

I remember once a man wanted
   to show me his hands
It was partly long solicitude in
the way "my people"   had subjected his

—"my people"   I say perversely
for that is what we saw
in the second instance if not the first
The sprawled foot of the wall
of the specific park we were in
   hidden by artful neglect
bramble of weed and thorny creature
and I in gentle cruelty saying *no*—

   This was already ages ago
Today scanning the dust-haloed trails
in front   or to the left   or behind me
the eyes that come do not
avert nor beseech nor linger
All around us spins the traffic
and the look's forever above or ahead

V

Some Notes on Race in the Ramayana

By the time you get to those Amar Chitra Katha comics for kids, the racial coding of certain old Indic stories becomes rather clear. Panel by panel we were fed this crap. And even there the strange wonder and terror of another history that would obliterate this one, that speaks through this one. A strange twist. The greatest gods and goddesses are many of them dark-skinned. Shiva wears locks. Traces of an earlier regime? A form of reconciliation in the war without beginning or end?

Yes, the British fed us the crap of narratives we took as our own, but the angry truth is Indic representations before the Brits were also clearly racial, or perhaps proto-racial...? Stereotypes right in the *Ramayana*—those Valmiki mss. they found, the earliest of which dated back to the twelfth century. And illustrators of the Persian *Ramayanas* seemed to make a point of both confusing and re-opening questions of race. My thoughts to the Ethiopian philosopher Teodros Kidros asking, What if our current dominant and repeatedly entangling if profoundly nonsensical regimes of race and gender begin in early confused conception not in post- or pre-enlightenment Europe but in ancient Egypt then moving to India, China, and so on? And in Valmiki always that strange and continual doubling, ugly and beautiful, light and dark, other and ourselves, gods and alter-gods. What kind of apocalyptic violence are we trying to remember through an iconology of skin tone which in this context looks to be almost exactly the same as caste? What is it that Valmiki, by legend an outcast himself , wants to reconcile? And as we're dreaming untainted originals, what of the Simians—in the *Ramayana* they're strangely more thoughtful than the humans. More reflective, more capable of doubt, they're so beautiful and important to the book. Have to believe they're part of a very different continuum completely unlinked to the stupidities of nineteenth-century European "thought". And if the dark-skinned Rama moves through all of this as fury and flame perhaps what we now call "Valmiki" is also an appropriation of an appropriation of an appropriation. Perpetual outsider. Dangerous storyteller. Roaming epic bard. "Sage" you never actually see in the company of prominent Brahminish sages like Agastya and Vishwamitra. And the real Rama is not at all who we think he is and Valmiki no longer the ridiculous lily-white Vaishnavite with the pedantic look. Instead, that sole rare poster you saw once in a side room of a temple dedicated to him in Delhi: young, angry, and already with the glare and hurt of true witness.

At Valmiki Sadan

In memoriam Guru Cheena Ji Maharaj

Valmiki   great visionary of the "outcastes"
  Poet of compassion for all beings
    How I wish to honour you
      and not the usurpers
among the claims of your people
      their artistry   their survival

Sentences Toward Another Manifesto of Translation Practice

Our central anxiety about translation today is our (relatively recent) anxiety over authorship.

Long live the wonderful friendship between translation and hoaxes! *Every* translation is a hoax at least in the sense that it is not what it claims to be: the author's "own words."

A new translation should be seen as an addition, not a replacement: translation is additive.

Every work of translation begins as a study. No translation is innocent.

"Faithfulness": a foil, a cover, an alibi. "Accuracy": when examined, always a term of imprecision.

But translation is *always* possible. Translation is the new art of the possible.

And translation *is* originality. Commentary, transcription, and calligraphy are allied original arts.

Part of the (relatively recent) conspiracy of nations in poetry is the fencing off of translations, suppressed or repressed as if they belonged to *other literatures* and not ours. (A few token exceptions to help police the line).

In 1857, the native sepoys of the colonial army plotted rebellion "behind the back" of the administration, in languages it hadn't bothered to learn well enough. In the wake of this surprise—after a spell of brutal, even mindless retribution against the native city—the colonists famously set about bringing the natives fully into English. They embarked on perhaps the widest, most intricate effort of translation ever. Land tenure, customary law, you name it. Nothing should escape the predatory eye of English, no "inaccurate" or freely improvised translation should ever be allowed or admitted to. It was a task of gathering but also fixing. The technology of the dictionaries they compiled helped them in this; but it also helps us, today.

And the boundary between languages no longer clear.

If translation can no longer be a consolation, what kinds of pressure and investment must it be willing to undergo? Under what terms do we endure mediocrity?

True translation is soul-fusion technology. Technology: i.e., techne.

Every translation is a collaboration among many, including all those who have come to this terrain before you. I am indebted even to those translations whose approach I reject because they gave me the benefit of having something to reject.

If nothing is to be lost, something must first be gained.

All poetry is translation.
All translation is not poetry.

Translation is movement not equivalence.

Count me out—from the translation that seeks to exile the source.

Alpasamkhyi

The first time I ever had to face my fit-as-a-fiddle yoga-breathing father in the hospital was when he was eighty-two and getting heart surgery at the strangely named OMIT hospital on the fraying skirts of South Chennai. Blitz of traffic, flashes of yellow uncultivated military land. Cross an improbable late-industrial interior bend of the Adyar river and you're there. Each afternoon on a post-lunch walk or occasionally at the very crack of dawn, I'd wander out past the bridge into a well-kept but solitary wartime cemetery. Then I might, for perversity's sake, run or negotiate across the highway to see the other side of the river split by the bridge. Then back to the medical complex—its regions for foreign and local patients, its "nature-zones," the levels of its low- and high-rises restricted by how much you were ready to pay, its basements for treatment of the poor, its distant lab rooms and featureless restaurants where the evening's menu had to be contemplated.

I learned quickly that in an Indian hospital at least you can get top-notch operative care and tech but it's in the post-operative hotel-end of the business that corners are cut. Sharing a private room, a bed across from his, I became the default night-and-day assistant. The overworked shift nurses were quietly thankful and I was grateful too for the intimacy with my father who'd become vulnerable in ways I didn't think possible. One of those nights, on a visit to the bathroom, my hands supporting his elbows, he suddenly grew contemplative, brow-furrowed, eyes askance, as if plagued by a sudden misgiving.

He said, "I had to take care of my father once in his last days."

He said, "Father called out to me in a desperate voice in the middle of the night. Needed to take a piss, for which you had to go right to the back of the yard, out past the well."

This was probably in the years after electricity had come to their village, but I imagine it still pretty dark. Not as dark as city folks tend to think but, let's say, that blue glow full of shadows. You could trip and fall out there, or get bitten by a rodent. My father said, "While I held my father on the precarious walk, he suddenly leaned closer and brought up a Sanskrit word, *alpasamkhyi*. Do you know what that means, Vivek?"

I didn't, of course, know what it meant. I had grown up in Africa far away from Sanskrit grammar or certain board exams and had, by then, been running from that upper-caste language for whole decades of my life. My father seemed to be making it very clear, and I couldn't quite understand why, that it was a kind of *secret* word, the kind with an esoteric meaning exchanged exclusively between father and son. Kept my ear close and strained to discern him. I can't promise you I heard it right. He was being elliptical and soft as if it were impossible to speak louder.

I'm pretty sure I heard him say, "It means: piss." But also, "remainder."

Perhaps I know a little better what it means now: hence the fancier transliteration. Inching up the substrings of the Monier Williams, I see that *alpa* is all things minute and trifling, whether attaching to the voice, or the body, or to money, to poverty, or to slender plants and the scantness of clothing, or to intelligences or wills or descendants or properties or of breath or of speech or of pain or of insect-like annoyance or of a little thing of value or above all just of . . . *stuff*. And indeed could the other part of it, *samkhyi*, just mean in some way—*stuff*? If, as I'm surmising, the word here is linked to *samkhya*—lit., enumeration, number, but also a school of philosophical thought which presupposes both a temporal body and a body of "subtle" matter that persists after biological death?

My father's giving me this word I did not want to let go of was a prelude to something else, completely unexpected. He said, "My father brought up something he had neglected to teach me when younger: to pull the foreskin back and wash the nub every time you take a bath. Vivek, I fear I must have also forgotten to tell you this. It's extremely important." I wanted to laugh, but my father's face grew serious and stern.

I'll admit that I have since been paying even closer attention to the care of my foreskin and what it covers. And yet I know in my heart the story means something more. The next time I faced my father in the hospital was a bare two years later. By the time I arrived he was already on a respirator, speech close to impossible, eyes attempting the bridge. But his face was expressive as ever.

The doctors and specialists—hematologists, for instance—were best accosted in the hallways. They were being elliptical too. "Do people ever leave the ICU alive?" This was asked to me by a kin of one of the other patients in the room, with genuine and almost-innocent wonderment, or perhaps just to ask it aloud. Her youngish mother was suffering from total sepsis. An odd and sometimes suspicious friendship, even community, developed among us patient-kin. Sometimes we were allies, sometimes competitors. Each night we had to decide whether it would be worth it for us to try and bribe or bluster our way past visiting hours.

As with the earlier time, I was a little frustrated and self-conscious about not being able to write anything at all in the notebook I kept with me, especially when it seemed the activity could do me some tangible good, help me reflect, or simply record all the details I would want to call up later, as a reassurance or as heavenly remainder. There was a girl—a young woman really—who sat in the waiting room and methodically filled page after page of her notebook in a neat script. I would stare at her and grow intensely jealous—she who was probably not even a *true* writer! Then I would blame myself: my callousness, my inability to feel when it was properly required of me, my lack of resourcefulness. Finally, after days of this I couldn't resist a peek. I looked in her notebook and it was the same name, line after line, in the Devanagari alphabet: a god's name on endless repeat.

This time my father was again desperate to tell me something, but his gestures had failed him comically. I was terrified of acceding to his request to remove the respirator from his mouth. How far or close was a nurse? How right or wrong was an action, any action? It was the first time I'd seen him really angry at me in a very long while.

The weekend arrived. We'd decided to bring him home, to have him back among us, but on the Monday the nurses called us from the hospital. We arrived and held his hands for hours and hours. Did he, like Lakshmana, stop his thoughts and then his breath? The evenness of the pace at which he eventually left, the slow dimunition into something that felt like silence.

The Final Asana

The *Smriti-sthana*, now lost to us, was a 5th century Sanskrit practical manual and critique of Patanjali's *Yoga Sutras* that, according to certain accounts, contained a detailed classification of several aspects of memory (relating to the memory of both texts and life experiences), as well as a series of asanas graded to train the practitioner's skills in each of the enumerated categories.

In the tenth century philosopher and writer Abhinavagupta's account of this book, he notes that there is one asana—a posture or an exercise—in particular that should be considered the most difficult, dangerous, and powerful. The details of this exercise, presented in the very first pages of the work, were apparently not obvious on initial reading, but instead encoded in a series of word and letter games, including but not restricted to puns, similes, extended metaphors, and symbolic tales that appeared to be nonsensical until one had finished reading the entire text, performed the other exercises, and returned to the first page. The authors of the *Smriti-sthana* believed that this was the best way to protect their last exercise from inadvertent or inexperienced practitioners.

Abhinavagupta does not give us much by way of specific examples. He does, however, provide a gloss on the final asana, which is simply this: if, in each of the previous sets of asanas, the student is asked to receive information, either by instruction or in the rawer state of sensory input, imprint it on the structures of the brain, and recall it in various forms, this last set asks the student to *resist*: that is, to actively push away any kind of sensory input or data (first from the forebrain). The principal metaphor used here is: *push away the sea waves with your bare hands*.

vi. After

◆　◆　◆

Let us praise also language
instrument deathless of the soul
for making more possible
after the abduction and the war
after the Simians had reveled
and returned—and the rakshasas upon
the rebuilding of their comprador city—
after Sita's trial by fire
and the bittersweet homecoming—
with quiet in the palace　After multiple state banquets
and the elders off on
assorted pilgrimages and errands and
with them tight
knots of attendants & advisors &
pundits & petitioners

Rama and Sita at the window watched
the capital's lamps go out in clusters
They were almost children again then
They climbed up to the terrace
as night spread itself
over the houses of the city
and the huts that ringed the houses　And out
beyond the light-eating river
and far into the hills where jackals and tigers
still roamed　chastened　the terrain
exceeded the people　the Kosala kingdom frayed
Ayodhya disappeared

For days the two relearned
one another　They fought
with unchecked fury
Distance and unknowing though hard
can be complacent　Closeness
offers no luxury　Still he
entered her　and she him

Token of verbal art:
The lotus pond Maybe   *Most often*
I am in the darkness of
my desire good itself
        an evil But sometimes too
    the night of non-meaning
    the dark transluminous

After weeks of night   the air
    crisp   The kingdom reawakened
            slowly from after-festivities
        but still ran reliably as if by wheels
        on a compliant sanded road
        Rama and Sita visited the royal gardens—
    the Ashokan grove—with the beauty
    of the forest but drained
    of fear   Even as you
    approached the gates
    the scent of the place took you:
    frangipani   big-leaved mahuas
    sandalwood eaglewood &
    mango trees   coconut   red sandal
    & deodar groves   champaka
    sita-ashok   pumnaga   madhooka   asana
        parijata   The pomegranate
    the rose-apple the overlappling
    waves of colour   flowers
    fruit dropped to ground
    pecked at by drunk birds
Sun-gold fire-flame or kohl-dark
    Raucousness at dawn
    or on evening's hem   Gardeners
darting about   And parting some foliage
the surprise of an illuminated pond   little
pagodas little overnight cottages   Inscribed
    stone bridges   frilled borders and low
    fences positioned so as to fuse
    with the whole   the whole

to be read and read
with the seasons
   Retinues of divine musicians
  and dancers join   they tap
the toddy brew from flowers
a divine Maireyaka wine   Rama takes
  a sip then makes Sita drink it just
     as Indra does Saci

offering her the wine intermixed with the scents and sounds of the grove. The tender would-be lover couples are on stage or down below on cushions. The old plan: lick, squeeze, hold on, exchange our glances and our juices but with, so we're told, not a trace of guilt or anxiousness. When I think of what happens there I can only think of the distance with which I am forced to tell it. That our bodies might be as readily offered to life

     as they are to the final fire! Winter inside
      winter light bristling winter   went
    and returned   the pleasure that cancels
       memory only after
        those winters have become
      points in the past And the endlessness of ritual
      observance locks up

the days of the pious like the life of a horse dragged by the traps it carries. Before long Rama had to reattend to the anxious boom of his court and Sita had to check in on her mother-in-laws. Though it was weeks before she or anyone would know, twin fresh branches of atman were growing in her. One dream of the stasis of the State: not the hell of repetition but a life made secure by routine, even war mellowing to myth. And violence where it struck occasionally mostly for the poor, those of "lowly" birth . . .

  Many would prefer to stop here

for who would wish misery on a royal hero and heroine in their old age? Who would wish on our king the raging madness that befell his own father? Who would not despair of Rama losing Sita a third time, bolted in place but shaking as if he'd been sliced everywhere? It's just life: even

<pre>
        apart   tearing me
    as I
                    speak
</pre>

for you can't take away anything. Not a thing. There's no unplucking the arrow of disownment. Your head as if in a cloud of smoke. You can't even walk, need the help of a stick but so angry you'd curse the Earth because she happened to be your wife's mother

> *I'll strip*
> *and scar your mountains I'll dam*
> *your rivers and flood the villages*
> *I'll leach you till you're dry*

I'm Rama king of Ayodhya and rightful ruler of worlds. Not a single living thing will be spared

And ruler of the worlds it is, make no mistake, who also in the next moment swoons in a pathetic craven heap saying only

> *Janaka's plough found*
> *your daughter among*
> *the furrows in his field*

avoiding eye contact, grinding in the mind and drowning in sweet-cruel pain. And even your well-wishers begin to retreat from consoling you. *Mother-in-law is hard as stone hard as the rocks that cover her And I can't even look at the friends & subjects who used to cheer me up.* Love is memory, sorrow a revelation.

> *As a jealous man*
> *I suffer from being common*

Springs a new fount of rage: he curses his arm, his famous arm. And not only that. *Curse the hand and fingers that direct the arm. Curse the torso, the legs, the face with its cold imperviousness. Gnaw yourself. Rip the infected body apart.*

I'm like a man who butchers a pet bird
I'm no sandalwood but a noxious poison tree
Push her away from my chest where she sleeps

My truest enemy   is far from glittering Lanka

And we are old, our sons grown—

I make myself cry
to prove
that grief is not an illusion

Readying for war
would bring shame on us both

And she poured herself like ghee into the fire...

◆   ◆   ◆

—Wha...?
—But *how* can you ask that
as if you haven't already read it in the *Ramayana*?

To preserve harm, give up your love. It's no secret we learn to grieve from
movies. Ramu, if you're out there, you forget as each one of us forgets what it is
we're watching. Seen here, staring at the screen, putty for the portending music.
Uncomprehending, as some *other* sinister king's brother & best friend helps an
unsuspecting pregnant queen into a chariot bound for the hills...

—But wait how
did we come to this desperate end?
—I'll tell you

◆ ◆ ◆

The powers of a moon on a cloudless winter night have nothing on her that woman heavy with child. As far as she's concerned, her brother-in-law's just taking her for a pre-birth round in the hills—fresh air, prayer, sightseeing. Lakshmana has the strictest of instructions from Rama not to tell her anything.

And yet this woman, daughter of the Earth, blind to her fate, feels a tremor.

Lakshmana why am I shaking? Why does
my right eye tremble so? And why my heart
unsteady in the faultless morning air? Our planet feels
like a great rising zero we're pouring ourselves
into it Brother—defender of brothers—I hope the king my husband
is ok I hope my mother-in-laws
and their families are ok I hope the kingdom's safe

Lakshmana stiffens. He can feel his heart drying up

like a pond in the heat
of an approaching drought   A smile wanes
on his lips *Everything's fine Sita Don't be silly* He helps her

into the car gets in signs to the driver

Half an hour just to get out of the city with its stirring businesses and early snarls of traffic. Someone spots the cab with the royal seal and little groups gather to try and glimpse who might be inside. Past the first agricultural enclaves and weekend homes, miles of prosperous farmers' lands along the highways forged by the Ikshvaku clan. Hours later, first hints of woodland

from where the shadows
began to chase them

Night's halt an ashram on the banks of the Gomati. Eat a simple dinner as the guests of the rishi there, sleep. At dawn the king's loyal brother wakes

like a coiled spring   Calls for the charioteer   Swift as thought
Sumantra's hitched the horses
        and is entreating a sleepy Sita

    Sita of the shining eyes
        & Lakshmana son of Soumitra
    climbed into that fancy transport and
Sumantra was its driver

    The road narrows, increases its appetite. Woods in green
unknowing blur. Names, particulars of places through without stopping

    just as a life learns to hold onto less and less
and eventually hears only the sound of its own transit   Half

            a day more they've reached the
                Bhagirathi
            (aka Ganges Ganga Jahnu's daughter)
            wide dark-grey pulsing steadily
            with the myriad little creatures
            living in her   briefly visible

    Seeing the river, wretched Lakshmana feels cold guilt-spasms. A
yelp slips his mouth. *What's wrong Lakshmana*, Sita asks.
                At this long desired hour we finally
                got to the banks of the great Ganga so what
                makes you upset? You're too used
            to following the footprints
            of your brother aren't you? It's
            the same for me obviously
                Rama's dearer than life Don't
            be childish Take me across the river show me
            the various kinds of sadhus
        meditating or begging on the opposite bank
        I'll distribute the cloths and gifts
            and after a few nights' stay
            we'll head back My own mind also
                hurries to the spouse

lion-breasted one with a slender waist

Having heard these
                    trusting words   suppressing his thoughts
              that great killer of enemy heroes

    calls for the ferryman: We'll   cross The river
laps the shore He's ready   The   cozy
boat   Helps Sita
            in gets in himself Boat rocks gently
in the late afternoon light   To
      the charioteer Stay Grief-gripped
      then to the boatman Go

    The boatman   his oar a dance
  They course gently across the water
When they've stepped on the opposite bank
    Lakshmana's own limbs
          object to him   Turning to Sita
  confessing through tears:

            Skiver my heart that
        I'd be the one forced to this deed
            that all the people
      will speak ill of me
                that the generations to come
      will judge me for what I've done

        Please Sita—you whose word
          is bond—don't hate me

Seeing him like this, death-dreaming with his head in restless hands, Sita feels cold as stone. *I don't understand. Just tell me the truth. I command you to tell me what your orders are.*

The sun's dipped a little. Hour of roselight soon upon them. A passing cloud with the faintness of its shade. Lakshmana straggles to the base of a peepal. Sita follows him there. The spear-tips of its leaves.

Very simple: people have been making jokes about whether the queen is really pure. The truth, it turns out, is a joke, but a consequential one that has festered in rumour, the rumour made real even if untrue by the indexical duties of our king. Lakshmana reveals a logic neither can fathom nor refute: concerning a woman's place in the ambit of statecraft, whether she should be killed or spared, whether she can ever be taken back.

Centuries of theoreticians have tackled these questions. None have found an answer. Sita listens, her womb grown large, blind to its own audition. Listens to the scheme so carefully stepped even while she'd been merely imagining a few days strolling in the hills.

The forest suddenly hollow. Not a bird chirps. Wait—except—somewhere far away—

a single bleating krauncha   Lakshmana can't
bring himself to look up
so looks—as he's always done—
at her feet: subtly lined but still
their long slim taper   the sloping curve in the arch   the flaring of
the bone under skin And the calves
and ankles sturdy

Opening his mouth to speak but not succeeding, Lakshmana of the tormented mind backs away, facing her. And when he's reached the tethered boat, climbs in. Spots his charioteer waiting for him on the other bank, the steeds restless.

She hasn't moved. Then turning, turning, again, again on the journey back across the river. *Did you see her? Did you also undergo treatment?* Widens to take in the whole of the bank: Sita an orphan silhouette growing smaller, indistinct.

And then the perspective from the bank, trying to get a glimpse of the chariot as it speeds out into the dwindling wick of the day. Again, again. It grows small, in a quick second isn't there.

Not a thing familiar. In the forest, Sita's cries amplified by the calls of peahens.

◆ ◆ ◆

Let's say it's still the late '80s, and we're in one of those grand old movie halls with names like Paras, Eros, Liberty, Rivoli. I miss them. Packed, the front benchers are whistling, clapping, jeering. Rama's sitting midway in the lower section with the seat next to him empty, worrying his hands, utterly alone. *Sita!* he shouts to the screen. *Don't trust your husband!*

Funny coincidence about the names in the movie. The script's long been locked, the movie cut and released. But something , someone must be doing the telling. So

who are they, these two handsome young brothers? Each wears black buckskin and a maddered purple-red cloth tied with murva grass. Each carries a bow, a rosary, a staff of peepal wood, and a saung between them.

They've been singing their epics for years to the accompaniment of this harp-like instrument, wandering through little jungle villages. Kosala, Rama's kingdom, is far away. The last time the big boss was here, he killed a meditating monk. That was just before our Lava and Kusha had come of age. So for instance they've never seen a horse before—

> *from behind a thick swatch of tail*
> *constantly swishing   long*
> *neck it has and hooves that number*
> *precisely four   an eater of grass it scatters*
> *yellow shit the size*
> *and consistency of mangoes*

—until none other than Rama's tasseled royal animal, the black horse meant for the sacrifice, arrives in their parts, daring any challenges.

They love the stories they sing, these young men do. It's their life and livelihood. And they sing their own father's tale, so they've been told. Yet is it wrong to hear in certain passages a barely concealed rage, even contempt for the patria? Doesn't the humiliated soma stone reply at least with a few spits of fire—after a whole day of the Daymaking God tirelessly bombarding it?

(Twins singing)

Rama great king—but not without the faults
he gets away with every time
See how even his snuffing
of Sunda's wife didn't make
a dent in his cred! And if
facing the fearsome Khara
He took those three coward steps back
he still—
that's how it is!—gets to be
the king! Rama great one
not above taking shortcuts   His "great skill"
in the blatant kill of Vali from behind—
everyone knows that score   And then
there's what he did to our mother

Well he's old and useless now what's even
the point in talking about it!
Rama   great king not without his faults

Rama thinks, *They're pretty boys and there's a sweetness in their recitation*
that's hard to resist. Before he's grasped who they are or what they're telling
he's seen with obscured heartbreak their mother's beauty in the eyes the jawlines
the outlines
of necks and hands

The stream when aware
of being listened to
gurgles incomprehensibly
How do I listen
sans the watchfulness
I thought of the other things
I am asked to provide

Many many days Rama was rapt to the tales the boys sang, rapt to sages &
lovers & kings & Simians. At first, only unmitigated strangeness ruled though
he felt some pity for the poem's lonely *kshatriya* protagonist. Then little snips

of further recognition little shocks. Rama trapped in Valmiki's lustrous poem
just as he, Rama, round and round his royal enclosure.

> And when The End came
> it was a massy smothering bow-curved
> tongue smacking on champers
> with a gurgled clangourous rout an
> event horizon so be it
> And after even the End
> had come and gone it became
> all too clear
> who the narrators were

He scans their faces with an intensity of wanting he's never known before.
Stiffens a little.

But law must intervene, the state must intervene. So he puts it like this in-
stead: *The sovereign has a message for her his wife their mother*
> *and for the poet Valmiki*
>> *If Sita's still pure of conduct*
> *might we hold the ritual of fire a second*
> *time? Duplicate? then why not just go ahead and ask*
>> *for it three times or four?*
>>> *—tomorrow morning*
>> *before the assembly And if she*
>> *should pass that test I request*
>> *she might join me by my side again...*

Asked as if it were a stain he'd thin out, his declaration by some awful trick
of transference still the words of a supreme ruler.
  The next morning she was there. She so long in the mansions of the rakshasa
and then so long in exile in the hut of the poet was come.
  Gladness, misery, anger clumped in our Raghava's heart. So he starts again
in that toneless voice, as if he had not much need for a wife but

> like sore eyes hating the lamplight
> like guilt and regret squinting baffled at the pyre

◆   ◆   ◆

Initially *we* heard it as good news
  First light the arena's packed
   The humans & the celestials & the animals
& the former enemies
& the noblemen & the peasants
  in their best clothes
& the pundits & the vow-takers & the seers
& the ones who knew & the ones who understood
& the ones who thought they knew
   the casual spectators
  the accidental spectators

        …For who could not love Sita?
        And who could know her mind?

      "mortals & gods & antigods men &
                women &
        animals   along with the beings of
    the middle space both
            moving and unmoving
      Brahmins Kshatriyas people
        of the city"

The crowd continues to thicken, but is hushed, motionless with news of her arrival. First poet Valmiki walks into the parting crowds. Sita's behind him looking down face averted choking on tears. The boys are grown. All of them so many years older. Upon seeing her, cries of
      "Bravo!" Then:
  "Halahala!" a kind of noise sloppily churned

Blameless Sita. Black-ringed eyes. Some praised her, some praised Rama.

Valmiki speaks. *I am the descendant of Prachetas, composer of the poem* Ramayana.

*Sita whom you abandoned—your instincts ruined by fear—knowing well she
was pure of heart—she's no less now than she was then.*

The sons are yours.

And Rama says: *I abandoned that blameless woman, it's true, for fear of what
some would say!*

Palm pressed to palm. Voice for once like his own.

There's proof in the poet's speech.

Remove the errors of the past and let love between Sita & me start again.

> The wind god surged
>   a promising breeze through
> the minds of those inconceivably gathered there
> from every country in the world—the Unbounded Era
>   faintly remaindered   like the faded   brownish cloth
>   that hung on Sita's bones But
>   she spoke: almost illegibly   still looking down

> > *As all are agreed*
> >   *If I have spoken the truth*
> >   *let my mother the Earth*
> >   *take me back into her*
> > *As all are agreed   Let the Earth*

> . . . nothing to say and the nothing
>   in it to say.
Pure of heart and nothing to say.

> The spine is a cable that connects us to ground.
The body dressed for cremation   the clothes cut lengthwise.

> > the stage
> > all those come

                    raja or saddhu
                  not one dare stand
              between Sita & her decision
                    In the sky
                  or on the ground
                       each
                  passing through
                   or immotile
                in the underworld
               in the coiling beneath
Some look at him   some at her
   Some are making what
     seem to be cries of joy Others
           just transfixed by
             the sight that
           stupefying *muhūrtam*   (moment)when
          when she returns herself to
          the black soil that bears us
               bears our crops &
                  trees alike

              she claims the earth
              the earth claims her

◆ ◆ ◆

The question of who Sita is, so central to Valmiki's *Ramayana* and the thousands of *Ramayanas* that both spring from and surround it, return to it. A problem for the eyes and ears. The Simians and the humans and the pandits all shouting, we're told, *Sādhu!* (i.e., *Bravo!*), aware, as the lines of a poem must be, of the king's presence among them. But Valmiki, we suspect, was on Sita's side. Some would even insist on her character as a free agent, a proto-feminist. "At first fate was like a congenial friend who went along with her every whim."

The poet's Sita in rags, bruised and blue, stretched taut on the rib, the scene of her final disappearance. And the alternative? The Sita of Ravi Verma's (and Tulsi's?) wishful, wonderfully willful imagination: oval-faced in a green-bordered sari, demurely braided hair, contentedly sitting on Rama's lap , the twin boys held on either side?

A happy family!

Once I learned to scratch I found unfailingly those layers that in their wild sympathies ran exactly counter to everything I thought I knew. A vague sense of having been lied to by one's elders. Rama, who flies into a complicated but brutal rage, rampaging through the forests in his conquest of the South. The suffering blameless rakshasas who take off their monster masks, look to the sky. The Simian inclined to devotion stopped in startling moments of doubt, of skepticism.

But if Sita is the seed of outrage—for Sita, at several points, certainly is the seed of outrage—why does she always paint me into a corner? Why does it slowly become impossible to speak for or through her, like a throat gone rasping dry? Is this finally when we must speak of my limitations?

On one side the body proper—skin eyes—tender warm   and on the other side the voice—abrupt reserved subject to fits of remoteness

Alas, even in Valmiki Sita must always carry the burden of being "good" and "pure." This is also the Sita who even in the midst of extreme sacrifices in the forest seems to like "nice things" and is not above fending off Ravana with a crude casteist slur. She never enjoys the freedoms known by the women of the forest. If she is furrow, she is also supporter of the plough. In her final moments powerless to change the epic's course, why bother to speak at all?

Then again, Sita *is* the seed of outrage, in her very person the violated one, the still daughter of the Earth in its conversations with us. And the loved, the longed-for, the reciprocal, the one who dreams of Simians bringing tokens as if it were she and none other who had composed the epic.

Wait. If Ravi Varma and Tulsi can have their fantasies of order, I'll have mine. Sita as the author writing herself in at every turn as a kind of magnetic absence, much like the sinkhole into which she goes, into which go all the lives we've lived and their scratchy self-congratulating mirrors, the rudraksha malas of ethical decisions we believe ourselves to have made. What if Sita removes herself so we are forced to look:

like a clay pot baking in embers
like a bud sheared from the stem
like the autumn heat parching
a ketaki leaf
like the reminiscence of a word
in the rumble of a cloud
like a peahen before the approaching storm
folded smoke
wasted disk of alabaster

.

To resemble the mother
  since I imagine her
regretting me eternally:
  the others are not the mother:
for them mourning
  for me depression . . .

"the way a crumb of magnet
  could force a great lump of iron . . ."

      The version of Sita
    he had so painfully made
    inside him—unlike the cold
        replacement idol fashioned
      from gold or kusha grass—
    begins to fade and "the heart . . . feels . . .
        as if burning
      on a fire of chaff"
                        "Their
      legs gripped by old age"
    the ashram far   bodies
    slow minds racing ahead

      and my breath
    a trembling evil
    does not stop no

  Poi come nel percuoter dei ciocchi arsi
  surgono innumerabili faville

"*as when burning logs are struck*
  rise innumerable sparks"

      And here again back in the forest Dandakaranya

in some of the same places where all those days we
      lived together and
                  long after
     we'd returned home
        talked so much about

    How does even the guy
    who shares my name
   moves in my body—
     Evil Ram let's call him
  completely alone now he's left
his lover to die—how does he
  just walk on by and not
   feel anything?
             Remember
the fresh waters of the Godavari
    The strolls we took on its shores

       —itchy lumpy-cheeked elephants rubbed up
     against heat-loosened heaps of their own branches'
  flowers falling in impromptu puja to the river and in their shade
    birds wobbling about with beaks peeling insects off the
    bark and cooing from sheer fatigue flocks of doves
           and wild cock against the heavy nesting
               trees on the bank—

               everywhere flowers
      raining from the keshara tree
       as if put there on that rock
        ledge just for me—

     that time you held a palm leaf
      to shield me from the sun

     those days we used to be kind to guests
     even if living on handfuls of grain

Ramayana equals
obstacle to study

The "wilderness in the middle distance"
"rose-apple trees dark with fruit"
"succulent shalaki leaves
                cool & sharp & tangy"
    "on the lower slopes our
        leaf-thatched huts"

        And the dusk rolled
        to one side a little

                    ◆

        ... well if it's too painful why not
        like Bhavabhuti   go see a show?

    They have a bunch of *Ramayana* paintings on
        at the National Museum though

        careful when you pay homage
        to the drawings of weapons:

        they'll hear your call and come alive

    Nice exhibit though. What's the period again‽

                LAKSHMANA:
        [clears his throat points to a painting]

        Friends here's where the rakshasas with
        their tricky magic glitter-deer
                did the dire deed

that continued to hurt
long after we'd won
the war to avenge it

Sita the forest of Janasthana
was zeroed by your absence
and my brother's killing frenzy

It made the watcher feel
like iron pulverized to a core
like tears drawn from stone

RAMA:

I like how the painter captures the psychology of all that

LAKSHMANA:
[next painting]

Here Rama and I without you on Mt. Prasravana where caves echoed with
the sound of the river that made a ring around them the white peak shot
from lush black forest thickets of trees & the mountain darkness thickened
more by the gathering clouds—

RAMA:

The white lotuses swaying
turn dark blue in the lens
of my tears

*

RAMA:

Where once a bracing current
now the river's sandy bed

the thick bush I knew has become sparse
and the arid areas are overgrown

Seeing it after so long doesn't
even seem like the same forest

Only by the mountains
do I know where I am

◆　◆　◆

RAMA:

"the peacock is surely remembering her"
　in treating the tree as her kin

and in a far canto somewhere
　we're still together my love

for something happens when
　you touch me:

I don't know if I'm
　happy or sad or

blissed out or asleep
　I can't quite tell if

　　　　I'm high
　　or drunk or sick

All my senses are in it
　and worthless

　　in the self-same
　　tide pool   it

stimulates and dulls
　my recognition

　and your ears only more
　lovely without the earrings...

　　　　And the hand I first held
　　　on our wedding day

a long-familiar hand by sight
when I was

allowed to touch it:
the faint veins under the skin

the flower of the palm its slender
fingers Graceful

as a lavali stalk a hand by which
to love all hands

SITA:

The day of our betrothal, we were peering over into adulthood's threshold.
Father was still alive and our stepmothers worried themselves sick over us.
Our bond was fresh. Those days won't be coming back. Heart brave body
shy. How we just lay there cheek to cheek talking about trivial stuff holding
each other into the hours until we'd outlasted the night

and I've put my head
where no other woman has
in the nest of Rama's arm
no greater pleasure
than to close my eyes there

RAMA:

I was the first one to find
—feeling carefully for it under
your fuzzy belly skin—
the double knot
in your womb I told you
only a few
days later

And remember that time when from long walking your feet were tired
and puffy and sore and I lay them on my lap massaging them until lost in
the work of my own fingers? When I looked again you were asleep. Your
neck sweat-beaded, from effort or anxiety who knows—tender, glistening
wet

      as a row of moonstones in
     the moonlight's eager kiss

                        *

      Coming across your personal effects
       knowing how fond you were

        of some of these things
           this or that an object

         of endless conversation Looking at it
         when all that's left of you is
          your name

         To discover one day on the
         skin of the relationship
          a tiny stain
             (Barthes)

         The resistance of the wood
         depends on where we drive
           the nail
            (ditto)

    . . . in which the loved person shows up
       with the lower part of his
         face erased
        and I whose soliloquy
       makes me a monster one
         huge tongue
           ( )

like an old tree
the fire eats
from the inside first—

SITA:

That time that time
in the forest so far away now
in the living morning you still sleeping
and I back from my river bath
a single towel tied around me
Hair still wet
& all I could think
was the pull of you

RAMA:

To be woken
by the smell of your hair
the freshness of
wet skin to my face
that light summer morn
joy floating
in and out of sleep
drowsing then rousing again

...and into that came a single jet black crow
Cocked his neb   He wanted
you too my sweet
I'd gone back to sleep
dreaming of your nipples
when your screams
as if far from
the rim of a village well
in its oval of sky
called me back

You'd shooed the crow away
but he'd swooped in for a snip
   drawing blood
 and I opened my eyes to that
   rivulet trickling
past the blue veins around
   your breast Just
   that Just that—
And your towel
   slipped I had to take
in the gorgeousness
 of your body first—
that body once so effortlessly mine—
   and I had to laugh
though gradually that
   little blood-trickle
would become all
   that stayed

SITA:

You were angry You
 drew a sharp stiff blade
of grass and pierced
that crow—a storyteller
 himself—in one eye
blinding it forever

RAMA:

The crows they've followed
us my love. Faces expressionless their
 bills like accusations eyes
fixated intent upon you
 or some part of you

BOTH:

When I fell for you we were strangers, only strangers fall in love. Then we were in the forest, far from the tentacles of relatives. We became like enemies, like enemies intimate. In a second's distraction you were gone and I yearned so long and hard I could no longer tell if the idol I'd fashioned in me was you. Then we were back, hard to say who the returning one. Already old joints creaking, limbs ready to reentangle, heat-seeking. We no longer had to tell the thing: it told us, or rather it pieced us together, like an album we'd lost or left. In the dark one reached for a simple glass of water.

Each day a knot on the mnemonic rope toward the final alvida. What did it feel like then? Something like the next train approaching in a tunnel—
>   first the light
>   then the sound
>   then the strenuous forgetting

◆ ◆ ◆

We do, without exception, what we feel we have to. Who escapes criticism's claws? No matter how faithful the victim how guileless the words— always the nasties arriving, the ill-speakers. When she was taken, all he wanted was her.

Now he wakes. It's as if only a single second has passed. She lies next to him in a soft huddle. A breath is once is there. Checks his phone, goes to the window. His legacy: unfinished terrain.

> "The sun: god
> who burns beyond the dust."

There is only one rasa but like water it is changeable and has many moods.

And back with his "colleagues"—his ministers and assorted advisors. The morning of the news that seemed so trivial: a few people were making jokes about the king and queen.

We who are not the king are not destined to understand his decisions. But the fact remains he smoked it out of his informants when it was not readily given; it was he who had wanted such an account of what "the people" felt. It was he who had pressed the point, he who picked the scab. And it started with one advisor, Bhadra, and the sweet words he spoke with a concentrated look, with palms clasped.

BHADRA:

> *Well this is how the citizens talk for good or ill sir*
> *at the main intersections or*
> *in the town squares in the crosshatching*
> *markets or gated enclaves*
> *and shabby resorts alike and along*
> *our wide highway trickling*
> *into hill and forest where*
> *despite the laws they like to make up for themselves your name definitely*
> *still holds sir it rings and rings out And trust me they're all saying*

The Great Rama did what no one else could:
brought peace and unity
forded the ocean with a bridge
killed the ruthless Ravana
decimated his army and his machines
subdued both the rakshasas and the Simians
established our tribute colonies there and

And what? Rama listening half-bored leans in, studies the silence even harder.

BHADRA:

A few rascals are found to be saying

"How generous of our king to take Sita back
after Ravana had carried her off winding
a free arm around hip and ass—"

(how they talk   sir)

"I guess Rama was just a little too grateful
I guess we'll all have to forgive our wives now!"

[you could almost hear someone from
   the next gully over—]

Such is the rough speech sir
from a few worthless fellows
in the taverns of our towns

As your minister I can only be
faithful in my reports

Bhadra smiles   shrugs withdraws

Rama's face completely
   without expression

*

How from poison's long seep comes
the sudden sharp spike that gets you or
how a hard-risen scar
on the quick of the heart
bursts so quick when

Rama whose teacher was the sun
who'd once killed the son of the sun

And walking back through
the far wilds of his conquest
years and years later   searching now
not for her but
for another who'd
also died by his unshakeable
arm   who in
going   had infused
into the very smoke
we breathed into
the material of the worlds
we lived in:
Shambuka
whose only fault had been
to aver his caste
when asked of him by Rama

There are no
places to escape to
my love we've taken
every one Deep
in an inhuman grove
the boughs founded
on the stock roots
a grounding
web the thicker
branches gams and

the long-fingering
  vines Grove
  after grove like
this he expects to
  somehow find
  at least evidence
of those dead by his sword
  his arrows He expects their
  plasms in hidden
   places Unsteady
   feet stumbled
  on rocks gashing
himself Like a madman
  staring at drops
of his own blood in awe

                    *

            But where
are they the departed from whom
     we seek forgiveness?

        Ah for
they have vanished led
  away deaf and blind
  by Yama's loyal servants

For they are restored and look upon the light of another sun
  for they bathe among the male and female waters
 where meet the westward waters and the eastward waters
    the waters of whirlpools and embryonic waters
 the caught rainwater or the sapwater or water that on windless days
            might pool
        and stand with sunglazed skin
for they wade where the sea and freshwater meet And he somewhere else
    stumbles on
Walks in black mist where twigs are shadows and knit
  in low light-green clouds

Someone takes his hand.

Is it—shuffling impatiently ahead—*Sleep*? The darling child of Yama and Varunani?

Must be. Could be. Further and further into the knotting of the trees beyond recognition

The grove of the severed head
Limbs of wood broken as if by a secret storm

And the fragrance of the crushed leaf   No not a trace of the dead
the Fathers and the Mothers—
it was he who had been killed   a group of men in spotless white with holes
for eyes   they'd chopped at him like patient butchers and
he felt nothing of it   looking down at the mortal part
and the men arrayed around the spectacle   The men are mist
arms and legs with multiplied
fingers and toes and his torso split in a V down the central axis
they all spin tenderly around
Or   do those charred limbs
haunches circling in the air
belong to the body of the black horse? In the centre
slowly visible
a head   hard to tell if this one is his own but it is unmistakably
a king's with crown
and golden earrings

In the next frame he wakes on the bed of stationary palanquin
If it's daytime he has no desire to know but

a new hand parts the curtain   an adolescent's   fresh fuzz
etched on upper lip   Ah vista

of the open road the grand trees
that give the traveler shade

That morning when at last it was truly the last thing he
was thinking about   he felt someone gently touch

him from behind   Turned around and there
Simple in beard close cropped hair   ragged mendicant's cloth

Shambuka! I've searched for you
so long and found no trace of you but for the dried tiger skin
you'd used as a seat I was certain finally that you'd reached
heaven I took comfort in that

The air's too thin to breathe there Rama I returned
to be among the plants and trees
and settlements I loved

Slim sharp-toned despite
his years of tapas As he'd been
when you first came to see him And now
because he was no longer sitting cross-legged
one noticed his feet were immaculate
and did not touch the ground

And Rama full of innocent questions again

breeze a booby trap   ringed in violet haze

Always straying from guilt into a garbage of language

SHAMBUKA:

You'd like the past to be done again. It is so, Rama, a thousand thousand times
over in all the worlds that continue beside us. Not alas in the one in which we
converse. Here it is given to us that the task of undoing our actions will be the
hardest of all. They'll kill and kill in the centuries to come, Rama, they'll kill
as you did, they'll cite you as example. They'll chop the hands, fingers, arms,
and feet. They'll gash the bellies, cut into wombs, mar the face anyway they can
They'll throw acid, burn villages.

Broke into sobs did Rama
He clutched and clutched
the shudra monk's feet

And will they know
that we met like this? They will not   The living
are foolish   They'll listen
as if in half-sleep
to the song of the koel

Why does one despair in crowded places? Tell me. The whizz of glances so complete. You make eyes with the whole lot. But touch is taboo—why Rama? Because any connection of skin and you are another's forever. For faithless they marry the wetness of my tears

Then the monk turns away, not out of refusal but as if to follow the wing of a thought.

Not arrival, but return. Not action but the long dwindling cosine of repercussion—the fabric continually rent, long sharp rips by which it reveals more of itself.

Time, the long self-sex of the atman. The only thing you've seen of it with your own mortal eyes is the salt of its departure.

I, the knitting weave of qualities, gunas. *I*, the song the gunas sing. *I*, the sharpness of a stone. The shape, intact, of the cut orange, juice bleeding but white fruit-spine resistant. *I*, the instants camouflaging their birth.

For *I*, the vehicle by which the question is asked and the answer provided.

I, the spooned leaf that tips the oil of offering.

The figure is prostrate in a scene of its making. Remorse and sorrow arise there, like twins acquainted since the womb. Remorse—*anutāpa*—the heat that turns inward turns outward and emanates in tapas.

For the king relaxing in his boudoir shares in it
for the palsied pi-dog shares in it
for the blind monk in his innermost cave shares in it
for the Jain in the abhorrence of meat shares in it
for the celibate in the fear of skin shares in it
for the Brahmin with the ritual sword shares in it
　　for the calf his offering shares in it

Would you take away, in the eons of its accumulation, the ground on which we walk? Would you release the lava's frozen arabesque? You must. You could.

Under a sky, white but warm, two figures: one spectral and one still half-alive the first leading the second by the hand. In this version, it is only the two of them who enter the deepening water.

(The compulsive hand copies the tale again and again, hoping this time to get it right.)

The city we dream of is not the one
  surrendered to　The return of sullen ethics
  like a check long cashed　terse
  soliloquies　drum of moth trapped
 in the corner behind　When they gave me

   it I resisted a long time even
 to touch the leatherskin　And the taste just short
   or was it on the tooth's bruise
 already slipping from us　The hold's
membrane crossed　weight of humiliations

carried and unavenged　Dreams
  buzz saw in the ear
a stone around which
the pulp of me hung
Each wind　so hard to take
  Air of throbbing machines

No passage then unattended　Frictive
  hurt　the norm　Lion ever at throats
Think of the cases they file　fabricated
at ready-evidence factories　Truth only
  matters for the perversion

of it　What kind of life to lead　Which
  side of the fence　　to fund from
What soil to drink of　　Semaphore
 lingo by sight　　Now that end of work is near
  clear a ground　plant the next

  to get to know more of us　to see again
beggaring beetle-shoes　in a salt of pretending
Meet up there　or here white white white
slate slate slate　all is white or all is slate all is
     white slate white slate

"[and we are] gradually led into a twilight territory where
Time seems to merge or emerge into Eternity"

Dearest   I'm taking steps
into that unbinding dark

No sea except
   what swims in it
No river but for
   the beings rolling continuously
inside   and here or there a head
or a tail breaks the surface
…and "dead spots   where the sound
   fails to circulate"

ACKNOWLEDGMENTS

To the many whose friendship, comments, suggestions, encouragement, assistance, and—in a few cases—extensive, closely engaged, and illuminating critiques of drafts changed this work: Janani Ambikapathy, Jeebesh Bagchi, Aditya Bahl, Kurt Behrendt, Eric Bergqvist, Amy Best, Maaz Bin Bilal, Stephanie Burt, James Byrne, Vahni Capildeo, Rohan Chhetri, Peter Cole, Bahauddin Dagar, Veena Das, Priya Doraswamy, T. Marie Dudman, Iain Galbraith, Forrest Gander, Shumona Goel, David Herd, Madhu Kapparath, Prashant Keshavmurthy, Siddhartha Lokanandi, Robyn Marsack, Leeya Mehta, Anna Deeny Morales, Christopher Nealon, Magnus William Olsson, Rowan Ricardo Phillips, William Pierce, Sheldon Pollock, Mani Rao, Souradeep Roy, Chandramohan S., Arun Sagar, Rahul Santhanam, Sabitha Satchi, Shveta Sarda, Arshia Sattar, Michael Scharf, Irwin Allan Sealy, Priya Sen, Vijay Seshadri, Don Share, Deb Shutika, Richard Sieburth, Bhrigupati Singh, Sushil Sivaram, Rahul Soni, Heather Streckfus-Green, Peter Streckfus-Green, Anand Thakore, A.J, Thomas, Keith Tuma, Snehal Vadher, Ananya Vajpeyi, Maarten Visser, Rosanna Warren, Laura Weinstein, Caroline Widmer, Jeffrey Yang, and Raúl Zurita.

To Parvez Imroz, Khurram Parvez, P. Govindan Kutty and Ron Padgett, for permissions to quote from their work.

To the near family: Ambika, Harini, Alli, Gautam, Hema Chitthi, Chari Chitthya, Varun, Veena, and Suren. To Rashmi, first reader. To the memory of K. Seshadri. To the memory of R. I. Narayanan. To my mother, Padma Narayanan, who first taught me both the idea of literature and the sound of Sanskrit shlokas.

To the library of the Sahitya Akademi in New Delhi, where this project was first begun in earnest. To the Radcliffe Institute for Advanced

Studies at Harvard University and the Cullman Center for Scholars and Writers at the New York Public Library for fellowships that were essential for this work to form and come into being. A special thanks to the School for Advanced Research, Santa Fe, New Mexico, for their hospitality and loan of an office, where the last part of this book was written. To George Mason University, for research and institutional support.

At the Radcliffe Institute: Anne Monius (in memoriam) for a key insight, Judith Vichniac (in memoriam) for all her kindnesses. Tyler Neill and Ben Williams, both doctoral students in Sanskrit at the time, were my research assistants, spending invaluable hours with me across the full academic year, taking me into the Sanskrit in a process that would eventually transform my work. I'm grateful to Tyler for teaching me a tune by which to recite Valmiki's meter; the circular "Swayamprabha" diagram in the poem "Un Trou" quotes from one of Tyler's explanatory e-mails to me.

At the Cullman Center: Paul Delaverdac, Lauren Goldenberg, Julia Pagnamenta, and Jean Strouse, in particular, for their kindnesses.

At the School for Advanced Research: Michael F. Brown and Maria Spray, for their kindnesses.

New York Review Books, for Herculean efforts.

Thanks to the publications in which the following poems first appeared, sometimes in an earlier draft:

"Shiva," "Ahalya," and "Ahalya" [2]: *Granta.com* (July 18, 2020)
"Ravana": *Paris Review* no. 229 (Summer 2019)
"The Mountain": *Ambit* 228 (2017)
"Ayodhya," "Manthaara, the Hunchback," "Kaikeyi," "Lakshmana," and "Ram's Arm": *Indian Literature* 297 (January–February 2017)
"Ravana's Rooms": *The Wolf* (2016)
"They Saw No Longer the Battlefield": *Indian Cultural Forum* (November 2016)
"Dasaratha" [1]: *Granta.com* (2016)
"Un Trou": *Agni* 81 (2015, excerpt) and *Aroop* (2020, complete)
"Rama," "Rama's Servants," "Chitrakuta," and "The Jeweled Deer" [3]: *Oxford Poets 2013* (Manchester: Carcanet Press, 2013)
"The Final Asana": *The HarperCollins Book of English Poetry* (2012)

Notes and Sources

TEXTS AND TRANSLATIONS OF VALMIKI

There are several different Valmiki texts—the Baroda critical edition, the vulgate, the various recensions—that all count different numbers of verses because of, presumably, alterations, variations, and interpolations through the ages. Curious readers can compare my versions with two more traditional, close translations:

The Ramayana of Valmiki: An Epic of Ancient India, seven volumes, translated and annotated by Sheldon Pollock, Robert and Sally Goldman, Rosalind Lefeber, and Barend Van Nooten (Princeton, NJ: Princeton University Press, 1984–2016). A clear, straightforward translation based on the Baroda critical edition with wonderful, voluminous notes, which include summaries of the classic line-by-line commentaries and which I have relied heavily on. Referred to as *Critical Edition*, or *CE*, in the notes below.

Valmiki Ramayana, translated, transcribed, and annotated by Desiraju Hanumanta Rao, K. M. K Murthy, et al., available at valmikiramayan.net. The text here may be based on either the standard vulgate or the southern recension; in any case, it is a rigorous and thorough perspective on Valmiki from within the tradition. Referred to as *Online Edition*, or *OE*, in the notes below.

Three other editions have served as crucial touchstones for this project:

Valmiki's Ramayana, translated by Arshia Sattar (Lanham, MD: Rowman & Littlefield Publishers, 2018, and HarperCollins India, 2019). For me, this abridged translation is the most lucid and accurate English introduction to Valmiki currently available.

Srimad Valmiki Ramayana, three volumes, translated by N. Raghunathan (Madras: Vighneswara Publishing House, 1981–1982). Raghunathan gives a line-by-line translation that is tremendously vigorous from both a scholarly and a literary perspective.

The Gita Press edition translated and supervised by Chimanlal Goswami (Gorakhpur: Gita Press, 1969/2011), with prose translations below the original Sanskrit text.

The seven books of Valmiki's *Ramayana* are:

1. *Balakanda* (Book of Childhood)
2. *Ayodhyakanda* (Book of Ayodhya)
3. *Aranyakanda* (Book of the Forest)
4. *Kishkindakanda* (Book of Kishkinda, the Simian Kingdom)
5. *Sundarakanda* (Book of Beauty)
6. *Yuddhakanda* (Book of War)
7. *Uttarakanda* (Book of What Comes After)

The word "rakshasa" (feminine form: rakshasi) is generally not translated in the poems of *After*. Many modern writers give it as "demon," but I want to argue that its use in Valmiki is more complex and multilayered. Rakshasas have other identities and become rakshasas at specific moments. In my mind, the closest translation of the word would simply be "other."

"Sarga" is synonymous with "canto" or "chapter"; "kanda" with "book."

BOOK ONE: CITY AND FOREST

The first book of *After* covers Valmiki's first three kandas, each section roughly corresponding to the respective kanda.

Balakanda (Book of Childhood) begins with an appearance by the epic's author himself. Valmiki discovers/invents the shloka meter when an inadvertent curse escapes his lips; the god Brahma informs him that he will use this meter to tell the whole of the *Ramayana*. Then, as the story proper begins, the screen splits. Above, the gods are searching for a way to check Ravana, an ambitious and increasingly powerful mortal who has been challenging their authority; below, King Dasaratha yearns for an heir. Rishyashringa—an ascetic with little horns who has grown up entirely in the forest and has never known a woman— must now be enticed back to the city, into marriage and a life as a priest to the kingdom. He performs the Ashwamedha, the crucial horse sacrifice, with King Dasaratha's hopes of resetting the royal state and producing an heir. As part of the ritual, Dasaratha's senior-most wife, Kausalya (later the mother of Rama), has to lie for a night with the sacrificed horse. By an inevitable chain of consequences, four brothers are born from three wives. A few years later, the warrior priest Vishwamitra comes to train and recruit two of them, Rama (the crown prince) and Lakshmana. He takes the boys into the forest, where a rakshasi woman, Tataka, must be destroyed. This is Rama's first kill, his first true test, and afterward Vishwamitra gives him his divine weapons. Later, walking the landscape, Vishwamitra tells the two brothers troubled tales of the forest's genesis. They visit an ashram, where an unfaithful wife, Ahalya, has been trapped in a limbo; Rama's arrival releases and redeems her. Eventually they reach the kingdom of Videha, where Rama wins Sita's hand in marriage by breaking Shiva's bow.

Ayodhyakanda (Book of Ayodhya) begins a few years later with impossible praise of the city of Ayodhya, then talk of King Dasaratha's retirement and Rama's impending coronation. Given a king's many wives and many princely siblings, deadly palace intrigue is never far away: Manthaara, the "scheming hunchback maid," convinces her mistress and Dasaratha's youngest wife, Kaikeyi, that her son Bharata must be made king; Kaikeyi then sings Manthaara's erotic praises. Kaikeyi uses her wiles and an old debt between herself and Dasaratha to force Rama into exile for fourteen years. Bound by duty to his father, Rama accepts the decision despite long arguments from Lakshmana and others to not do so. Much of *Ayodhyakanda*, in fact, is dedicated to various people, even desperate crowds, who try to convince Rama not to go into exile, with seemingly little effect. Notable among those is Jabali, an atheist and empiricist resident in Dasaratha's court. Eventually, Rama, Sita, and Lakshmana cross into the forest and exile; Dasaratha, in a Lear-like moment, goes to pieces and dies; messengers are sent to fetch Bharata, who has been at his uncle's palace and knows nothing of his mother's actions.

By the beginning of *Aranyakanda* (Book of the Forest) Rama, Sita, and Lakshmana have journeyed a little way into the forest, built a place for themselves, and made peace with the spirits. However, the landscape is rife with rakshasas, who are disturbing the Brahmins' sacrificial fires. Rama is inevitably drawn into the role of protector, the one who must mete out justice and ruthlessly kill the offenders, whether actual or potential. Surpanakha is one such rakshasi, a widow and a temptress with form-changing powers. Her infatuation with Rama ends badly, with Lakshmana's cruel amputation of her nose. She is Ravana's younger sister and eventually compels the Lankan king's intervention. Indeed, Ravana has his eye on Sita himself, so he convinces his uncle Maricha to transform into a magical deer that draws and mesmerizes Rama into the hunt. After he has been gone for a while, Sita in turn forces Lakshmana to go looking for him; Ravana appears as a humble but decorous Brahmin wandering the forest, stopping at Sita's hut for water. Soon Ravana is completely besotted. He discards his disguise but still fails to win Sita over. He then abducts her and carries her away in his flying chariot that is pulled by ghoulish asses. They are intercepted by Jatayu, prince of the vultures, who battles bravely at the cost of his own life. While this is happening, Rama and Lakshmana meet and realize that Sita is gone; Rama, both god and human king, flies into a state of pure madness and rage, total power and total uncomprehending vulnerability.

7　*To Valmiki*: After a prayer to be recited before a ritual reading of the Rama-yana.

11　*Valmiki Discovers the Shloka Meter*: Valmiki's second canto contains "Maa Nishada," perhaps the best-known verse in the entire epic. Translated here, this is the inadvertent curse that marks the ambiguous invention of the shloka meter.

　　The canto also includes the famous formulation of meter as the link between shoka (pain, sorrow) and shloka (verse), the two simultaneously joined and separated by a single lateral consonant. An alternate translation of this particular verse appears in an epigraph to Book One.

　　According to many thinkers, including Abhinavagupta, the separation of the lovemaking birds at the beginning is meant to be an echo of Rama and Sita's final separation at the end of the epic.

14　*Ganga*: After *Balakanda*, sarga 42 in *CE*. Ganga is the river Ganges; the narrative refers to her first descent to earth from the heavens, when she had to be poured through Shiva's dreadlocks.

16　*Shiva*: After *Balakanda*, sarga 35 in *CE* and 36 in *OE*.

18　*Song for the Horse Sacrifice*: In the Ashwamedha ceremony, a horse, treated in a way as the king's envoy, is made to wander for a year, meeting challeng-ers and thus marking out and reconsecrating the territory of the kingdom. Later, as part of a ceremony where at least three hundred other animals in different categories are also sacrificed, the horse is strangled to death. The king's wife then lies with the horse for a night.

　　In Valmiki, the Ashwamedha at the start of the book is performed with Dasaratha's hopes of producing an heir for the kingdom; at the close of the epic, we see a second Ashwamedha that ends up uniting Rama with his es-tranged sons.

　　In the fourteenth canto of his first book (sarga 13 in *CE*), Valmiki de-scribes the ceremony and sacrifice in detail; but what he does *not* tell us are the words that might have been said by the queen (in this case Kausalya, Rama's mother), or by an officiating priest on her behalf, during the night with the dying horse.

19　*Rishyashringa*: Loosely after *Balakanda*, sargas 9 and 10 in *CE* and *OE*.

23　*Rama's Servants*: After *Balakanda*, sarga 27 in *CE* and *OE*.

25　*Tataka, Tataka*, and *Tataka, the Yakshi*: After *Balakanda*, sargas 23–24 in
to　*CE* and 24–25 in *OE*. Viswamitra, the warrior priest, takes the young Rama
28　and Lakshmana into the forest with him for a period of instruction and training. As part of this, Viswamitra guides Rama in his first kill, of Tataka; later, Viswamitra gives Rama the divine weapons mentioned in the poem "Rama's Servants." Rama's targets, broadly, are the rakshasas who have

been, among other things, disrupting the ritual fires that the Brahmins tend in the forest.

Tataka is a rakshasi. However, with a characteristically contradicting sense of multiplicity, Valmiki also supplies her with another identity, another story, that of a yakshi, a benign and beautiful earth spirit. In telling of how Tataka went from being a yakshi to a rakshasi, Vishwamitra notes her antagonism toward the Brahmins and that her husband was killed, but does not elaborate the story further.

There is evidence to suggest we should *not* take Vishwamitra's injunction at face value, that the problem of women in war remained unresolved in the classical texts. Accounts of Vishwamitra elsewhere and in Valmiki too—in the stories of his rivalry with other sages, for instance—subtly show him to be an ambiguous figure. Many classical Indian texts explicitly forbid the killing of women in war; Rama himself is at first hesitant, typically circumventing the rule against femicide by disfiguring Tataka instead. Much later, in *Yuddhakanda*, Vishwamitra's words seem to be echoed in the words of an *enemy* of Rama and are used by that character to support the killing of Sita, the great heroine of the epic. Compare with the notes to the poem "Not Sita, but a Phantom" in Book Three.

My specific picture in "Tataka, the Yakshi" doesn't quite appear in Valmiki and instead owes something to the scene of her with a toddler among the *Ramayana* murals of the Mattancherry Palace in Kochi.

29 *Ahalya*: After *Balakanda*, sargas 47–48 in *CE* and 48–50 in *OE*. Ahalya is seduced by Indra, who is often presented as "king of the gods" but in practice is more of a trickster figure in the epics. When discovered, both Indra and Ahalya are cursed by her ascetic husband, Gautama. Much later, she is redeemed when Rama's feet touch the place where she has been made immobile and/or invisible.

"invisibleliving on airsleeping in the ashes": Closely paraphrased from the translation of Valmiki by Sattar. The second Ahalya poem owes something to the imagery in Kamban's medieval *Ramayana* in Tamil.

33 *Ayodhya*: After *Balakanda*, sarga 6 in *CE* and *OE*.

35 *For the Crowning of Rama*: After *Ayodhyakanda*, sarga 3 in *OE*.

36 *Manthaara, the Hunchback*: After *Ayodhyakanda*, sarga 9 in *CE* and *OE*.

39 *Lakshmana*: After *Ayodhyakanda*, sargas 18–20 in *CE* and 21–23 in *OE*.

41 *Dasaratha*: After *Ayodhyakanda*, sargas 56–58 and 63 in *CE* and 62–64 and 69 in *OE*. I have folded together the account of Dasaratha's death and funeral with Bharata's nightmare, which seems to reflect a mirror image of the same event.

43 *the gold censer that catches fire*: The concluding lines of my poem draw
    from Masih of Panipati's seventeenth-century *Ram Wa Sita*, which is con-
    sidered the greatest of many *Ramayanas* that exist in Persian and, accord-
    ing to Prashant Keshavmurthy, merges Sanskrit and Persian poetics. The
    entirety of this work has never been translated into English; here I borrow
    and rework a few lines of Keshavmurthy's translation.

45 *Bharata's Arrival* and *Bharata*: After *Ayodhyakanda*, sargas 64–65 in *CE*
to and 70–71 in *OE*. Bharata is Rama's younger half brother, the son of Kaikeyi,
46 Dasaratha's youngest wife who is responsible for Rama's exile. He has been
    living with his uncle in a distant town, so knows nothing of the events.

48 *Ayodhyakanda, Canto CXIV*: Quoted directly from *Srimad Valmiki Ra-
    mayana, Volume 1: Balakanda and Ayodhyakanda*, translated by N. Raghu-
    nathan (Madras/Bangalore: Vigneswara Publishing House, 1981), 423–25.

49 *Jabali*: Jabali is a respected adviser in Dasaratha's court, an atheist and ma-
    terialist. We hear his arguments in *Ayodhyakanda*, sarga 100 in *CE* and 108
    in *OE*. See the philosopher Ramkrishna Bhattacharya's essay cited here. A
    translator homage is buried here as well, as Bhattacharya quotes exten-
    sively from Pollock's pellucid translation of the sarga.

57 *Chitrakuta*: After *Ayodhyakanda*, sargas 48–50 in *CE* and 55–56 in *OE*.

59 *The Jeweled Deer*: There are three different poems under this title. All are
    after *Aaranyakanda*, sargas 40–42 in *CE* and 42–44 in *OE*.

62 *Surpanakha*: Surpanakha is the forest temptress whose nose is cut off by
    Lakshmana as cruel punishment for her jealous infatuation for Rama. In
    the last book of Valmiki, we also learn of how Ravana, her elder brother,
    kills her husband.
        The temple to Lakshmana that is mentioned is in Nasik, a city in Maha-
    rashtra suffused with references and apparent locations from Tulsidas's sev-
    enteenth-century version of the *Ramayana* in Awadhi, a dialect related to
    Hindi. According to legend, Nasik got its name because it was the place
    where Lakshmana cut off Surpanakha's nose.

64 *Aaranyani*: The speaker of this poem is the *Ramayana* character Surpana-
    kha—"of the long nails"—but I have renamed her Aaranyani by linking her
    to the forest spirit from the ancient Vedas. The poem draws freely from
    Aaranyakanda and also contains elements from the traditions of erotic po-
    etry written by women and men in later Sanskrit poetry.
        The last stanza retranslates a famous line from the ninth-century poet
    Vijjika, who is taking issue with the writer and literary critic Dandin's char-
    acterization of Saraswati, the goddess of poetry, as "fair-skinned." By con-
    trast, Vijjika presents *herself*—dark as a blue lotus bud—as the true
    Saraswati.

65 *Sita's Arguments*: After *Aranyakanda*, sarga 8 in *CE* and 9 in *OE*.

73 *Nasik*: See note to "Surpanakha" above.

74 *Ravana, Ravana, What Ravana Said, What Sita Said*: After *Aranya-*
to *kanda*, sargas 44–46 in *CE* and 46–48 in *OE*. See note to "Surpanakha"
76 above.

80 *Rama to the Mountain, Its Reply*: After *Aranyakanda*, sarga 64 in *OE*.

   kaccit kṣiti bhṛtām nātha: This line can actually be parsed in two different ways: first, as Rama's question to the mountain, and second, as the mountain's reply to Rama. Rama is extremely frustrated by this answer, in which the question cannot be distinguished from its echo, the landscape responding with the only utterance it's capable of. When I first read this it seemed like the earliest proto-example of *slesha*, a more poetic cousin of double entendre that is taken to extreme levels in later Sanskrit poetry. Pollock, however, tells us in his notes (*Kishkindakanda*, 338) that it is in fact a line from the play *Vikramorvaśīya* by the fourth/fifth-century "new wave" Sanskrit poet Kalidasa that has been retrofitted, as it were, into Valmiki.

82 *Theological Reading*: After *Aranyakanda*, sarga 60 in *OE*. I quote directly here from the incredibly valuable word-for-word translation (with occasional commentary) by Rao, Murthy, et al.

   "Did Rama really weep?" is one of the traditional questions engaging with the scene where, having lost Sita, Rama appears to lose his mind, at once infinitely powerful ("I'll destroy the universe") and infinitely vulnerable ("I'll die"). Yes, Rama did in fact weep, this theological account goes, despite his being at once Vishnu's incarnation. Rama's tears are precisely what prove him to be both god and man, flawed. This insistence on Rama's humanity may even have been instrumental in his being more of a personal god to figures like Kabir, the boundary-crossing fifteenth-century North Indian mystic poet, or Thyagaraja, the influential nineteenth-century Telugu composer and lyricist.

83 *Winter*: After *Aaranyakanda*, sarga 15 in *CE* and 16 in *OE*. This famous but oddly transferred simile is quoted and discussed in detail in Anandavardhana's great work of literary criticism and philosophy, *Dhvanyaloka*, with a commentary by Abhinavagupta.

85 *Jatayu the Vulture*: After *Aranyakanda*, sarga 64 in *CE* and 68 in *OE*. Jatayu is the vulture (some translators would prefer to see him as an eagle, but that's another matter) who intervenes in Ravana's aerial abduction of Sita, and pays for it with his life. As it turns out, Jatayu is an old friend of Rama's father, Dasaratha.

BOOK TWO: DREAMS AND NIGHTMARES

The second volume covers the fourth and fifth kandas of Valmiki.

Kishkindakanda (Book of Kishkinda, the Simian Kingdom) is set in a monkey kingdom in the forest. Rama and Lakshmana have traveled there to make an alliance with the exiled Simian king-in-waiting Sugriva, who with his army will help in the defeat of Ravana, but first, Sugriva and Vali have an uncomfortable history to be resolved between them.

Vali, the elder brother, is by rights the king of Kishkinda; yet once while Vali had chased a monster down a cave and fought with it for long years, Sugriva had apparently abandoned Vali for dead, closed the mouth of the cave, and come back to usurp the kingdom. When the more powerful Vali did return despite the odds, he was furious at Sugriva. Vali took his kingdom back; Sugriva fled to the single mountain where Vali was forbidden and from there plotted his revenge. Rama, who has also lost a wife, arrives rather conveniently into all of this; Hanuman, Sugriva's general, is sent as an envoy. Sugriva quickly convinces Rama into a mutually beneficial contract and even tests the hero's power to boot; soon Sugriva is luring Vali away from his palace while Rama hides in the bushes with bow and arrows. The brothers' first fight has to be abandoned by Sugriva because Rama cannot tell them apart; in the second fight Sugriva wears a garland of champak flowers, and Rama shoots Vali from behind.

On his deathbed, with his son Angada and his weeping wife, Tara, by his side, Vali offers a long critique of Rama's actions and, regardless of the neatness of Rama's reply in the next canto, this passage has troubled and obsessed commentators for millennia. How could the virtuous Rama have ignored the rules of combat and killed the noble Vali by stealth? Moreover, without ever quite saying so outright, Valmiki seems to offer several clues as to the strong-necked ally Sugriva's unreliable character: He is a cowardly, self-obsessed, power-hungry showboat; later, sometimes he is depicted as turning cruel tyrant to make up for his insecurities. Rama also has something practical to gain from the alliance: an army that will fight the war with Ravana.

After Vali's death, Sugriva conscripts his Simian soldiers from villages far and wide, and sends them out in search parties to find Sita, whose whereabouts are still not known. The soldiers have a month to find Rama's abducted wife or, under Sugriva's harsh commandment, they will be executed. Surviving a series of harrowing events, one search party accidentally meets the vulture Sampati, king of the vultures and elder brother of Jatayu, who has also been a witness to Sita and Ravana flying through the air, and knows Sita's location. Sita is being kept by Ravana in Lanka, his island across the sea; Hanuman, the strongest and most powerful of the Simians, leaps across the waters on a reconnaissance mission. *Sundarakanda* (Book of Beauty) is set in Lanka. At the beginning of the kanda, Hanuman has shrunk himself to the size of a cat and snuck into the city. He can't help but be struck by the opulence and virtue of Lanka and its inhabitants going about their daily lives, even if it is a rakshasa city. Inevitably, he strays into Ravana's palace, and thence into Ravana's bedrooms, where a massive orgy has just taken place among Ravana and his countless lovers. Hanuman is the only Valmiki character, to my knowledge, who is given a true internal monologue; he finds out what it is to be a voyeur and explores the question of complicity. Later, he finds Sita desolate even though she is being kept in a beautiful grove of asoka trees, surrounded by rakshasa attendants who are also her guards. Hanuman watches from the trees and frets about whether Sita will be startled by his perfect Sanskrit; eventually they meet and exchange news, tokens, and hope. On his way back to carry the news of Sita to Rama, Lakshmana, and the Simians of the opposite shore, Hanuman decides to leave a few bruises on the city of Lanka. He is captured. While maintaining the injunction against killing messengers, Ravana opts to merely set the Simian's tail on fire. By a prayer of Sita, Hanuman cannot feel the fire; he takes the opportunity to set the entire city of Lanka ablaze before dousing his tail in the water and leaping back to the old shore.

93 *To Crimson*: A microlevel study of an insect, a colour, a dye, and a word—*krmi*—of the quarter line in *Kishkindakanda* where it appears, and of the other worlds across the ancient world it links to through the commercial routes.

95 *To Amar Chitra Katha*: The comic-book series where so many of us gained an interesting but problematic education in Indian storytelling and thought. The particular Amar Chitra Katha title directly quoted from and referenced here is *Vali* (Bombay: India Book House, 1976).

99 *The Arrow*: The first poem under this title is a fairly close version of Vali's
to   death drawn directly from *Kishkindkanda*, sargas 16–23 in *CE* and 17–24 in
110 *OE*. The second poem called "The Arrow" is an exploration that ranges more freely across *Kishkindakanda* and the events leading to Vali's death, frequently lingering in footnotes, commentaries, insinuations, and scents. Principal sources for this poem include the footnotes of *CE*.

112 *Sample Direction: East*: After *Kishkindakanda*, sarga 39 in *CE* and 40 in *OE*. This is the first of four chapters dedicated to a dream geography of the directions. Sugriva is about to send his troops out in search of Sita.

117 *Un Trou*: After *Kishkindakanda*, sargas 49–54 in *CE* and 50–55 in *OE*. With a few inputs from Jean Améry in his *On Suicide: A Discourse on Voluntary Death*, translated by John D. Barlow (Bloomington, IN: Indiana University Press, 1999). The "bila" that is the focus of this incident can be translated as broadly as "cavern" or as simply as "hole." One French translation of Valmiki, by Alfred Roussel (1903), as Jeffrey Masson points out, elegantly folds in the different possibilities: "*une cave, une caverne, un trou.*"

143 *Sampati*: After *Kishkindakanda*, sargas 55–62 in *CE* and 56–63 in *OE*. Sampati, king of the vultures, is the elder brother of Jatayu, the vulture prince killed by Ravana in *Aranyakanda*. Sampati has lost his wings, for reasons narrated in the poem, and so has not eaten for thousands of years. He too had seen Ravana and Sita flying through the air, but his only thought had been that they would be tasty to eat. When he comes upon a beach full of death-fasting Simian soldiers (see the end of the previous poem, "Un Trou"), he thinks his luck has finally improved. The Simians see only death's arrival. As it happens, Sampati reveals Sita's location to the Simians and so saves them; and thanks to Rama, Sampati is given back his wings.

148 *Simians, Plural*: After *Kishkindakanda*, sarga 36 in *CE* and 37 in *OE*.

150 *Sugriva's Roar*: After *Kishkindakanda*, sarga 14 in both *CE* and *OE*.

152 *The Mountain*: After *Kishkindakanda*, sarga 66 in *CE* and 67 in *OE*.

157 *"Trijata's Dream," by Ron Padgett*: After *Sundarakanda*, sarga 25 in *CE* and 27 in *OE*. The poem excerpted here is, I believe, an uncollected translation of Padgett's. It was published in 1971 in the special Sanskrit issue of *Mahfil*, a now-obscure journal for Indian literature in translation.

164 *Ravana's Rooms (Take One)*, *Ravana's Rooms (Take Two)*, and *Ravana's*
to *Rooms (Take Three: In the Buddha's Unforgiving Sight)*: After *Sundara-*
177 *kanda*, sargas 7–9 in *CE* and 9–11 in *OE*. These are all multiple takes of the same passage, when Hanuman, on a reconnaissance mission, steals into Ravana's bedroom and finds a postcoital scene. "Take Three: In the Buddha's Unforgiving Sight" translates a passage from a later work, the influential *Buddhacharita* (Story of Buddha) by the great foundational Buddhist Sanskrit poet Asvaghosa (c. 80–c. 150 CE). Asvaghosa has clearly read and been closely influenced by Valmiki; the very first line of the later epic situates the Buddha in the same lineage as Rama. This particular passage of his very closely echoes the orgy scene in *Sundarakanda* but spins it in a slightly different way. My version is indebted to the bilingual Clay Sanskrit Library edition of *Buddhacharita*, translated by Patrick Olivelle.

183 *Sita / Hanuman*: After *Sundarakanda*, sargas 28–38 in *CE* and 29–41 in *OE*.

194 *The Password: 1*: After *Sundarakanda*, sarga 33 in *CE* and 35 in *OE*. Since they have never met before, Sita and Hanuman must provide tokens of secret knowledge to each other; this is what Hanuman has to offer. The intimate but exacting description of Rama's body also seems to draw on Indian traditions of physiognomy.

195 *Shloka / Shoka*: Partly after *Yuddhakanda*, sarga 5 in *CE*. See note to "Valmiki Discovers the Shloka Meter" at the start of Book One.

198 *Notes on the Burning of Lanka*: After *Sundarakanda*, sargas 52–53 in *CE* and 53–55 in *OE*. Hanuman's return flight from Lanka is after *Sundarakanda*, sargas 54–55 in *CE* and 56–57 in *OE*. As a child I had somehow been taught to understand this scene merely as an example of Hanuman's inventiveness and heroism; yet Valmiki's camera—at least in all the manuscripts of the southern recension (according to Robert and Sally Goldman) and in the Gita Press edition—quickly turns to the suffering of the innocent rakshasas. In particular, we see a woman with a child suffering in the flames, which seems a very pointed critique; indeed, in the next canto, Hanuman himself questions his decision to set the city on fire, and no less a political theorist than the ancient Kautilya advises against the use of fire in war, for reasons I quote as one of the epigraphs to this book.

In this sequence, I also I draw on a few "external inputs."

First, an unfinished eighteenth-century drawing attributed to the Family of Nainsukh, in the collection of the Museum of Fine Arts, Boston, which not only depicts but also explicates the scene—in the depiction of the woman with child in the lower left corner, we see just how closely the painters of the Pahari school studied and thought about the source text.

Second and third, from a series in *Ground Work: After the War* where Robert Duncan rewrites, sometimes translates, the metaphysical poets. Here I focus on his remixes of Robert Southwell's "The Burning Babe" in the context of a Vietnam-era image.

Fourth, the poems of Raúl Zurita in *Sky Below: Selected Poems*, translated by Anna Deeny Morales (Chicago, IL: Northwestern University Press, 2016) and his installation *The Sea of Pain* at the Kochi Biennale 2017, which, among other things, responds to the troubled, problematic status of images from the Syrian War with a pointed refusal of the image.

218 *Fernand Cormon's* La Mort de Ravana *(1875)*: Cormon was a research-based painter in nineteenth-century Paris and a teacher to Toulouse-Lautrec and van Gogh. His *La Mort de Ravana* shows, regardless of its restaging for a colonial era, a remarkably close reading of the passage of Ravana's death in Valmiki (*Yuddhakanda*, sargas 110–11 in *CE*) that, among other things, registers the "dark and light skins" of Ravana's consorts and shows the dying rakshasa—as I have tried to show him throughout this book—not as a demon but as simply other. Cormon must have read Hippolyte Fauche's lilting translation of Valmiki in nine volumes (1854–1858). A few years after his Ravana painting, Cormon created a scandal in the Paris salons with his radical, provisional, and disturbing scientifically influenced depictions of the human body in his version of the Cain story. See Martha Lucy, "Cormon's Cain and the Problem of the Prehistoric Body," *Oxford Art Journal* 25, no. 2 (January 2002): 109–26.

At the start of Valmiki's sixth kanda, *Yuddhakanda*, the Simian general Hanuman has confirmed Sita's imprisonment on the island of Lanka and returned to his old shore with the news. The preparations for war begin on both sides. Vibhishana, Ravana's younger brother, advises surrender; this infuriates Ravana. (Vibhishana will soon go over to Rama's side and be installed as the king of Lanka by the end of the war.) At first the problem for Rama is logistical: a sea keeps the Simian army from reaching Lanka. Eventually, a solution is found in a massive collective bridge-building effort by the army, carrying stones into the sea with the assistance of nearby creatures.

Once the crossing of the sea has been accomplished, the story turns rapidly to the strategies and action of war: spies, mutual assessment, deceptions—including a chilling sequence where Ravana's son Indrajit executes a "phantom" Sita on the battlefield to frighten the enemy troops—one-on-one combat, group fights, whole armies hurled at each other. After that, there are the final denouements and a sequence where Ravana is killed by Rama and mourned. It's much like any war or superhero flick in its ups and downs—and surely intended to provide the same kinds of thrills for its audience—but all the same it is relentless and unflinching in its brutality and phantasmagoric horror. The book is Valmiki's longest and most repetitive. Though the point is for Rama to win, there also emerges a deep pessimism and sense of mourning, similar to that found perhaps in *The Iliad* or many other classical texts on war. There are points where, blinded by the dark or the dust of the battlefield, the soldiers can no longer distinguish enemy from ally.

At the end of *Yuddhakanda*, after victory has been declared, there comes another shock: Rama's rejection of the woman for whom he has fought the war. But I've saved *that* episode for the next and final book, "After."

225 *Not Sita, but a Phantom*: After *Yuddhakanda*, sarga 81 in *OE* and 68 in *CE*. In order to frighten and psyche out the enemy troops, Indrajit, Ravana's eldest son, slays what appears to be an illusory Sita, somewhere between an effigy and a chimerical phantom, given Indrajit's knowledge of the black arts.

226 *Believe meI'd // never hesitate to kill / a woman*: Compare to the first "Tataka" poem in Book One. The discussion around whether it is acceptable to kill women seems to be an explicit throwback to Vishwamitra's insistence to Rama, his young princely ward, that the killing of women can be an acceptable part of a king's duties. Now that advice comes back to bite Rama, given that the woman being "killed" is Sita. As the translators and editors of the Princeton edition point out in notes to both scenes (1.25.15: 336; 6.68.21: 1162), there are extensive injunctions against killing women in the scriptures, despite apparent defences of such killing both by Rama's teacher and by his enemy. This echo, although separated by more than a thousand

pages, was not lost on traditional commentators. In fact, some of the manuscripts even insert the line, "Why did Rama kill Tataka earlier? So, I shall kill Rama's queen..." (*Yuddhakanda* in *CE*, vol. 2, 1164).

228   *Chalkfaceclown // headholy shroud*: A borrowing from the chapter on "faciality" in Gilles Deleuze and Félix Guattari, *A Thousand Plateaus*, translated by Brian Massumi (Minneapolis, MN: University of Minnesota Press, 1987).

232   *They Saw No Longer the Battlefield*: After *Yuddhakanda*, sarga 55 in *OE*.

233   *Coming Back*: A loose translation of the Hindi poet Shrikant Verma's poem in his last collection, *Magadh* (New Delhi: Almost Island Books, 2013), which is set in a series of ancient, now destroyed cities, and often assumes the voice of a sly but embittered adviser to a king.

235   *To Shrikant Verma*: Shrikant Verma was one of the key Hindi poets of the latter half of the twentieth century and a major Congress party functionary. He was reputedly a speech writer for Prime Minister Indira Gandhi and thus was implicated in various intricate ways with the authoritarianism and violence of her leadership.

235   *PatalipuraHastinapur // AvantiKosambi...*: Lost cities mentioned in Verma's *Magadh*.

236   *Rohitashva*: According to folklore, Rohitashva was the son of Harischandra, a king-turned-corpse-worker. In the poem "Corpses in Kashi," Verma writes (translation by Rahul Soni):

> Ask then, whose corpse is this?
> Is it Rohitashva? No, no
> all corpses cannot be Rohitashva
>
> His corpse, you will recognize
> from a distance
> and if not from a distance
>
> then from up close
> and if not from up close
> then it cannot be Rohitashva
>
> And even if it is,
> what difference
> does it make?

236   *"Fools! It was only / after losing // the nation / that I found this poetry // which can belong to anyone"*: A line from an early Verma poem translated by Vishnu Khare. I have changed the lineation. See Shrikant Verma, *Otherwise and Other Poems* (Calcutta: Writers Workshop, 1972).

237 *Relatives*: After *Yuddhakanda*, sarga 10 in *CE* and sarga 16 in *OE*. This is from a monologue by Ravana, when his younger brother, Vibhishana, sides with Rama.

238 *Kumbakarna Sound System*: After *Yuddhakanda*, sarga 48 in *CE* and 60 in *OE*. Kumbakarna is a fierce warrior and Ravana's younger brother. Thanks to a trick played on him by Saraswati, the goddess of speech, Kumbakarna sleeps for "six, seven, eight, even nine months at a time." The waking up of Kumbakarna is a popular episode often told to kids.

Maarten Visser, who composed the score, is a saxophonist and composer based in Chennai who works with contemporary music, often through improvisation. Visser began a collaboration with the contemporary dancer and choreographer Padmini Chettur in 2000 and has since then composed music for all of her productions.

248 *Mainda & Dwivida*: After *Yuddhakanda*, sarga 5 in both *CE* and *OE*.

249 *Know Your Enemy (KYE)*: After *Yuddhakanda*, sargas 17–20 in *CE* and 26–28 in *OE*.

253 *Note on Large Numbers*: After *Yuddhakanda*, sarga 28, lines 34–43 in *OE*. This passage doesn't seem to appear in the *CE*.

254 *Some Omens*: See for instance *Yuddhakanda*, sarga 23 in *OE* and elsewhere.

256 *From the Sukra-niti*: Adapted from *Sukraniti*, chapter 5, lines 140–160, in *Sacred Books of the Hindus*, various translators (Allahabad, 1914).

257 *The Bridge*: In perhaps the best-known episode from *Yuddhakanda*, Rama and his monkey army, faced with the problem of crossing the sea to Lanka, build a bridge of stones. In some variants, little squirrels help by rolling in sand and using it as sealant. This particular story of the squirrels, however, doesn't appear in Valmiki but in some of the other *Ramayanas*, in Telugu and Bengali.

263 *Poem Without Beginning or End*: The 2019 report on torture in Kashmir by the Jammu Kashmir Coalition of Civil Society (JKCCS) can be found online at www.jkccs.net. I am very grateful to Parvez Imroz and Khurram Parvez of JKCSS and P. Govindan Kutty, the former editor of *People's March*, for permission to use the materials herein.

269 *Martyrs of Dandakaranya*: This is meant to be the title of the second (Maoist-related) thread in the poem, but the title itself is taken from the title of an article in *People's March*. Dandakaranya, the forest where much of the action of the *Ramayana* takes place, is also a forested region in contemporary India that indigenous peoples and Maoist rebellions call their own.

Additional sources for the first strand of the poem (Valmiki and classical war):

301 The diagrams of *vyuhas* (military formations) that I have superimposed on each other are taken from G. T. Date, *The Art of War in Ancient India* (London: Oxford University Press, 1929).

Other texts consulted, reinvented, and drawn from include:

P.C. Chakravarty, *The Art of War in Ancient India* (Dacca: University of Dacca, 1941).

Gerard Chaliand, editor, *The Art of War in World History* (Berkeley: University of California Press, 1994).

G.R. Josyer, *Diamonds, Mechanisms, Weapons of War: Yoga Sutra.* (Mysore: Josyer, 1979).

S.N. Prasad, *Historical Perspectives on Warfare in India: Some Morale and Material Determinants* (New Delhi: Centre for Studies in Civilizations, 2002).

Additional sources for the second strand of the poem ("Martyrs of Dandakaranya"):

268 *Beyond is a zone* [. . .] *Hillocks are lovely things*: Sanjay Kak, "10 Years of the Chatthisgarh School of Insurgency," *The Caravan* (August 2015).

386 *Dekuna*: Ejaz Kaiser, "This tribal hamlet in Chhattisgarh sends youth to defend nation," *The New Indian Express*, March 4, 2019.

393 *On one side of the road / there was a community centre*: Debobrat Ghose, "Once a Maoist den cut off from mainstream, Palnar village is now a digital hub," *Firstpost*, July 9, 2018.

396 *Police first picked up R. K. M.*: Human Rights Watch, "'Between Two Sets of Guns': Attacks on Civil Society Activists in India's Maoist Conflict," July 30, 2012; available at www.hrw.org.

Additional sources for the third strand of the poem (torture in Kashmir):

273 *Photographs of mass graves in Kashmir*: From "Buried Evidence: Unknown,
and Unmarked, and Mass Graves in Indian-Administered Kashmir," a 2009 re-
283 port by the International People's Tribunal on Human Rights and Justice in Indian-Administered Kashmir; available at https://www.kashmirprocess.org/.

282 *"we Kashmiris / would often offer tea or lunch"*: Marouf Gazi, "Amid 'trying times' . . . ," *Free Press Kashmir*, February 28, 2019.

283 *"When you see 8–10 drunk / armed men"*: Priyanka Chandani, "Voices from the Valley," *Asian Age*, March 8, 2019.

283 *"The boys got it as a gift for the brigade" [and preceding lines]*: Barkha Dutt, "Confessions of a War Reporter," *Himal Southasian*, June 2001.

285 *The Indian army said / it had "not manhandled any civilians as alleged"*: Sameer Hashmi, "'Don't beat us, just shoot us': Kashmiris allege violent army crackdown," BBC News, August 29, 2019.

305 *B.W. appeared with his real name*: M. A. Mir, "Burhan Wani—an icon of Kashmir's Freedom Fight," *Express Tribune*, July 8, 2017.

305 *A. killed in an encounterhad / [...] Two rows of tombstones*: Ipsita
to Chakravarty and Rayan Naqash, "Valley of Martyrs," *Scroll.in*, July 9,
306 2016.

390 *At checkpoints throughout Srinagar*: Aijaz Hussain, "Kashmir's Main City a Maze of Razor Wire and Steel Barriers," Associated Press, August 13, 2019.

391 *"the Indian army came / and handed these photocopies / to us"*: "Month after abrogation of Article 370 in Jammu and Kashmir, Indian Army and terrorists wage 'poster war'," *Firstpost*, September 9, 2019.

395 *Trend Lines Constant*: Wikileaks / US Embassy Cables, as published in *The Guardian*, December 16, 2010.

BOOK FOUR: AFTER

This section begins with an exploration of Rama's rejection of Sita that happens near the end of kanda six, which eventually goes on to conclude on a happy note: Rama takes Sita back, after the intervention of the gods; the lost Simian soldiers are brought back to life; and Rama is returned and reinstituted to the throne.

The title of Valmiki's seventh kanda, *Uttara*, might be translated in several different ways, including simply *After*. It is considered difficult and problematic by many within the tradition; some would just wish it away as something that doesn't "count." Often, it is charged that it was added later. Nevertheless, this last book, a return and an unraveling, is included in the earliest available manuscripts of Valmiki and is an essential—even key—part of the long tradition of thought around the *Ramayana*, triggering such great later works as Bhavabhuti's drama *Uttararamacharita*.

The first third of the kanda comprises what some scholars have called a "mini-epic," focusing on the earlier misdeeds of Ravana, an enemy now dead. This is part of a long bit of a prequel, where sages tell Rama stories of how and why things came to be. There's an attempt to revisit certain questions raised in the earlier books of the *Ramayana*, and to answer any doubts the plot may have given rise to.

Then we return to the present: the erotic reuniting of Rama and Sita, and the conception of twins. Everyday life seeps back into the city, and Rama returns to his court; but there is trouble brewing. Rama learns from one of his advisers that "the people" have been joking about his reunion with Sita, how he took her back despite her long stay in another man's house. In a cold reversal, apparently done to protect his reputation as king, Rama instructs his brother Lakshmana to take Sita on a little trip without bringing her back. Especially terrifying is that Rama never tells his great love Sita, now pregnant with his children, the true purpose of the trip she is being sent on. Lakshmana has been given orders to keep her in the dark until the very moment of abandonment. Luckily, and apparently without Lakshmana's knowledge, Valmiki, the author of the *Ramayana*, is in the vicinity. He saves Sita and takes her to his ashram.

After this, some episodes unfold about Rama's now solitary life as king. Perhaps the most shocking and disturbing of these scenes is his assassination of the lower-caste monk Shambuka. Eventually, in the midst of another horse sacrifice to "reset" the kingdom, Rama is reunited with his twin sons. They lead him back to thoughts of Sita and a desire to be with her again. This time, however, it will be Sita's turn to reject him. If Valmiki's previous volume ended on a happy note, the abiding theme of the last book of the *Ramayana* is undoubtedly separation.

The *OE* does not include the *Uttarakanda*. So along with Raghunathan's edition, the Princeton translation of the *CE*, and the Gita Press edition, I also referred to Arshia Sattar's *Uttara: The Book of Answers* (Delhi: HarperCollins, 2019), which is a translation of Valmiki's entire seventh book along with some accompanying essays. Sattar's startlingly original essays in this volume, as with *Lost Loves*, her earlier book on the *Ramayana*, have had a deep influence on my thinking. I have not given separate chapter/sarga numbers for her *Uttara* because she, like the Princeton volumes, follows the Baroda critical edition.

415 *Dhvanyaloka 2.1*: This is a poem by Anandavardhana (9 CE), from his great work of literary philosophy, *Dhvanyaloka*.

421 *Rama and Sita, Just After the War*: The episode narrated in this poem actually comes at the end of Valmiki's sixth book, *Yuddhakanda*, right after the end of the war and before the ostensible happy ending which concludes that book. See *Yuddhakanda*, sargas 101–6 in *CE* and 113–18 in *OE*.

426 *Ganga: n Views*: The first part of the first section, "Not at Gaumukh," owes a debt to Pranay Lal's *Indica: A Deep Natural History of the Indian Subcontinent* (New Delhi: Allen Lane/Penguin Random House, 2016). See also the poem "Ganga" in Book One.

442 *Kashi*: Another name for Varanasi/Benares.

446 *Raasta nahi hai*: "There's no way here" (Hindi).

448 *Ila*: After *Uttarakanda*, sargas 78–80 in *CE*.

450 *Shveta*: After *Uttarakanda*, sargas 68–69 in *CE*.

452 *The Nobility of the Rakshasas*: After multiple sargas in the first half of *Uttarakanda*.

454 *Ravana's Earlier Career*: After multiple sargas in the first half of *Uttarakanda*.

457 *Hanuman vs. Rahu*: After *Uttarakanda*, sarga 35 in *CE*.

458 *Dandakaranya*: Partly drawn from *Uttarakanda*, sargas 71–72 in *CE*.

460 *Pushpaka Transport*: The wondrous "flying chariot" of sorts, first owned by Kubera, the god of wealth, then stolen and taken to Lanka by his step-brother Ravana, then finally the means by which Rama and Sita return to Lanka at the end of the war. *"Vimana"*—here translated merely as "transport"—are a whole genre of mythological flying vehicles.

463 *On Certain Illuminated Pages of Abdur Rahim's* Ramayana: Abdur Rahim (b. 1556) was not only the commander in chief of the Mughal armies but also a famed poet in multiple languages, including Sanskrit; a translator, most notably of *Baburnama* from Turki to Persian; and a patron of a bookmaking atelier that made the *Ramayana* in Persian that is now known as *The Freer Ramayana*. My sequence of poems draws on several illustrations in this work. Given that Rahim oversaw the project, had already translated works into Persian, and was well versed enough in Sanskrit to write canonical poems in the language, it seems very likely that he had a hand in the translation as well. This is one of three extant "Akbari *Ramayanas*"—illustrated *Ramayanas* in Persian translation commissioned by or at the time of the Mughal emperor Akbar (1542–1605) in a remarkable collaboration between workshops of Hindu and Muslim scholars, writers, translators, and painters.

For this sequence of poems, I am very indebted to John Seyller's *Workshop and Patron in Mughal India: The Freer Ramayana and Other Illustrated Manuscripts of 'Abd al-Rahim* (Zurich: Artibus Asiae, 1999).

474 *Sunashepa*: An uncomfortable and ultimately forestalled story of human sacrifice, retold by Valmiki.

478 *Kumbhakarna*: Ravana's younger brother, who also appears in *Yuddhakanda*. In Valmiki's seventh book, we hear the backstory of how Kumbhakarna, after great penance, is tricked by the goddess of speech into asking for long sleep as a boon instead of other powers.

479 *Hanuman's Uncertainty Among the Magic Plants*: In an episode that I don't cover elsewhere, Rama and Lakshmana are mortally wounded and Hanuman is dispatched to collect magic healing herbs from a mountain. When he gets there, Hanuman is not sure which herb is the right one, so he brings back the whole mountain.

480 *Not Sita, but a Phantom*: See the poem of the same name in Book Three, as well as the notes to that poem.

485 *Ram's Arm*: This poem is stitched together from different lines in praise of Rama throughout Valmiki but also incorporates Bhavabuti's reminders of what the tradition itself saw as his two most problematic actions.

486 *Shambuka*: After *Uttarakanda*, sargas 64–67 in *CE*.

487 *At Ramtek*: I went with the photographer Madhu Kapparath to visit this town in eastern Maharashtra where, according to a local legend, Rama killed Shambuka. A notice at the temple there indicates that a shrine to Shambuka and his resting place could be found next to the main altar for Rama, but we weren't sure if we found it.

489 *Valmiki's Students*: Partly drawing on *Uttarakanda*, sargas 84–85 in *CE*, but also heavily influenced by the corresponding scene in Bhavabuti's *Uttararamacarita*.

490 *A Knock on the Door*: After *Uttarakanda*, sargas 93–96 in *CE*. The Gillian Rose quote is from *Mourning Becomes the Law* (Cambridge, UK: Cambridge University Press, 1996).

495 *Collective*: Partly after *Uttarakanda*, sarga 100 in *CE*. This poem and the previous poem were also heavily influenced by the corresponding scene in G. Aravindan's film *Kanchana Sita* (1977).

500 *Ramnagar*: The Indian government's Citizenship (Amendment) Act (CAA) discriminates specifically against Muslims and sparked one of the most widespread and widely attended peaceful protests by students, civil society groups, and lay citizens in recent years. Ramnagar, across the Ganges from Varanasi, is the site each year of one of the largest *Ramlila*s (*Ramayana* plays that are performed often in the streets, sometimes extending over several days, by amateur thespians). Ramnagar and the CAA are not directly related in any way apart from the coincidence of my having been in Ramnagar on the day the CAA was announced.

501 *In Memoriam Mohammed Akhlaq*: Mohammed Akhlaq was lynched by a Hindu mob on the (false, it turns out) charge of keeping beef in his refrigerator in 2015. This poem has been heavily influenced by the reporting of Mohammad Ali and Rohini Mohan (the latter in *Harper's Magazine*).

504 *Chandramohan S.*: An Indian Dalit poet who writes in English. His books of poems include *Warscape Verses*, *Letter to Namdeo Dhasal*, and *Love After Babel*.

507 *Shaheen Bagh*: Neighborhood in New Delhi that was the site of sit-ins from December 2019 to March 2020 in protest of the Citizenship (Amendment) Act.

508 *Maitreem Bhajata*: A song in Sanskrit composed by Chandrasekharendra Saraswati (1894–1994), the sixty-eighth Shankaracharya (head guru) of the Kanchi monastery and, famously, sung by the Carnatic singer M. S. Subbalakshmi at the United Nations in 1966.

509 *Ayodhya*: The exact factual/archaeological relationship between today's pilgrim town of Ayodhya in Uttar Pradesh and the Ayodhya of the *Ramayana* is not known. Present-day Ayodhya is revered by Hindus, especially supporters of the Hindu right, as Rama's birthplace. In December 1992, the destruction of a mosque by Hindu activists—at, so they claimed, the site of Rama's birth—became a galvanizing moment for the resurgence of Hindu right-wing activism and state capture. I visited the town in early December 2019, exactly twenty-seven years after the demolition. This is an account of what I found then. I am especially indebted to an under-recognized classic, Scharada Dubey's *Portraits from Ayodhya* (Chennai: Westland, 2012).

521 *A Ramayana on the Delhi Ridge (2)* and *(1)*: The Delhi Ridge—which can be
to found on Google Maps—is a vast, various, and fragmented forest in and
534 around the city of Delhi. Since many different places have laid claim to being the "actual" locations of the *Ramayana*, these two poems begin with the imagining of the ridge as the location of the epic.

The "Krishen book" is Pradip Krishen's lovely and groundbreaking *Trees of Delhi: A Field Guide* (New Delhi: Dorling Kindersley, 2006). I am also indebted to Amita Baviskar's *Uncivil City: Ecology, Equity and the Commons in Delhi* (New Delhi: Sage Publications, 2020) for thoughts about the ridge and the term "Budget Bauhaus."

537 *Some Notes on Race in the Ramayana*: Teodros Kiros's brief discussion of his theories about the origins of our current racial and gender regimes can be found in an episode of the *Africana Philosophy* podcast at https://historyofphilosophy.net.

538 *At Valmiki Sadan*: The Valmiki community is a large cluster of Dalit (that is, "untouchable") castes and groups in North India that claim direct descent from Valmiki. Valmiki Sadan is a large residential colony in Delhi where members of the Valmiki group live; many of them work in sanitation. Next to Valmiki Sadan, on the edge of the Delhi Ridge, is a temple to Valmiki originally built by the community and later renovated by the Birlas. I am very indebted to the scholar Ajayraj and to Guru Cheena Ji Maharaj, guru and social activist of the Valmiki community, for their kindness and conversation. This poem is dedicated to the memory of Cheena Ji Maharaj.

544 *The Final Asana*: To the best of my knowledge, Abhinavagupta does not give an account of any such book; the poem is a fiction.

545 *After*: This poem draws principally on the following sources: *Uttarakanda*, sargas 82–89 in the *CE*; Bhavabhuti, *Uttararamacarita*, translated in a bilingual edition by Sheldon Pollock as *Rama's Last Act* (New York: Clay Sanskrit Library, 2007); and Roland Barthes, *A Lover's Discourse: Fragments*,

translated by Richard Howard (New York: Hill and Wang, 1979). Any direct quotations from Pollock's translation appear in quotation marks; in other places I have adapted, retranslated, or imitated. Direct quotations of Barthes appear in italics, although italics are used for other purposes as well throughout the poem.

564 *Poi come nel percuoter*: Dante, *Paradiso* XVIII. Translated in the line below it.

566 *And the dusk rolled*: Ezra Pound, Canto VIII.

584 *"[and we are] gradually led into a twilight territory where"*: From K. Seshadri, *Heritage of Hinduism* (Madras: C. P. Ramaswamy Aiyar Foundation, 1977).

111 *The Monkey King Vali's Funeral Pyre*: Circa 1780, Kangra Court. In the collection of the Metropolitan Museum of Art, New York. Accession number: 2004.367. Photograph is in the public domain; with kind thanks to the Met.

116 *Searching the Forest*: Folio from the "Shangri"-Ramayana. India, Pahari region, Bahu or Mandi, 1700–1710. Permanent Loan Collection Eberhard and Barbara Fischer. Courtesy Museum Rietberg, Zürich | REF 15 © Photo: Rainer Wolfsberger, rietberg.ch.

130 *The Monkeys Visiting the Ascetic Svayamprabha*: Folio from the small "Mankot"-Ramayana. India, Pahari region, Mankot or Guler, circa 1720. Permanent Loan Collection Eberhard and Barbara Fischer. Courtesy Museum Rietberg, Zürich | REF 25 © Photo: Rainer Wolfsberger, rietberg.ch.

137 *The Monkeys in Despair Meet Sampati* (detail): Folio from the small
and "Mankot"-Ramayana. India, Pahari region, Mankot or Guler, circa 1720.
142 Collection Eva and Konrad Seitz. Courtesy Museum Rietberg, Zürich | 2005.86 © Photo: Rainer Wolfsberger, rietberg.ch.

182 *Hanuman Discovers Sita in the Asoka Grove and Gives Her the Ring* (details): Indian, Pahari, circa 1780–1790. Kangra style, Punjab Hills, Northern India. Attributed to: The Family of Nainsukh. Ink and opaque watercolor on paper. Overall: 26 x 37 cm (10¼ x 14⁹⁄₁₆ in). Image: 20.6 x 31.6 cm (8⅛ x 12⁷⁄₁₆ in). Courtesy Museum of Fine Arts, Boston, Ross-Coomaraswamy Collection 17.2435. Photograph © 2022 Museum of Fine Arts, Boston.

204 *Hanuman Sets the Demon Capital on Fire* (complete, then various de-
to tails): Indian, Pahari, circa 1790. Punjab Hills, Northern India. Attributed
208 to: The Family of Nainsukh. Ink on paper. Overall: 26 x 36.7 cm (10¼ x 14⁷⁄₁₆ in). Image: 20.4 x 30.8 cm (8¹⁄₁₆ x 12⅛in). Courtesy Museum of Fine Arts, Boston, Ross-Coomaraswamy Collection 17.2437. Photograph © 2022 Museum of Fine Arts, Boston.

211 *Sea of Pain*. Installation by Raúl Zurita, Kochi Biennale. Photograph credit: © Yosha Gupta, founder, memeraki.com. By kind permission.

214   *Hanuman Leaps Across the Ocean*: Folio from the small "Guler"-Ramayana series, circa 1720. India, Pahari region, Guler. Courtesy Museum Rietberg, Zürich | RVI 840 © Photo: Rainer Wolfsberger, rietberg.ch.

217   *La Mort de Ravana* (1875): By Fernand Cormon. Oil painting on canvas, 260 x 341 cm. Public domain. Courtesy Musée des Augustins, Toulouse. Photo credit: © Bernard Delorme; © Daniel Martin; © Photo STC-Toulouse City Hall.

273   Mass graves in Kashmir. Photographs © International People's Tribunal on
and   Human Rights and Justice in Indian-Administered Kashmir (IPTK). Used
283   here with due acknowledgment and gratitude.

465   *The Freer Ramayana* (1597–1605). Pages from the manuscript. Patron: Abd-al
to   Rahim (Abdur Rahim); various artists. Photograph in the public domain,
473   with kind thanks to the Freer Gallery of Art, Smithsonian Institution, Washington, D.C. Gift of Charles Lang Freer, F1907.271.1-172; F1907.271.173-346.